SYLLABUS

SUBJECT 1 : INTRODUCTION TO FINANCIAL PLANNING

CHAPTER 1 : INDIAN ECONOMIC ENVIRONMENT

Introduction to Economics and Indian economy

- What is economics?
- Objectives of economic policies
- Indian economy today
- Economic growth & national income
- Inflation
- Role of money in inflation, money multiplier
- Business cycles
- International trade and balance of payment

Economic policies and tools

- Monetary policy
- Fiscal policy

Economic indicators and value of investment

Media and information sources

- The financial press
- Research papers

- Company reports
- Official sources of data as per economic calendar

CHAPTER 2 : OVERVIEW OF INDIAN FINANCIAL MARKETS

Basic concepts

- Money
- Financial assets
- Securities
- Debt securities
- Equity
- Risk
- Primary and secondary markets

The Financial System

- Economy and financial system
- Functions of the financial system
- Facets of market malpractices and asset bubbles

Types of Financial markets

- The equity market
- The debt market
- The foreign exchange market
- The money market
- The derivative market
- Insurance and mutual funds

Features of Financial markets

- Primary and secondary markets
- What makes a market tick?
- How securities are bought and sold?
- Investing in securities and financial markets
- Impact of globalisation of financial markets

The flow of funds

- Intermediation
- Disintermediation

CHAPTER 3 : PARTICIPANTS, INTERMEDIARIES & REGULATORS OF THE INDIAN FINANCIAL SYSTEM: INSTITUTIONAL & NON- INSTITUTIONAL

Participants in the finance industry

- Participants and the flow of funds
- Who is an intermediary?
- Intermediaries and financial markets
- Role of intermediaries
- Intermediaries in the Indian financial system

Types of financial services

- Retail financial services
- Wholesale financial services
- Mutual funds

CHAPTER 4 : BASICS OF FINANCIAL PLANNING

Introduction

- What is financial planning?
- The importance of risk profiling
- Pre- and post-retirement planning
- Users of financial planning services
- The role of a financial planner
- Who provides financial planning?
- Increasing professionalism of financial planners
- Remuneration
- You and your client
- You and your dealer

Regulatory controls and practices

- Regulation of the Indian financial system

- Regulatory authorities
- Self-regulatory bodies
- Reasonable basis for recommendations
- Limited advice
- Disclosure requirements
- Documentation
- Advertising and projections about securities

A brief overview of advisers

- Liability
- Basic field audits
- Basic licensing review

The consumer life cycle

- Stages of the life cycle
- Non-traditional life cycle stages
- Demographic trends underlying the life cycle
- The changing workforce
- Variables that influence financial behaviour over the life cycle
- Stage by stage analysis

The wealth cycle

- Accumulation
- Preservation
- Distribution

CHAPTER 5 : THE FINANCIAL PLANNING PROCESS

- Various views of financial planning
- The evolution of financial planning as a profession
- Good practices in financial planning
- Content of a comprehensive financial plan

Appendix: Preparing financial statements

CHAPTER 6: TOWARDS A FINANCIAL PLAN

Working with clients

- The client introduction
- The financial services guide

Gathering initial information from the client

- Data collection

Additional information

- Financial goals
- Assessing risk tolerance
- Analysis of insurance needs
- Analysis of retirement savings
- Analysis of investment preferences
- The conclusion of the first interview

Meeting the client's objectives

- General requirements
- Disclosure
- Recommendations

Asset allocation

- Selection of investment and insurance products

Implementation

- The written plan
- Your action plan

Ongoing service

CHAPTER 7 : RECOMMENDING FINANCIAL PLANNING STRATEGIES TO INVESTORS

- Financial planning strategies - Investing for the long term
- Asset allocation - The strategic tool
- Comparison of products

CHAPTER 8 : EFFECTIVE COMMUNICATION IN FINANCIAL COUNSELLING

Introduction

Three types of structured communication

- Interviewing
- Counselling
- Advising

Essentials in financial counselling

- Structure
- Rapport
- Recognizing resistance
- Common areas of resistance

Profile of the effective counsellor

- Unconditional positive regard
- Accurate empathy
- Genuineness
- Self-awareness

Elements of non-verbal behaviours

- The body
- The voice
- Interpreting the meaning of non-verbal behaviours

Attending and listening skills

- Physical attending
- Active listening
- Responding during active listening

Counsellor leading responses

The questioning process of a Financial Counselling

CHAPTER-HEADS

CONTENTS

1

INDIAN ECONOMIC ENVIRONMENT

2

OVERVIEW OF INDIAN FINANCIAL MARKETS

3

PARTICIPANTS, INTERMEDIARIES & REGULATORS OF THE INDIAN FINANCIAL SYSTEM : INSTITUTIONAL & NON-INSTITUTIONAL

4

BASICS OF FINANCIAL PLANNING

PAGE

5

FINANCIAL PLANNING PROCESS

6

RECOMMENDING FINANCIAL PLANNING STRATEGIES TO INVESTORS

7

TOWARDS A FINANCIAL PLAN

PAGE

8
EFFECTIVE COMMUNICATION IN FINANCIAL COUNSELLING

1 CHAPTER

Indian Economic Environment

ABOUT THIS TOPIC

An understanding of the basic economic principles, and how the economy works, will be important for you as you design and present portfolios to help your clients toward their goals.

You will need to explain, for example, how the portfolio has been put together in the context of current and anticipated economic and financial conditions, including prospective interest rates, dividend yields, inflation and income and capital gains tax.

This understanding will also be important in enabling you to discuss how the portfolio will need to be reviewed and altered as these and other economic conditions change.

Some of the important concepts are:

- *What is economics?*
- *Objective of economic policies*
- *Indian Economy today*
- *Economic Growth & National Income*
- *Inflation*
- *Role of excess money in Inflation*
- *Money Multiplier*
- *Business cycles*

- *International trade and balance of payment*
- *Economic Policies and tools including monetary policy, fiscal policy*
- *Introduction to macroeconomics*
- *Economic indicators and value of investments*
- *Media and information sources*

TOPIC OBJECTIVES

- *At the end of this topic, you should be able to:*
- *Explain the relevance of the economy and economic analysis to investment decisions*
- *Outline the major influences on interest rates and the impact of inflation on investment decisions*
- *Explain Government budgetary, monetary and regulatory policies*
- *Describe how these policies, along with international influences, can affect investment values*
- *Outline the economic information the Financial planner can obtain from the media*
- *List sources of detailed research applicable to the financial planner*
- *Identify and describe business and economic cycles and their effect on investment values.*

1. INTRODUCTION TO ECONOMICS AND INDIAN ECONOMY

1.1 WHAT IS ECONOMICS?

Economics surrounds all of us and many of our decisions are influenced by the system of economy around us. We will aim to demystify some of the economic concepts to get a better understanding for the purpose of financial planning. Economics is said to be a study of the relationship of matching infinite needs and finite means. It is a study of how society uses the 'resources' of labour, capital and land to meet its 'wants and needs' of the various goods and services of food, shelter, transport, security, entertainment, etc. and how those goods and services are 'distributed' within society.

This, in turn, leads to an analysis of the questions of what is to be paid to the owners of the various resources — *i.e.* wages and salaries to those in employment; interest and dividends to the owners of capital; and rent to the owner of land for the use of those resources.

There is also the analysis of questions about the prices for the goods and services to be produced — whether same should be encouraged or discouraged, through subsidies or taxes, if society wants more or less than the market might decide. And there are the questions of how these goods and services are distributed — *e.g.* if individual or groups in society should be given preferential treatment through Government subsidy or direct access, or taxed to reduce their disposable incomes.

There is also the analysis of how much should be allocated to consumption now as compared with investing for future consumption.

From these questions, varied analyses have developed the study of economics and of particular relevance to financial planners, analysis of how interest rate, share prices, exchange rates, property yields, etc. are determined.

An important part of this study has been the development of the concept of the 'economy'. Many Economists and Economic reporters speak of the economy as if it were a real thing with power to move and to impact business and personal actions. Almost every day, the media comments on how the 'economy' is performing.

The study of economics is broadly divided into macroeconomics and microeconomics. Macroeconomics is the study of very large economic aggregates including national income, investments and savings, markets, imports and exports, balance of payments, and Foreign Exchange rates, These are influenced and may be governed by monetary and fiscal policy. Macroeconomics also includes the following:

> *The terms of trade,* which measure the ratio of the prices of India's exports of goods and services to the prices of India's imports of goods and services. It is one indicator of the real spending power of India's international trading effort.
>
> *Inflation,* which is the rate of change of the general price level in the economy. It is important in understanding what is happening to real spending power or investments and India's international trade competitiveness.
>
> *Household savings ratio,* which is how much of the income that flows to the household sector that is left after tax and debt service, is not immediately consumed. It is a measure of the savings that the household sector can make available to the rest of the economy.
>
> *Profits share,* which is the share of gross domestic product that remains with business after the various payments have been made for the labour inputs - such as wages and salaries and superannuation. It is often used as an indicator of the health of the business sector and what is available for business investment.

Microeconomics usually looks at sectors in the general market, individual companies and the impact on individuals. Microeconomics explores the impact of macroeconomics on the bottom line — the profitability, productivity and lifestyle of the end purchasers — the consumers of the goods and services provided in a nation. Included, under this heading, are the changes to industry regulation by the government, such as the privatisation of the telecommunications and insurance sectors in the recent past.

Changes in both macroeconomic and microeconomic policies significantly change investment opportunities, outlook and returns. An understanding of economics will, therefore, help financial planners better appreciate why such changes take place, how they might affect investment performance and how they might be anticipated.

Each country develops an institutional and ideological arrangement for solving the major economic problems, which, in short, can be called "Economy". Over the ages, contrasting type of economies have evolved. On the one hand, we have "free enterprise" economy and on the other "planned" economy. In India we follow a mixed economy as operating philosophy, which incorporates elements of free economy and planned systems.

In a free enterprise economy, there is little or no regulatory interference. The main axiom is interaction of demand and supply forces of the market. Free and fair competition is supposed to work for consumer. Regulator's role is limited to ensure fair competition between producers and take steps to avoid collusion between producers

In a planned economy, the "state" decides the direction of economy. It decides, by allocation of resources to various sectors, pricing and distribution. There is limited role for free and open competition.

1.2 OBJECTIVES OF ECONOMIC POLICIES

The main objectives of economic policies are:

(*a*) Guide growth while controlling inflation

(*b*) Achieve full employment

(*c*) Steady growth in national income as measured by output of goods and services

(*d*) Improve balance of payments by guiding foreign trade (imports and exports) and investment

(*e*) Reduce regional imbalances

(*f*) Reduce economic imbalances in society

(g) Ensure efficient, articulate and advanced financial system.

1.2.1 The relevance of Economics to financial planners

The study of Economics is fundamentally about how people interact as consumers and workers, as managers of businesses and, as Government policy makers, in trying to use the resources available to them to meet their varied and changing objectives. These interactions occur principally through a uniquely human construction known as 'the market'. Markets largely undertake the matching of the resources of labour, services and capital to the making of the goods and services that we use/avail. In a mixed economy like India's, the Government tries to influence the flow of such resources through:

Public sector companies, where the Government has a controlling stake

Policies that serve as incentives or disincentives for private sector to operate in a particular direction or manner.

For financial planners, the markets of most interest are those that deal in capital — the money, share, foreign exchange and property markets. The focus is movement of prices— the interest rates, share prices, exchange rates, rents and capital values — of what is traded in these markets.

An understanding of economics can help the financial planner better understand how and why these markets and their prices can be affected by underlying economic changes and the Government policies — monetary, budgetary and regulatory — used to influence understanding of how these changes in the economy and Government policies might impact the performance of investment portfolios and how and why they should be structured and reviewed.

Such an understanding is often complicated, however, by the difficulty of knowing what is happening in the economy today, let alone trying to forecast what will be the impact of current and future economic events and Government's policies on financial markets today and tomorrow. To help this understanding, economic analysts use a variety of economic and financial data and tools, including trying to find 'leading indicators'. These are statistics or events that usually signal a change in economy or Government policies.

Economic factors form a vital part of investment analysis and strategy formulation. They are part of the external or environmental considerations that you will analyse when making recommendations to your client. In addition, when your clients ask, 'Where is the share market going?' or, 'Are interest rates going up or down?', it will be helpful for you to have at least a basic understanding of how recent and prospective developments in the economy might be affecting financial markets and the investment outlook.

REFLECTION

The Indian economy is showing definite signs of an upturn. How would an upturn in the Indian economy impact the financial plans you create for your client?

1.3 INDIAN ECONOMY TODAY

Today, India is amongst the top 10 economies of the world in terms of GDP. For the year 2014-15, India's GDP, at current market prices, was Rs. 125412 billion. In the past, India had been, primarily, an agricultural economy. The share of agriculture and allied activities, in the total economy, has been continuously declining and now stands at around 16% of the GDP. However, agriculture still supports more than half of India's population. This implies a high degree of backward and forward linkage between the agricultural and industrial sectors. It has been observed that agricultural performance tends to have a bearing on the industrial performance with a year's lag.

India is a developing economy. However, the structural change, noted in the growth dynamics of the economy, is a sustained higher growth in the services sector, propelled by trade, transportation and communications, financing, insurance and real estate and business services (including software services).

India is rich in natural resources excluding natural gas and crude oil. About 80% of India's crude oil requirements are met through imports. India has an abundance of cheap and skilled labour. However, India still tends to export raw materials and import finished products, leading to a balance of payments deficit, despite growing foreign exchange flows from intangibles. This, coupled with higher inflation (compared to that in developed countries), has resulted in sustained depreciation in the value of our currency.

India is now seeing an increase in various areas of manufacturing and services. Privatisation has aided competitiveness and India is getting globally competitive in many industries and services.

With China emerging as a major economic power, comparisons are quite often made with India. Infrastructure is one area where China scores. In the power sector, using the commercial establishments to subsidise politically sensitive constituencies, has pushed power tariffs sky high. Experts are of the view that inefficiencies, taxes on inputs, cost consequences of inadequate infrastructure, and cost equations arising out of political factors are affecting India's emergence as a global manufacturing base. On account of the availability of a cheap labour force, western countries are outsourcing work from India, particularly in the software sector. Modern means of communication have dispelled the tyranny of distance and the world grows smaller day by day. This has aided India's growth in the services Sector.

India has always required substantial money to further its development. India has had to borrow abroad to fund its financial requirements. In 1991, India faced a balance of payments crisis, reflecting a deteriorating fiscal position, rising external debt (especially short-term debt), a surge in oil prices and a sharp decline in external remittances. As capital flight accelerated and official reserves rapidly declined, the Indian Government entered into a stand-by arrangement with the International Monetary Fund (IMF). Subsequently, India launched a package of comprehensive macroeconomic and structural adjustment policies along with a shift in the development strategy in favour of market orientation and provision of appropriate incentives.

Indian economic era, since independence, can be divided in two parts i.e. pre 1991 (pre-reform period) and post 1991 (reform period which led to liberalization of Indian economy). Since independence Indian economy was highly regulated. The private sector had to obtain licenses for making investments in any industry/service facility from authorities. Foreign collaboration and direct investment were also restricted. Foreign trade and movement of foreign exchange were also tightly controlled. Economic reforms since 1991 are guiding towards structural adjustment programme with the twin objectives of preventing recurring macroeconomic imbalances on the one hand, and acceleration of long run growth of income and standard of living, on the other.

The financial market reforms comprised of the banking and capital market reform. They included implementation of Narasimham Committee report and loosening of government control over the public sector banks by way of divestment of ownership. Capital market reform included strengthening Securities and Exchange Board of India (SEBI), guidelines for mutual funds and venture capital funds, permission to raise funds from abroad, and attracting Foreign Institutional Investors (FIIs) to Indian capital market. The objective of economic reforms is market orientation and competition.

Two decades of economic reforms have altered the structure of the Indian economy, making it more resilient to external shocks than before. However, the reform process is far from complete and needs further deepening to consolidate economic growth.

The rate of economic growth of India declined in last few years but the growth in previous few quarters has been encouraging. The latest figures of GDP growth have been around 7.5%. It is the aim of the Government to sustain the GDP at around 7.50% for the year 2015-16 and at around 8% during the next year.

As mentioned above, India has seen a higher inflation compared to that in the developed economies of the world. In order to contain the inflation, RBI adopted the monetary policy of high interest rates, adversely affecting the growth of the economy. With declining prices of crude oil and commodities, the inflation has been under control in recent times and RBI is gradually lowering the policy rates.

REFLECTION

Who benefits when the Indian rupee is weak against the American dollar? Who benefits when the Indian rupee strengthens (appreciates)?

1.4 ECONOMIC GROWTH & NATIONAL INCOME

Economic growth is measured by comparing the total output of the economy at different periods of time. In market economies, the cost of different goods is reflected in their prices. True measure of economic growth will be growth in output at constant prices (i.e. base year's price). This method of measurement is also called index number method, which allows measurement of a total output of different goods and services. Nation's output (Gross Domestic Product "GDP") is the total market value of all the final goods and services produced within the territorial boundaries of the nation and may be measured either by way of summing the value of final products (ready for consumption) (receipts from sales plus change in the value of inventory) or as summing the cost incurred in producing that production (counting profits as factor of production cost).

Both methods are supposed to give the same result.

Gross National Product (GNP) is equal to GDP plus total capital gains from overseas investments minus income earned by foreign nationals domestically.

To measure real GDP, we factor in price comparison with base year, to get real GDP at base year's price from nominal GDP.

Not all transactions in the economy are covered in the GDP accounts. One major example is gains and losses by way of transfer of securities or land. Other examples are non-marketed final products (for example, the wheat consumed by the farmer himself) and the parallel economy transactions. It is said that GDP gets reduced when you marry your maid as her work becomes now that of a housewife which is not paid for. The GDP does not reflect the measure of change in the welfare of the population.

The uses of GDP accounts have increased over the years as it provides information about major industry groups and several sectors by functions. The GDP figures have to be adjusted for population to account for the growth of the population. Thus, we calculate per capita GDP by dividing the figure of GDP with average population. India's Per Capita GDP, for the year 2014-15, was Rs 98,983.

The current scope of India's statistical publications needs to be viewed against the vast expanse of the country that makes the task of collecting micro-level data an extremely difficult and costly proposition. The Indian economy is also characterised by the high share of the unorganised and unregistered sector that is not strictly captured by published data on various economic parameters such as production, national income, employment, etc.

Despite difficulties, steps have been initiated for better collection, compilation and dissemination of data: The Statistics Wing in the Ministry of Statistics and Programme Implementation is the apex body in the official statistical system of the country and consists of the Central Statistical Organisation (CSO) and the National Sample Survey Organisation (NSSO). The wing prepares annual estimates of national products, Government and private consumption expenditure, capital formation, savings, etc.

The Reserve Bank of India (RBI) is responsible for publishing data on the monetary, banking and financial sectors and the balance of payments. The RBI publishes its *Weekly Statistical Supplement,* which provides wide ranging data on money supply, reserve money, trade in Government securities, business of scheduled commercial banks, etc.

To adhere to the international norms of data dissemination, India publishes data on:

Gross domestic product (GDP) estimates at current and constant prices

Monthly index on industrial production

Price indices

Employment, unemployment and wage rates.

1.5 INFLATION

Inflation is the rate of rise in money prices of goods and services. Goods and services do not refer to capital market securities or financial assets but to the tangible and intangible commodities that economic agents produce and sell to one another. While money price refers to the amount of money in local currency per commodity unit, inflation does not refer to the movement of the relative prices in barter system but to the movement of absolute prices.

As is the case with measuring change in GDP, measuring inflation rate also have issues of quality of goods and change in product design. Inflation is measured with help of price index. In price indexes, commodities are weighted by their importance in consumer budgets, depending upon the area. Indexes with weights differing in concept or in base data will give different results. While measurement of inflation is inevitably imprecise, the standard price index numbers capture the major changes.

Cost of living index is one measurement of movement of prices of goods and services, which is normally used in wage settlements to provide protection to salaried employees.

Rate of inflation, in India, is measured by the Wholesale Price Index (WPI) or the Consumer Price Index (CPI). There are three CPIs in India - the CPI for Industrial Workers (CPI-IW), the CPI for Urban Non-Manual Employees and the CPI for Agricultural Labourers. In India, the Ministry of Industry makes available the WPI, while the Ministry of Labour brings out the CPI. The WPI represents the weighted average of the wholesale prices of a 'basket' of over 400 manufactured goods.

1.5.1 Effect of inflation on asset prices

Assets such as bonds, debentures, bank accounts and fixed deposit accounts fall in real purchasing power, or value, during inflationary periods. While such investments earn interest, which provides some protection against the effects of inflation, many investors in an inflationary environment find it hard to protect the real value of their capital, particularly when taxation of the interest is taken into account.

In contrast, the value of other investments, such as shares and property, broadly track or do better than inflation over the medium to longer term. Table I shows the impact of inflation on the real value of investments over time.

TABLE I : IMPACT OF INFLATION

INCOME AND CAPITAL GAINS (AFTER 12 MONTHS)

Tax rate	Return on investment	Post-tax return	Real return at inflation rate of		
			2%	5%	10%
0.00%	5.00%	5.00%	2.90%	-0.25%	-5.50%
	10.00%	10.00%	7.80%	4.50%	-1.00%
	15.00%	15.00%	12.70%	9.25%	3.50%
30.00%	5.00%	3.50%	1.43%	-1.68%	
	10.00%	7.00%	4.86%	1.65%	
	15.00%	10.50%	8.29%	4.97%	

Tax rate	Return on investment	Post-tax return	Real return at inflation rate of		
42.00%	6.00%	3.48%	1.41%	1.69%	
	8.00%	4.64%	2.55%	-0.59%	
	10.00%	5.80%	3.68%	0.51%	

Thus, tax and inflation have a significant impact on effective return, irrespective of whether the investment is held for income or capital gains.

1.6 ROLE OF MONEY IN INFLATION

Money is a unit of account standard & measure of value and store of value. It is a commonly accepted medium of exchange and a unit of account for calculation. We store value by way of money, as we cannot store in all the commodities which we are going to consume in future because we are exposed to price risk of variation in prices of these commodities and services in future.

Inflation is said to be a state of affairs when "too much money is chasing too few goods". In old times inflation raised its head when state power i.e. government wanted to consume more than what it had with it. Presence of government in the market squeezes out other private citizens specially when the economy is operating at near full capacity. Government, to finance its consumption, can impose higher taxes but there is a limit to which the taxes could be increased and actually collected. The other option is to borrow, but there also has to be a reasonable limit as it entails obligations to pay the interest as well as the principal at the end of the loan period. Government finds it much simpler to print money to cover up the gap in revenue and expenditure.

However, production does not increase in the same proportion as the increase in government expenditure in a short time frame. It contributes less to GDP and more to inflation. The price rise puts pressures on private citizens, especially those dependent on fixed rupee income (the salaried class without inflation protection) and financial assets (the pensioners). Easy monetary and credit policy may act as a source of excess demand. People tend to borrow more when the interest rates are low.

It is possible to have inflation and excess supply, as was the case in world economy throughout much of the 1970's. This was a context of stagnation in output and inflation in price, which was called 'stagflation'. Any modern economy seems to have an inflationary bias. Inflation rates rise more easily and more quickly in response to excess demand and they tend to fall less in response to excess supply.

1.7 MONEY MULTIPLIER MODEL

All market economies experience cycles or swings in business activity when unemployment increases during depressions or when excessive demand leads to inflation. Multiplier model is a theory used to explain how output is determined in the short run. The name multiplier comes from the finding that each rupee change in certain expenditures (such as investments) leads to more than a rupee change (in short, a multiplier effect) in the GDP. The multiplier model explains how shocks to investments, foreign trade and government tax and expenditure policies can affect output and employment in an economy with unutilized resources.

The Keynesian multiplier model shows that an increase in investment will increase GDP by an amplified amount by an amount greater than itself. Suppose investment increases by Rs. 50 crores and this causes an increase of Rs. 100 crores in the GDP, the multiplier is 2. The size of the multiplier (k) depends upon the marginal propensity to consume (MPC) and the marginal propensity to save (MPS). K= $\frac{1}{1-mpc} = \frac{1}{mps}(mps)$. If mpc is 80%, mps will be 20% and k will be 5.

1.8 ECONOMIC OR BUSINESS CYCLES

There is one certainty in economics: the status quo will not remain, and the more that people expect it to do so, the more likely it is to change. A trough in the share market is a classic example. The fluctuations in economic activity between boom times and bad times are known as business cycles (also called economic cycles or trade cycles, because they are cycles of economic activity). The term cycle also implies that the fluctuations are fairly regular.

One difficulty in the study of cycles is that there are cycles within cycles. Some shorter cycles are more commonly referred to as technical corrections when a market 'is overbought' or 'oversold'. Longer economic cycles such as the 50 year Kondratieff cycle are still somewhat of a question mark. The cycle that most economists talk about is usually thought of as occurring over four years from peak to peak or two years from peak to trough. The amplitude of cycles is usually consistent around what economists call a trend line, with declines from peak to trough of around 25% to 35%.

1.8.1 Stages of business cycles

It is generally accepted that there are four stages to a business cycle:

1. Peak to contraction
2. Contraction to trough
3. Trough to expansion
4. Expansion to peak.

Understanding these cycles, and their impact on investment strategy, will help you keep your client's portfolio up to date.

Underlying the trends, the following fluctuations in economic variables are identifiable:

Peak to contraction: GDP falling, industrial production falling, capacity utilisation falling, labour productivity increasing, unit labour costs decreasing.

Contraction to trough: WPI falling, retail sales declining, unemployment rising, housing starting to fall, home lending falling, consumer sentiment decreasing.

Trough to expansion: WPI falling, resulting in consumer real income increasing, interest rates falling, consumer sentiment increasing, consumer demand increasing (car sales increasing, consumer credit increasing, retail sales increasing, housing starting to increase).

Expansion to peak: GDP increasing, resulting in industrial production increasing, capacity utilisation increasing, unit labour costs increasing, WPI increasing owing to excess demand, production at maximum, labour market tightening, growing expectations that boom cannot last.

Economic fluctuations refer to increases or decreases in the magnitude of economic variables such as national income, national output, employment, national consumption, investment, saving, and general levels of prices and wages.

As all the economic variables are interdependent, a change in one affects the others. Thus, economic fluctuations involve a series of changes in the economy, which affect the total level of aggregate demand.

While we use the term cycle in the context of economic fluctuations, it should be understood that these fluctuations do not follow an exact, regular or repetitive pattern. Furthermore, economic growth does not proceed in a regular or steady pattern.

However, there are periods in an economy's growth that are recognisable as belonging to identifiable stages of business cycle activity.

Periods of growth, decline and stagnation in an economy

Expansion

Expansion or upswing is usually marked by the following economic characteristics:

increasing investment spending

increasing consumer spending

increasing price levels

increasing money wages

rising employment

increasing national income.

Peak or boom

A peak or boom is usually marked by:

economic indicators reaching a maximum level before declining a high level of employment faltering of business optimism a slackening in the rate of investment activity higher costs for business firms the occurrence or indications of unfavourable trends in international trade.

While a peak or boom might be a period of inflation, it is possible for a peak in economic activity to occur without inflation. Inflation occurs when demand in the short term cannot be satisfied by supply, so, that excess purchasing power is used to bid up the prices of goods in fixed supply. While supply might not be expanding as fast as demand in some industries or sectors of the economy during the expansion or peak phases, general inflation occurs only when this condition is evident in the majority of the sectors of the economy.

As a consequence of high costs for export industries and their need to increase prices to maintain profit levels, there might be a decline in the volume of export sales. The excess spending during the expansion stage might be channelled into increased imports, with the consequence of an unfavourable balance of trade.

The level of imports and exports is closely associated with the general climate of economic activity in an economy. The fluctuation of either export or import payments plays an important role in the business cycle of an economy that is greatly dependent on its export sector for income, and whose bank liquidity is greatly influenced by the balance of payments.

Contraction

Contraction or downswing is usually marked by:

a decline in the level of national income

a decrease in aggregate spending

a decrease in the level of spending

decreasing prices

decreasing wages.

Trough

Trough or depression is usually marked by:

- a low level of investment
- reduced output levels in secondary industry, although outputs in primary industry might increase
- excess capacity in the majority of industries
- a high level of liquidity preference

- a lack of investment opportunities because profit expectations are low or non existent
- (sometimes) a failing birthrate
- high level of unemployment

This period of economic stagnation might last for months or even years if the level of spending is very low and fails to increase. Consequently, we see government expansionary policies during these periods.

You need to distinguish between a depression, which is a time of low economic activity, *i.e.* an economic trough, and a slowing of the rate of economic expansion, generally - referred to as a recession.

Note: Share prices, first to fall in a downturn, are first to recover in an upturn. Real estate which is last to fall, is the last to recover. Compiled by the *Evening Standard,* London, from a study of trade cycles over a period of 150 years.

1.9 INTERNATIONAL TRADE AND BALANCE OF PAYMENT

Balance of trade is the difference between the exports and imports of a nation for a given period. It is a trade deficit when imports are more than exports and trade surplus when imports are less than exports. A country with a trade deficit, has to either borrow internationally or sell its stock of equity. Developing nations typically experience deficit, as they have to import capital machinery and equipment that increase productivity, in turn, help them attain rapid growth through industrialization. If the deficit is on account of large import bill of consumption goods, which are meant for direct consumption by the consumers, payment of interest and repayment of the principal amount becomes rather difficult.

Balance of payments is balance of trade plus trade in services, invisible flows and net investment income from rest of the world. In capital account, we have on credit side investments from abroad by way of portfolio investments as well as direct investment, while on debit side, we have our investments in rest of the world by way of portfolio and direct investment.

2. ECONOMIC POLICIES AND TOOLS

2.1 MONETARY POLICY

2.1.1 The objective of the monetary policy is to foster monetary and financial conditions that will help to promote growth in output on a sustainable basis and control inflation. The essence of monetary policy is to control the growth in money supply in such a manner, which stimulates bank lending for consumer and business spending, and at the same time, controls inflation. Monetary policy impacts the level of employment, the volume of output and its growth and the rate of inflation and serves as a major tool for influencing economic activity. In India, RBI is responsible for framing and implementing the Monetary Policy, independent of Government interference. As announced in the Union Budget for 2015-16, decision making by an empowered monetary policy committee (MPC) would require amendment of the Reserve Bank of India Act, which the Government intends to do in near future.

2.1.2 Policy Framework

The framework aims at setting the policy (repo) rate based on a forward looking assessment of inflation, growth and other macroeconomic risks, and modulation of liquidity conditions to anchor money market rates at or around the repo rate. (Repos are collateralised short term borrowings and lendings from/to commercial banks by RBI). Changes in Repo rate (presently at 6.75%) transmit through the money market to alter the interest rates in the financial system, which in turn influence aggregate demand - a key determinant of inflation and growth.

Once the repo rate is announced, the operating framework on a day to day basis is implemented through proactive liquidity management, which aims at anchoring the operating target – the weighted average call rate (WACR) – around the repo rate.

2.1.3 Instruments of Monetary policy

There are several direct and indirect instruments that are used in the implementation of monetary policy, like:

- **Cash Reserve Ratio (CRR):** The share of net demand and time liabilities (deposits) that banks must maintain as cash balance with the Reserve Bank. The cash reserve ratio is currently at 4.00%. RBI can change it, if it wants to change the state of money supply quickly.
- **Statutory Liquidity Ratio (SLR):** The share of net demand and time liabilities (deposits) that banks must maintain in safe and liquid assets, such as, government securities, cash and gold. Changes in SLR often influence the availability of resources in the banking system for lending to the private sector. Currently, SLR is at 21.5%
- **Refinance facilities:** Sector-specific refinance facilities aim at achieving sector specific objectives through provision of liquidity at a cost linked to the policy repo rate. The Reserve Bank has, however, been progressively de-emphasising sector specific policies as they interfere with the transmission mechanism.
- **Liquidity Adjustment Facility (LAF):** Consists of overnight and term repo/reverse repo auctions. Progressively, the Reserve Bank has increased the proportion of liquidity injected in the LAF through term-repos.
- **Term Repos:** Since October 2013, the Reserve Bank has introduced term repos (of different tenors, such as, 7/14/28 days), to inject liquidity over a period that is longer than overnight. The aim of term repo is to help develop inter-bank money market, which in turn can set market based benchmarks for pricing of loans and deposits, and through that improve transmission of monetary policy.
- **Marginal Standing Facility (MSF):** A facility under which scheduled commercial banks can borrow additional amount of overnight money from the Reserve Bank by dipping into their SLR portfolio up to a limit (currently two per cent of their net demand and time liabilities deposits) at a penal rate of interest (currently 100 basis points above the repo rate). This provides a safety valve against unanticipated liquidity shocks to the banking system. MSF rate and reverse repo rate determine the corridor for the daily movement in short term money market interest rates.

- **Open Market Operations (OMOs):** These include both, outright purchase/sale of government securities (for injection/absorption of liquidity)
- **Bank Rate:** It is the rate at which the Reserve Bank is ready to buy or rediscount bills of exchange or other commercial papers. This rate has been aligned to the MSF rate and, therefore, changes automatically as and when the MSF rate changes alongside policy repo rate changes.
- **Market Stabilisation Scheme (MSS):** This instrument for monetary management was introduced in 2004. Surplus liquidity of a more enduring nature arising from large capital inflows is absorbed through sale of short-dated government securities and treasury bills. The mobilised cash is held in a separate government account with the Reserve Bank. The instrument thus has features of both, SLR and CRR.

2.1.4 Interest rate regulation

RBI has historically regulated the financial markets by limiting interest rates. RBI used to decide interest rate for various maturities, types of accounts etc. Currently, RBI has liberalized the rate fixing on deposits though some of the controls on tenure remain. In other words, banks are free to decide their deposit rate structure as well as lending rates. Even the Government of India borrows at market-determined rates by auctioning its papers.

2.1.5 Using monetary policy

RBI controls money supply by various tools mentioned earlier. Let us assume that the RBI is concerned about inflation and has decided to slow down the economy. It may start the process by aiming to reduce bank reserves by selling securities in the open market. Each rupee reduction in the bank liquidity produces a multiple contraction in current deposits, thereby reducing money supply, which in turn will raise interest rate and tighten credit conditions. In addition, the amount of credit (loans and borrowings) available also will decline. This, in turn, will reduce long-term investments. Spending, as well as consumer credit related consumptions. Thus, businesses will scale down their investment plans. High interest rate, depending upon linkage with external world, will raise exchange rate, depressing net exports. Finally, the pressures of tight money, by reducing aggregate demand, will reduce income, output and price level. As output and employment falls below the levels that would otherwise occur, prices tend to rise less rapidly or even tend to fall.

2.2 FISCAL POLICY

Government raises its resources through taxation, borrowing and other revenue sources. The Governments have to incur expenditure at union, state and local levels in order to achieve and sustain economic growth.

Fiscal policy refers to the use of government spending and taxing power, to achieve macroeconomic objectives. Government expenditure influences both private investment and private consumption.

Taxation reduces private consumption besides influencing investment and potential output. Fiscal policy affects total spending and thereby influences real GDP and inflation.

Trade policies, exchange rate policy, monetary and fiscal policies make an attempt to keep imports in line with exports and stabilize foreign exchange rate. In post reform era since July 1991, Government of India has initiated a number of measures to open up the foreign trade sector and has announced massive import liberalization measures. The changes in economic policies have affected the direction, structure and magnitude of foreign trade. India's foreign trade has increased significantly and has undergone structural changes in the post reform period.

Reflection

How could an independent RBI affect the Government's monetary policy? You need to be aware of the Government's monetary policy, since a tight monetary policy usually results in higher interest rates. Conversely, a relaxed stance might result in either a fall in interest rates or, in the worst case, no change.

Fiscal policy affects tax rates and thresholds, and also welfare benefits. Investment advisers need to be aware of the tax implications for their clients, and recommend investments accordingly.

Much international concentration in the early to mid-1980s centred on monetary policy to limit inflation. The emphasis then shifted to fiscal policy, where it was aimed at correcting the balance of payments problem. The future path of monetary and fiscal policies will be dependent upon the outlook for both the domestic and world economies.

The two policies (monetary and fiscal) never operate in isolation. Financial, deregulation, both internationally and in India, has greatly complicated the interpretation of the fundamentals. Comprehensive inflation and interest rate data are available on the following three websites:

http://www.rbi.org.in

http://eaindustry.nic.in

http://mospi.nic.in

Use these to check the latest figures and for comparative analysis.

Apart from the Monetary and the Fiscal policies, mentioned above, the policies relating to the wages and Exchange Rate Policy also have important influence on the economy.

In economics, wages are regarded as another measure of inflation, being the price of labour. Therefore, low inflation implies a low rate of increase in wages. Thus any Government policy formulated to control inflation cannot ignore wages. In India, a series of Pay Commissions give recommendations based on which the levels of pay in the government sector are decided. Increase in pay, in both the government and non-government sector, is by way of a dearness allowance (DA), which is linked to the rise in CPI. Trade and labour unions are recognised under Indian law and they too have a say in the fixing of wage levels. Increasingly, the bargaining strength of unions is diminishing.

The value of the Indian rupee against the USA Dollar, is often viewed as an indicator of the economy's strength. When the world sees the economic situation in India as strong and productive, the value of the Indian Rupee increases. If it sees India as economically weaker, the value of the Rupee drops. These swings in value have major implications for:

Government debt repayments. The lower the value of the Indian Rupee, the more Rupees, both the government and businesses have to pay in order to meet debt denominated in another currency.

Import and export balances. The lower the value of the Indian Rupee, the more- attractive Indian goods and services become to the rest of the world — they are 'cheaper'.

The float of the Indian Rupee is not a 'clean' float, but a 'managed' float, *i.e.* it is not only the market forces that determine the Rupee value, but also the active intervention of the Reserve Bank of India (RBI).The RBI has various tools at its disposal to contain sharp volatilities and speculative activities in the currency market. RBI uses both direct and indirect measures to intervene in the forex market:

Direct intervention refers to direct purchases and sale of dollars in the open market. This is mainly intended to correct the sharp demand supply mis-matches in dollars

Indirect intervention strategy includes various measures such as quantitative, restrictions on open positions, changes in the reserve requirements on various categories of non-resident Indian (NRI) deposits, reducing the period within which foreign exchange earners are compelled to bring the foreign currency back into India, and monetary policy measures such as raising short-term interest rates by changing the bank rate and repo rates.

The RBI is also in certain cases able to cool the market by verbal interaction with the participants, whereby it enquires about the positions with RBI and indicates its willingness to intervene directly in the forex market.

SELF ASSESSMENT EXERCISE 1

1. The overall economy is an important consideration when making investment decisions. Briefly explain how the following affect the economy:

Supply versus demand

The value of money

Global economic forces

International influences

....
....
....
....
....
....
....
....
....
....
....

2. Why do you need to be familiar with RBI's and Government's monetary and fiscal policies?

....
....
....
....
....
....
....
....
....
....
....
....
....
....
....
....
....
....
....

3. Which policy (fiscal or monetary), do you believe, will more effectively control domestic inflation and improve India's international competitiveness?

....
....
....
....
....
....
....
....
....
....
....

3. ECONOMIC INDICATORS AND VALUE OF INVESTMENT

Investment adviser has to take into account the economic cycle while considering various alternate investment decisions. He also needs to adjust existing investment with expected movements in economic cycles, as they impact the investment value. To determine the economy's position in the economic cycle, a variety of partial economic indicators are followed. These can be grouped into leading, coincidental and lagging indicators. Example of each are as follows:

Leading Indicators

Leading indicators lead the business cycle by about six months. They include:

Consumer sentiment

Consumer purchases around festivals

Movements in realty sector

Automobile sales

Sales of residential housing

Coincident indicators

Coincidental indicators are concurrent with the business cycle. They include:

Job advertisements

Credit off-take by private sector

Retail trade

New motor vehicle registrations

Credit provided to the private sector

Lagging Indicators

Lagging indicators trail the business cycle by about six months. They include:

Unemployment rate

Employment growth

Job advertisements are a leading indicator for the employment report. However, the employment report lags the business cycle (*i.e.* GDP). These partial indicators, along with broader measures, such as the national accounts, the consumer price index (inflation), the balance of payments and government policy statements, provide information about the current state of the economy and likely directions. As a result, their release is a dominant feature in financial market trading and can influence the value of investment.

Reflection

For each of the following indicators, consider what type they are: WPI, balance of payments, government policy statements.

Example — influence of broader indicators

The release of inflation data, for example, will have a direct bearing on debt and equity instrument values: a high inflation rate might imply monetary policy will be tightened, which will produce a softening in bond prices (higher interest rates), with the prospect of higher interest rates negatively impacting on company borrowings, and therefore company balance sheets, producing a fall in share prices.

Release of the data, which provide details about economic growth, might also impact on investment values: stronger than expected growth implies greater prospects for company balance sheets, thereby making share prices firmer, but might also imply rising inflationary pressures, which will result in weaker bond prices. However if the economy has underutilised capacity, inflationary pressures will not be immediately seen.

Example — influence of partial indicators

While the broad economic indicators will play a larger role in moving investment values, partial indicators will also impact. For example, strong retail sales imply that economic activity is strong, which will positively impact on balance sheets, which in turn might provoke a rally in share prices. But bond prices could well be weakened by such news, which could raise the likelihood of the Government tightening monetary policy.

Consequently, it is important for the investment adviser not only to take into account the economic climate when making investment decisions, but also to be aware that investment values can be positively or adversely affected by the trends indicated by the economic indicators.

4. MEDIA AND INFORMATION SOURCES

4.1 THE FINANCIAL PRESS

Today, investment advisors are flooded with data on streaming basis from Internet, fax, television, SMSs and radio. Fortunately, data from press still has limited frequency. However, differences in opinion and objectives also have widened. One needs to be cautious with regard to a number of matters while relying on reports in the press for:

- Correctness of factual information
- Sources of information
- Relevance of information
- Degree of opinion
- Frequency of information
- Usefulness of information
- Reliability of interpretation, known biases and unnecessary emphasis

Markets are often driven, not by known facts but by perceptions of the future in light of past events. These perceptions are guided in a complex manner by publicly available information and opinion. Media provides a cheaper source of information.

4.2 RESEARCH PAPERS

Advisors do study more detailed research and information from wider sources. They may include trade journals, fund managers' commentary and reports from independent research companies.

4.3 COMPANY REPORTS

Fundamental analysts evaluate company shares based on an examination of the company's financial statements as presented in the annual report. A summary of a listed company's financial performance is compulsorily printed in the business press. Detailed Annual Reports of all important listed companies are available on the internet.

4.4 OFFICIAL SOURCES OF DATA AS PER ECONOMIC CALENDAR

Analysts follow a calendar of the major official data and economic release during the year. The various releases relate to inflation measurement (CPI) as well as WPI. Information on production comes by way of Index of Industrial production. Every week RBI releases data on bank deposits, credits, foreign exchange reserves etc.

The calendar provides broad details of the timing and interpretation of the official data releases most watched by financial markets. Unlike some of the developed markets, the timing of data releases in India is unpredictable. There is no fixed scheduling for most releases.

The official statistics are released by various agencies such as CSO, NSSO, RBI, the Ministry of Finance and the Ministry of Industry. The information can be classified under four headings:

1. Prices and wages growth
2. Economic growth
3. External sector
4. Monetary growth.

Considerable information is also available from other official and private sector agencies. Much from the latter source is interpretive or of more limited market interest. Of some value are the various surveys of economic conditions and 'composite' indices of leading indicators published by private agencies.

SELF ASSESSMENT EXERCISE 2

1. You acquire a large quantum of information through scanning the media. Why should this information be treated with caution?

   ....
   ....
   ....
   ....
   ....
   ....

2. What are some useful sources of detailed research available?

   ....
   ....
   ....
   ....
   ....
   ....

REVIEW

QUESTIONS

The purpose of these review questions is to give you experience in applying your knowledge. After you have finished a review question, check your answer with the suggested answer provided. If you have given the wrong answer or if your understanding is still unclear, refer to the relevant parts of this topic.

1. What are the objectives of economic policy?
2. Explain how discount rate policy works?
3. Give examples of leading indicators.

ANSWERS

1. The main objectives of economic policy are;
    (*a*) To promote growth while controlling inflation
    (*b*) To achieve full employment
    (*c*) To achieve steady growth in national income as measured by output of goods and services
    (*d*) To improve balance of payment by promoting foreign trade (imports and exports) and investments.
    (*e*) Reduce regional imbalances
    (*f*) Reduce economic imbalances in society
2. When commercial banks are short of their own reserves as they are not able to raise short term resources, they approach the RBI as a lender of last resort. Obviously, rate at which RBI is willing to lend to commercial bank would act as floor rate for lending by the banks. It may also use repo rate to signal to market desired short end market rate. Discount rates are not changed frequently, thus, they provide medium term signal to the market.
3. Examples of leading indicators are:
    - Consumer sentiment

- Consumer purchases around festivals
- Movement in realty sector

IN SUMMARY

Before analyzing investments, it is essential to understand the environment within which these investments operate. We began this topic by understanding key economic concepts. We saw how the financial system facilitates the interaction of various sectors of economy. We noted important roles of government and RBI and how they influence the economy through their monetary, fiscal and expenditure policies beside understanding various tools they use to crank up or cool down economy.

Investors and advisers need to analyse the prevailing economic situations, formulate economic conclusions and then allocate an appropriate degree of possibility to various scenarios. Investments portfolios need to be designed with appropriate features to accommodate these situations.

There is more information available from the press, journals and research papers and various publications.

SUGGESTED ANSWERS TO SELF-ASSESSMENT EXERCISE 1

1. Discussion of:

   Market forces - the balance between supply and demand determines price variations

   Inflation and how it erodes the value of money over time

   India's own features and how they play a part in economics, e.g. land mass, population, natural resources, geographic location, environment etc.

   How overseas influences affect the Indian economy

2. Your response should include reference to the way such policies affect:

   Interest rates and, therefore, return on investment, credit off take, etc.

Tax rates and thresholds

Social benefit policy

Inflation

Employment, expenditure etc.

3. There is no single correct answer to this question. Answers should discuss why and how fiscal and monetary policy are applied, and what effect they have.

SELF-ASSESSMENT EXERCISE 2

1. You need to be certain of the value of the information - accuracy, source, relevancy, bias, currency and usefulness. It is better to combine the information, one obtains from any source, with more detailed research, so one can judge the usefulness/validity of the information. Generally, media information is a useful starting point for research or a further confirmation of other sources.
2. Answer should, at least, include

   Research papers

   Company reports

   Official statistics from Government sources, RBI and other sources

   Secondary sources of research department

CHECKLIST

Below is a checklist of main points, covered by this topic. Use this checklist to test your learning.

The government is a source, user and intermediary for funds

The government exercises economic policy through its fiscal policy (budgeting, expenditure, taxation, etc.). RBI uses its monetary policy to control of money supply and influence interest rates.

Economic fluctuations are observed to follow cycles

The economic/business cycles do not follow an exact and regular pattern and there are cycles within cycles

The value of the Indian Rupee against other world currencies and, more importantly, with major trading partners is an indication of the economy's strength

Economic growth is a rise in the level of goods and services without the influence of inflation. It is measured as a function of GDP

There are four identifiable stages of a business cycle: peak to contraction, contraction to trough, trough to expansion, expansion to peak

Fiscal and monetary policies affect investments, e.g. fiscal policy affects tax rates and welfare benefits, while monetary policy influences interest rates

Investment values are affected by the economic climate and you must take this into account when making investment decisions

Poor investment performance can be the result of wrong timing or macroeconomic factors rather than the selection of the poor investment products

Leading indicators lead the business cycle by about six months

Coincident indicators are concurrent with the business cycle

Lagging indicators trail the business cycle by about six months

Economic indicators, coupled with broader measures, such as the national account, CPI, balance of payments, etc., provide information about the current state of the economy.

2 CHAPTER

Overview of Indian Financial Markets

ABOUT THIS TOPIC

This chapter gives an overview of the functions and operations of financial markets

It focuses on:

- *Financial systems*
- *Types of financial markets and instruments*
- *Features of financial and securities markets*
- *Flow of funds through the financial system*

Topic Objectives

At the end of this chapter, you should be able to:

- *Define the basic terms like "money", "financial assets" and "securities" in the context of financial markets*
- *Differentiate clearly between debt and equity*
- *Describe the functions of the financial system in the modern economy*
- *List and briefly describe the major markets that form the Indian financial system*
- *Distinguish between the primary and secondary markets*

- *Identify the characteristics of securities, considered by Investors*
- *Explain the impact of globalisation of financial markets*
- *Differentiate between intermediation and disintermediation*

1. BASIC CONCEPTS

A financial system is a web of relationships between various markets and institutions that facilitate the flow of funds between the various sectors of the economy. The movement of funds may take many forms, including money/cash, financial assets and securities (like debt, quasi-debt and equity).

There are people(suppliers) with surplus funds and there are those with a deficit (seekers). A financial system or financial sector functions as an intermediary and facilitates the flow of funds from the areas of surplus to the areas of deficit. A Financial System is a composition of various institutions, markets, regulations and laws, practices, Money managers, analysts, transactions and claims and liabilities. Financial System consists of financial markets, financial intermediaries and financial instruments or financial products

Let us understand these basic concepts, which help us traverse the financial system's web with considerable ease.

1.1 MONEY

In modern times, it is difficult to imagine a world without the use of money. Money is the life-blood of the present day world and all our economic activities are carried out through the use of money. For carrying on business we need resources which are pooled in terms of money. It is primarily required for obtaining physical resources, carrying out productive activities and business operations that affect sales and pay compensation to suppliers of resources.

Money is anything that is accepted as a store of value, which can be exchanged for payment of debts and purchase of goods or services. Money is a medium of exchange and acts as a common denominator or unit for valuing goods and services for the purpose of exchange. Many articles have acted as money; for example, before the origin of metal and metallic coins, ordinary articles such as seashells were used. Articles got acceptance as unit of money or measurement on account of being durable, easily storable and portable. It is a matter of confidence that a paper currency represents something of value. Confidence is vital, as can be seen in foreign currency market, where two paper currencies strive to find equilibrium like price *i.e.* exchange rates.

Legal tender (*i.e.* notes and coins) is still commonly used form of money. They are getting replaced by plastic money (debit card, smart card and credit card) and electronic money by way of electronic funds transfer. These are all "liquid assets", and are so called as they can be quickly converted into performing the function of cash. (In addition to coins and currency notes, demand deposits are also considered as constituting Money). The concept of money also includes other forms of the "financial assets".

In recent time, concepts of virtual money and e-wallet have also gained ground. Virtual money or currency is unregulated digital money, issued and controlled by its developers. It is used and accepted only by members of a specific virtual group. It can be used as a means of payment and can be transferred, stored or traded electronically. Virtual currency does not have legal tender status in any country. Bit coin is an example of such digital currency.

An e-wallet refers to an electronic system that allows an electronic transaction. This can be purchasing items on-line or using a mobile phone to purchase an item at a store. There is an increasing use of e-wallets not only for basic financial transactions but for authenticating the holder's credentials, like verifying the age of the buyer by the seller, while purchasing alcohol. Bank account of the holder of e-wallet can also be linked to it. It can also contain the holder's driving license, and other ID documents. It is possible that the mobile phone e-wallets will replace physical wallets. These have already gained popularity in some of the developed countries.

1.2 FINANCIAL ASSETS

A financial asset is a document or certificate of title which represents the underlying physical asset. Example of financial assets (with their respective obligations) includes: Fixed Deposit Receipt (liability of bank to pay after the fixed period at contracted rate of interest), RBI Relief Bond (Liability of Indian Government towards the holder) and shares (Company shareholders' funds).

Currency (notes and coins) is the most liquid form of financial asset, while investment in a long-term loan to a company is comparatively illiquid. Liquidity refers to ease of conversion to cash with little or no cost (at fair valuation of the assets) and minimal delay.

1.3 SECURITIES

Securities are documentary evidence (including electronic one) of ownership of financial assets. In India securities are defined by Securities Contracts (Regulation) Act, 1956 ("the SCRA"). As per SCRA, securities include:

1. Shares, scrip's, stocks, bonds, debentures, debenture stock or other marketable securities of a like nature in or of any incorporated company or other body corporate;
2. Derivatives;
3. Units or any other instrument issued by any collective investment scheme to the investors in such schemes;
4. Government securities;
5. Such other instruments as may be declared by the Central Government to be securities; and
6. Rights or interest in securities.

Thus, we see that the distinguishing feature of securities is that they are tradable or exchangeable or salable in the market place.

Major classification for securities is nature of reward for that investment. It can be fixed like debt or variable like equity.

Debt: It is the obligation by a borrower (person or company or legal person) to pay a specific amount of money to lender (another party). This obligation may include manner of repayment, term of loan, interest rate, and underlying security (or collateral guarantee). It may also provide for terms of takeover of security or invocation of collateral in the event of default by borrower and prepayment options.

Equity: Equity stands for ownership. In the context of financial markets, the term equity' is used interchangeably with shares. When shares are purchased, you acquire part ownership in the issuer of the shares (such as company). This means you share in its profits (through the receipt of dividends) and the rise or fall in the market price of its shares.

1.4 DEBT SECURITIES

The debt market brings together households and institutions with surplus funds and those with shortage of funds.

Debt is an obligation of one party to pay a specific amount of money to another party. A simple case of debt involves the lender advancing a sum of money (the principal) to the borrower for a specified period of time. In returns the borrower pays the lender an agreed rate of interest (the charge for the borrowing) at specified intervals, and at the end of the agreed period, repays the original sum borrowed.

Both Governments and companies issue debt securities:

Government debt securities : Governments are major issuers of debt securities; by issue of bonds they finance the gap between expenditure and income. The Government of India borrows money by issuing both short term debt securities (Treasury bills) and long-term debt securities (as those for period one year and more). These bonds are held by banks, financial institutions, household investors and also corporates.

Corporate debt securities : Companies also borrow to meet their funding requirements. They issue short term debt securities in the form of bills of exchange, Commercial papers and Certificate of deposits, and are increasingly also issuing long term paper by way of debentures.

1.5 EQUITY

Investing in companies *via* shares gives investors opportunity to receive a capital gain or loss. If company prospers, it will grow large and the value of its shares will rise. The investor will be able to sell the share at higher price than cost price and make profit by way of capital gain. Company may also pay surplus of profits by way of dividend to holders of shares. In case of poor performance companies may skip dividend payment and investor may also face prospect of booking loss in case the share price falls below the cost price.

Limited liability means the liability of shareholders is limited to the issue price of shares (generally the face value). If the company was wound up, shareholder who held partly paid shares would have to pay any unpaid portion of those shares. Limited liability has made investment in equities considerably attractive compared to partnership where liabilities are unlimited.

SELF-ASSESSMENT EXERCISE 1

Complete the table below by highlighting the basic differences between the debt and equity.

Feature	*Debt*	*Equity*
Capital/Principal		
Repayment		
Return		
Participation in profit of venture		

1.6 RISK

"Risk" stands in financial markets for the possibility of potential loss arising from uncertainty. Several of risks in financial markets are given below :

Market risk

The risk of adverse movement in the price of securities due to the change in the market dynamics. *E.g.* an increase in the interest rates in the market will result in prices of existing bonds and debentures (fixed income securities) coming down.

Credit risk

The risk that a counter party will default its obligations in whole or in part. *E.g.* a company , which has issued debentures, may not pay the interest and/or the redemption amount partially or totally.

Liquidity risk

The risk that a market may lack sufficient depth to facilitate efficient and inexpensive entry into and exit from the market.

Funding risk

The risk that a participant may be unable to meet its payment obligation when they are due.

Operational risk

The risk that inadequate internal controls or failures of risk management systems through human or technological error may lead to unexpected losses.

Legal risk

The risk that a counter party's performance obligations may not be legally enforceable or legal process to ensure enforcement takes too long time

Reputation risk

The risk that a company's reputation may become tarnished through imprudent or ill-considered practices.

1.7 PRIMARY AND SECONDARY MARKETS

Market is a place where buyers and sellers of goods, services, assets and instruments come together and interact. In emerging environment such places are more likely to be electronic rather than physical to ensure gathering of larger sets of buyers and sellers.

Primary market is where corporate and government entities can raise capital and where the first transactions with the new issued securities are performed. If a company's share is traded in the primary market for the first time this is referred to as an initial public offering (IPO).

Investment banks play an important role in the primary market:

- Usually handle issues in the primary market;
- Among other things, act as underwriter of a new issue, guaranteeing the proceeds to the issuer.

Secondary market - where previously issued securities are traded among investors. Generally, individual investors do not have access to secondary markets. They use security brokers to act as intermediaries for them. The broker delivers orders received from investors in securities to a market place, where these orders are executed. Finally, clearing and settlement processes ensure that both sides to these transactions honor their commitment. Types of brokers:

- Discount broker, who executes only trades in the secondary market;
- Full service broker, who provides a wide range of additional services to clients (ex., advice to buy or sell);
- Online broker is a brokerage firm that allows investors to execute trades electronically using Internet.

2. THE FINANCIAL SYSTEM

2.1 ECONOMY AND FINANCIAL SYSTEM

Economy is made up of a number of sectors, owning, producing or purchasing resources, goods and services flowing throughout the system. These sectors include the following:

- Household sector - consumers of goods and services
- Business sector - producers of goods and services
- Government sector - includes central, State, local Government as well as public sector institutions
- Financial sector - includes all banks and financial intermediaries
- Rest of world sector - where imports and exports take place.

Every modern economic system has a financial system ensuring that people can exchange their resources (*e.g.* labour, goods or services) for output of other sectors. The financial system facilitates this exchange process. The flow of resources, goods and service throughout the economy is matched with a flow of payments to the owners of resources.

Thus, householders supply labour to business in return of wages or salaries. With these payments, they are able to buy goods and services manufactured by business sector or Government sector. Business uses this sales revenue to buy more raw materials to continue to produce goods and services. Government also gets its share of revenue by taxing these transactions by way of taxes. Householders do not spend all their income on goods and services and it denotes the savings component. Business on the other hand requires extra short-term sources of funds to finance the production or to grow at the desired rate. The financial system, with the help of intermediaries, stands between savers and borrowers and channels funds from one sector to another. Financial Systems are crucial for capital formation and promotion of investment climate in an economy. Adequate capital formation is indispensable to a speedy economic development.

An example of this function of the financial system is when individuals deposit their surplus funds with a bank. The bank in turn is approached by a business seeking funds (debt) to buy new equipment or to finance inventories. The bank lends funds (pooled from depositors) to the business, which is then able to put these funds to use in expanding the business. Another example is the sale of shares by companies acquiring ownership funds directly from households with the help of financial sector.

2.2 FUNCTIONS OF THE FINANCIAL SYSTEM

The financial system provides for:

Mobilization of funds : it aids in the mobilization of the country's savings and the transfer of these savings to sectors, which make productive use of it

Flexibility in investment : financial markets also allow people to alter their existing investments by selling shares/debentures, earlier purchased by them, and buying those of another corporate

Implementation of monetary policy : through the financial system, Government authorities can influence holdings in financial assets by exerting an influence on interest rates and ultimately the level of activity in the economy (*i.e.* spending on goods and services)

An efficient saving process : by providing savers with a safe avenue for their surplus funds, the financial system encourages savings and so increases the volume of resources available for investment in productive assets like plant and machinery.

A financial system enables lenders to use their excess funds to produce more funds by way of earning interest. It also increases the pool of money available to borrowers and enables to aim for higher level of outputs rather than being restricted with their own sources. In short, the financial system encourages more productive use of funds and resources.

3. TYPES OF FINANCIAL MARKETS AND INSTRUMENTS

Financial markets are where securities and other financial instruments are issued and traded. Financial markets are designed to allow corporations and governments to raise new funds and to allow investors to execute their buying and selling orders. In financial markets funds are channeled from those with the surplus, who buy securities, to those, with shortage, who issue new securities or sell existing securities. A financial market can be seen as a set of arrangements that allows trading among its participants.

Financial market provides three important economic functions:

- Financial market determines the prices of assets traded through the interactions between buyers and sellers;
- Financial market provides a liquidity of the financial assets;
- Financial market reduces the cost of transactions by reducing explicit costs, such as money spent to advertise the desire to buy or to sell a financial asset.

The major markets in the Indian Financial system are:

- Equity market
- Short term debt market (Money market)
- Long term debt market
- Foreign exchange market.
- Derivatives market
- Insurance and Mutual funds

3.1 THE EQUITY MARKET

The equity market is a major segment of the financial system. It consists of both the primary and the secondary markets. The types of securities and financial assets, classified under the equity market, are given below:

Shares: the most common form of share trade on the share market is the ordinary share, which represents a share in ownership of the company.

Hybrid securities: A hybrid security is a security, which has characteristics of both equity and debt (*e.g.* convertible debenture has the characteristics of a debt security as regular interest payment is made, but unlike other debt instruments, a convertible debenture does not involve the repayment of the principal upon maturity. At the maturity date these debentures convert into shares).

Warrants: A warrant provides holder with an option to purchase a company's share at predetermined price at a future date without any obligation to actually purchase the share on that future date. Warrants not exercised turn into useless pieces of paper.

3.2 SHORT TERM DEBT MARKET (MONEY MARKET)

Institutions dominate the short-term debt market in India with hardly any role for individual investors due to the size of the transaction. The motivation to participate in this market is to deploy temporary surpluses of funds and those with temporary short-ages of funds. By convention, a security or loan with maturity of one year or less is called a short-term security. The money market also includes Commercial Paper (CP) issuances by corporates, PDs and financial institutions and Certificates of Deposit (CD) issued by banks to institutional investors. Un-collaterised call money market is restricted to banks and Primary Dealers subject to prudential limits. The collaterised segments include Collaterised Borrowing and Lending Facility (CBLO) and market repo transactions between banks and financial institutions. Just like the equity market, money market also has its own primary and secondary markets.

3.3 LONG-TERM DEBT MARKET

The long-term debt market also includes both the primary markets and the secondary markets. It has a large number of players like term lending institutions, banks, investors both individual and institutional, pension and mutual funds and insurance companies which are all engaged in providing long term debt capital to the industrial sector by way of securities.

Long-term debt securities include:

Government security - These are the major borrowing instruments used by the Indian Government when it wishes to raise funds. They are sold on the primary market by a tender system by country's central banker *i.e.* Reserve Bank of India (RBI) who acts as an agent for the Government. These include State Government bonds also. The Government securities market has seen significant growth in the last two decades. It has a sizeable primary and active secondary segments. Trading largely takes place on the Negotiated Dealing System-Order Matching (NDS-OM), an anonymous order-matching trading platform. The average daily trading volume in Government securities market has shown significant growth from Rs.32.15 billion in 2005-06 to Rs.433.12 billion in 2014-15. All the secondary market transactions in Government Securities are settled through a central counterparty mechanism under Delivery Versus Payment mode. Multilateral netting is achieved with a single funds settlement obligation for each member for a particular settlement date. The settlement is achieved in the RTGS (Real Time Gross Settlement) Settlement/Current Account maintained by the member in the Reserve Bank.

Debentures, corporate bonds, unsecured notes and asset backed securities : Companies can also raise medium and long-term fund by issuing variety of instruments. Debentures are usually issued by manufacturing companies and are secured by fixed or floating charges over the company's assets and offers are made through a prospectus.

3.4 THE FOREIGN EXCHANGE MARKET

The foreign exchange market can be defined as a market within which individuals; business firms, governments, banks and others purchase and sell foreign currencies. Residents can hedge their foreign exchange exposures through various products, such as, forward contracts, options involving rupee and foreign currencies, currency swaps and cost reduction option structures in the OTC market. Foreign investors can also hedge their investments in equity and/or debt in India through forwards and options. In addition, trading within specified position limits is permitted on exchange traded currency futures in four currency pairs and in USD for currency options. Residents are also permitted to hedge their commodity price risk, as per specific guidelines, in the overseas OTC markets and exchanges.

This is an important market which remains open 24 hours a day globally (but during business hours in India). Principal function of such a market is to provide a mechanism by which funds in domestic currency from one nation are transferred to another nation in its currency. Thus, it performs a clearing-house function. Over the years, the foreign exchange spot as well as forward market has expanded quite significantly. The average daily forex market turnover has grown from approximately USD 16 billion in 2005-06 to nearly US$ 55 billion in 2014-15. The average daily trading volume in the inter-bank USD/INR forwards was at USD 6.43 billion and that of the USD/INR futures was at USD 2.64 billion during the financial year 2014-15.

The foreign exchange rate refers to the price of one currency in terms of another currency. Assume that India is the home country and the USA is the foreign country. Also suppose that Rs. 49 exchanges for US $ 1. There are two ways of measuring the foreign exchange rate:

One being the price of foreign currency (US $ 1) in terms of domestic currency (Indian rupee) *i.e.* Rs. 68 per dollar while second being the price of domestic currency (100 Indian rupees) in terms of foreign currency (US $) or $ 1.470 per 100 Indian rupee.

Under the current international monetary system, nations have a great degree of flexibility in choosing the exchange rate regimes that best fit their economic conditions. At one extreme we have the fixed exchange rate system, where the exchange rate is stable and can fluctuate only within a very limited band. On the other extreme we have the freely fluctuating exchange rate system, where exchange rate is set by the free market forces of demand and supply.

3.5 THE DERIVATIVES MARKET

Derivatives are financial instruments whose value is derived from an underlying physical commodity or financial asset, *e.g.* stock futures are based on the price of the underlying stock in the securities market; 10-year bond futures are based on the price of 10-year bonds traded in the fixed interest market.

Unlike physical securities, the creation of derivatives is not intended to raise finance for the issuer, nor is trading in them usually intended to transfer ownership of assets. Rather, derivative instruments were developed as a means of transferring risk. Because they allow future prices to be set in the present, they permit market participants to protect themselves from the risk that market prices might change.

In the OTC interest rate derivatives (IRD) segment, interest rate swaps (IRS) and forward rate agreements (FRA) are permitted on various benchmarks where banks and primary dealers (PD) take hedging and trading positions. Other regulated entities like insurance companies, mutual funds, Non-Banking Finance Companies can participate in IRD for the purpose of hedging. The activity in IRS market has shown impressive growth with the average daily inter-bank trading volume (notional principal) in Rupee IRS at Rs. 88.60 billion in financial year 2014-15. In addition, there are exchange traded interest rate futures (IRF) which are also open to Foreign Portfolio Investors (FPI). Trading activity in the IRF market has picked up in the recent period with average daily trading volume of Rs. 19.18 billion during the financial year 2014-15.

The trading in the derivatives market is mainly in the form of Forward contracts/Futures, Options/swaps or Exchange Traded Funds (ETFs).

3.6 INSURANCE AND MUTUAL FUNDS

Insurance products available in the Indian market include those which provide either pure risk coverage or a combination of risk and investment. The insurance market in India used to be a monopoly of the public sector players, till a few years back. The insurance market was opened up in August 2000 and the foreign companies were allowed ownership of up to 26%. The FDI limit in insurance sector was further raised from 26% to 49% in July 2014. Liberalisation of the sector has resulted in many private players entering the field of both life and general insurance. Many of these private entities have entered into collaboration with large international players in the insurance field. The insurance sector, in India, is a quite large and is growing at a rapid rate of around 20%. An insurance service, together with banking services, add about 7% to India's GDP and provides long- term funds for infrastructure development. Presently, there are 28 general insurance companies including the ECGC and Agriculture Insurance Corporation of India and 24 life insurance companies operating in Indian insurance market.

An insurance repository has been set up on 16 September 2013, to help policy holders buy and keep insurance policies in electronic form, rather than as a paper document. It will hold electronic records of insurance policies, issued to individuals. Such policies are called electronic policies or e-Policies. Policy holders can hold all their insurance policies in an electronic format in a single account, called Electronic Insurance Account (EIA). Insurance Regulatory and Development Authority of India (IRDA) has issued licenses to five entities to act as Insurance Repository.

Mutual Funds: Like a company, a mutual fund also raises funds in the desired objectives sought by investors. Mutual funds have an asset manager who will invest the funds and distribute benefits as per terms of offer document. A mutual fund can be equity oriented fund or a debt oriented fund or a combination of both debt and equity. The units of a mutual fund are often listed and traded in stock exchanges to provide liquidity to these instruments.

Formation of the Unit Trust of India in 1963, marked the start of the mutual fund industry, in India. This was an initiative of the Government of India and Reserve Bank of India. This was the first phase of the development of mutual funds in India. The second phase (1987 to 1993), was marked by the entry of non-UTI, Public Sector Funds, set up by LIC and public sector banks. The third phase from 1993 to 2003, saw the entry of Private Sector Funds. The fourth (present) phase started in February 2003, when, following the repeal of the Unit Trust of India Act 1963, UTI was bifurcated into two separate entities. With the bifurcation of the erstwhile UTI and with the setting up of a UTI Mutual Fund, conforming to the SEBI Mutual Fund Regulations, and with many mergers taking place among different private sector funds, the mutual fund industry has entered its current phase of consolidation and growth. Today, there are large number of players in the MF industry and the assets managed by them reached the level of Rs 13.43 trillion in November 2015. This shows a growth of about 20% over the November 2014 level of 11.19 trillion.

4. FEATURES OF SECURITIES AND FINANCIAL MARKETS

4.1 PRIMARY AND SECONDARY MARKETS

Each type of financial market discussed in the previous section may be divided into two sub-markets: the primary market and the secondary market:

The primary market

The term primary market is used to describe new lending and borrowing arrangements and new equity issues.

An example of primary market activity is the issue of Government security on the long-term debt market by the Government of India. This transaction takes place directly between the borrower and lender.

Another example of primary market activity is the new issue of shares on the share market. Investors provide a company with funds, which are used to develop and grow the business. In return, they expect to receive a portion of the profits, which are paid in the forms of dividends.

The secondary market

The term secondary market is used to represent the subsequent buying and selling of existing securities. In case of debt securities, the bonds or debentures may change many beneficiary holders by way of trade in secondary market.

Similarly, investors in shares may not want to hold their shares indefinitely. They too can liquidate their investments by selling their shares in the secondary market.

Link between primary and secondary market

The success of a float or a security issue on the primary market is closely linked to expectations of activity in the secondary market. Many investors do not wish to hold debt securities until maturity, nor equities for a significant length of time or until the companies are wound up. Therefore, they will participate in the primary market only if they have a reasonable expectation of being able to sell their securities in the secondary market.

4.2 WHAT MAKES A MARKET TICK?

Where there is a significant number of active buyers and sellers in a market, that market is regarded as a deep market. The opposite of this is a shallow or thin market where there is very little activity, few sellers and few buyers.

A deep market offers the benefits of liquidity (*i.e.* the ability to buy and sell a reasonable number of securities readily), without undue disturbance to the market price. Securities traded in liquid markets are generally more attractive to investors than those available in markets lacking depth.

Lenders (investors) are able to liquidate (*i.e.* sell) their securities without undue delays, and borrowers have access to a wider range of lenders. Investors in illiquid markets hope to be compensated by higher returns.

4.3 HOW SECURITIES ARE BOUGHT AND SOLD?

Earlier, dealing system in Indian stock exchange used to be 'open outcry' system, or bid and offer. In an 'open outcry' lots are offered by the seller or bid by the buyer. Today, technology has automated the processes of the market place. Trading floors in India have been replaced by electronic trading systems.

4.4 INVESTING IN SECURITIES AND FINANCIAL MARKETS

Borrowers and lenders have different preferences in terms of risk, return, maturity, liquidity and marketability and will select securities, which match these preferences. For younger age group individuals since the investment horizon is long they prefer to invest in products which can offer capital appreciation or growth on investments. One should always check that he or she has allocated funds to spend on his or her immediate needs before investing. The preferences will be determined by the financial objectives of the borrowers and lenders.

Characteristics of securities:—

Risk: This is the chance you take that you will not get your money back or will lose a substantial part of it when, say, you deposit it with a bank or take debentures/equity in a company.

Return: This is the amount of interest earned, say, on an investment in the bonds of a company. In the case of a share, it is the dividend on that share *plus* or *minus* any capital gain or loss taken at acquisition price rather than face value.

Maturity: This is the period of time before which debt or borrowing is due to be repaid. Equity in a company is not normally repaid to shareholders, unless the business is wound up or there is a return of capital.

Liquidity: This is the capacity for a security or deposit to be converted quickly and easily into cash. Liquidity may depend on the length of maturity of the security or asset. A house has low liquidity as it usually takes a considerable time to sell. A deposit with a cash management mutual fund is highly liquid.

Marketability: This is the ability to buy or sell a security quickly and easily and get prompt payment when selling and prompt delivery when buying. Generally, the higher the risk of an investment, the less marketable and less liquid it will be and the more liquid and marketable the security, the lower will be the return (Other things being equal) on that security.

Table below summarizes these characteristics for three different types of securities :

Security	Return	Risk	Maturity	Liquidity	Marketability
Equity Share*	Variable	Medium	N/A	High	High
Treasury bill	Low	Low	Short	High	High
Debenture	Medium	Medium	Medium	Medium	Low

*This is subjective and will change depending upon the performance of the company, the outlook for the share market and economic conditions.

4.5 IMPACT OF GLOBALISATION OF FINANCIAL MARKETS

Globalisation refers to the integration of world markets as a result of the removal of economic restrictions and technological innovations that facilitate the trading of securities across all markets. It means that no market is isolated from developments in other markets.

The extent to which globalisation affects India's financial markets will depend upon India's linkage with rest of world by way of free convertibility of currency, extent to which permission is given to Foreign Institutional Investors (FIIs) to hold Indian securities and to Indians to hold foreign securities. We have seen in past impact of NASDAQ price movements in Indian technological sector. A fall in the international aluminium prices may result in lowering the value of specific aluminium producing stock in India.

Indian shares are traded on overseas markets in the form of Global Depository Receipts (GDRs) and American Depository Receipts (ADRs). These securities are affected by domestic factors, as well as trends in the overseas markets where they are traded.

International Investment

Recent announcements in policy have opened global market for Indian investors in a small way. International investment has a number of advantages for the investor:

- It enables investments in different markets and different currencies. Markets and currencies do not all move in unison and careful timing of when to be in or out of a market or currency can increase returns.
- It enables a spread of risk by being in a mix of markets and currencies but introduces currency exposure.
- It counters the limitations of the Indian market, which in terms of world stock market is relatively small and very much influenced by the inflow and outflow of overseas funds.
- It enables access to stocks and sectors not available in India.
- Investment in markets and economies with different cycles tends to reduce the overall volatility of an investment portfolio.
- It facilitates participation in economies which may be growing faster than India's economy.

SELF-ASSESSMENT EXERCISE 2

1. Complete the table below by matching the following securities and financial assets with the financial market in which they are issued and/or traded :

Securities/Financial asset	Financial market
Ordinary shares	Share market
Treasury paper	Short-term debt market/Money market
Foreign currency	Foreign exchange market
Mutual Funds	Capital market
Promissory notes	Short-term debt market/Money market
Preference shares	Share market
Company debentures	Long-term debt market
Bills of exchange	Short-term debt/Money market Commercial
Paper Short-term debt/Money market Treasury bills	Short-term debt/Money market

2. Distinguish between debt and equity

....

....

....

....

....

....

3. Describe the differences between short-term debt securities and long-term debt securities

....

....

....

....

4. The flow of funds

Within the financial system, there are two types of financial flows :

a. Direct funds flow

b. Indirect funds flow

DIRECT FUNDS FLOW

This refers to the flow of funds directly from savers to borrowers. This method of transferring funds is efficient only when the sums involved are large for both borrowers and lenders and where the needs of borrowers and lenders are exactly matched as to term, interest rate, amount and repayment arrangements.

5. INDIRECT FUNDS FLOW

Indirect financing refers to the flow of funds through financial intermediaries. Funds saved are pooled and packaged and are then further lent to borrowers for a fee. This is the commonly used process in today's financial system and is called 'intermediation'.

5.1 INTERMEDIATION

Intermediation refers to the activities of financial intermediaries in assisting the indirect flow of funds through the financial system. Financial Intermediaries Act as 'middle men', pooling the funds of lenders (savers) and passing that money on to end users (borrowers). Financial intermediaries also trade in financial assets such as shares and bonds through specific markets established for this purpose such as share markets, money market, long-term debt markets, foreign exchange markets etc. Examples of intermediaries include banks, life insurance companies, finance companies and mutual funds.

5.2 DISINTERMEDIATION

Disintermediation describes the process of companies arranging their own borrowings and placing their deposits directly in the market, without going through a financial intermediary. Acceptance of fixed deposits from the public/shareholders by a company is an example of this.

Today, many companies have their own traders or dealers for performing activities done by financial intermediaries. Companies are now developing sophisticated trading operations in currencies, interest rates and money market securities, bypassing financial intermediaries.

Disintermediation in the corporate market is restricted to very large, sound business that can access financial markets in their own right.

SELF-ASSESSMENT EXERCISE 3

You have inherited Rs. 25 lakhs. You must now decide how to invest these funds for a five-year period

List and explain five factors that you, as an investor, must consider in deciding how to invest these funds.

....

....

....

....

....

....

....

....

....

....

....

....

....

....

REVIEW

QUESTIONS

For each of the multiple-choice questions, select the best response.

1. A security:
   A. Represents the obligation by one party to pay a specific amount of money to another party
   B. Is the most liquid form of financial asset
   C. Could be either documentary evidence of ownership of an asset or acknowledgement of indebtedness and obligation to repay
   D. Is a piece of paper representing an underlying financial asset
2. Disintermediation refer to the trend towards:
   A. Fewer financial intermediaries in the financial system
   B. Bypassing intermediaries for lending and borrowing requirements
   C. Increased regulation of financial institutions and intermediaries
   D. Decreased regulation of financial institutions and intermediaries
3. Financial intermediaries exist because they match the needs of borrowers and lenders: They earn income by:
   A. Charging a margin on borrowings
   B. Charging a margin on deposits
   C. Charging a fee for services rendered
   D. All of the above
4. A list of the major markets in the Indian financial system would include:
   A. The intermediary market
   B. The debt market
   C. The foreign exchange market
   D. Both B and C
5. The equity market is commonly known as :
   A. The forex market
   B. The share market or stock market
   C. The short-term money market
   D. The authorized money market

6. An example of the primary financial market is:
   - A. The new issue of share on the share market
   - B. The sale of shares on the stock exchange
   - C. Any activity on the forex market
   - D. The sale of bonds to a merchant bank

Indicate whether the following statements are true or false:

7. Money is defined as anything that is accepted for payment of debts or purchase of goods :

   True/False
8. Debentures are equity securities, traded on the stock exchange :

   True/False
9. The primary financial market deals with buying and selling existing securities :

   True/False
10. Liquidity represents the capacity of a security to be quickly and easily converted into cash :

    True/False

ANSWERS

1. C	6. A
2. B	7. True
3. D	8. False
4. D	9. False
5. B	10. True

IN SUMMARY

This topic has been a broad introduction to financial markets. We began by examining two basic concepts - debt and equity. Debt is an obligation by an individual or company to pay a specific amount of money to another party. Equity represents the ownership interest in the company being normally referred to as shares. We saw that securities are written undertakings securing the repayment of money or evidencing ownership and are tradable in the market place. We then reviewed the Indian financial system, its role in the economy and the players. We also considered the role and the participants in each of the major financial markets.

SUGGESTED ANSWERS TO SELF-ASSESSMENT EXERCISE 1

Feature	Debt	Equity
Capital/Principal	This is the principal amount borrowed and does not vary unless you repay funds, borrow more or capitalize interest.	This the value of your shares when you purchase them and may rise or fall.
Repayment	Repayment arrangements are agreed at the time debt is drawn	Most types of shares don't have any repayment arrangements. The shares exist until such time as the company is wound up. Selling your shares is the means by which you convert your investments back to cash
Return	Returns on funds lent are through interest. Interest can be either fixed or floating or a combination of both	Dividends - Payments from profits on a per share basis. Capital gain - The change in value of your holding as compared to your cost price. The gain or loss happens only at time of selling
Participation in profit of venture	If you lend money, the borrower is obligated to repay funds under the agreed terms. One can have a mortgage over assets owned by borrower but not the ownership right	When you purchase shares in a company, you own a portion of that company

SUGGESTED ANSWERS TO SELF-ASSESSMENT EXERCISE 2

1.

Securities/Financial asset	Financial market
Ordinary shares	Share market
Treasury paper	Short-term debt market
Foreign currency	Foreign exchange market
Mutual Funds	Capital Market
Promissory notes	Short-term debt market
Preference shares	Share market
Company debentures	Long-term debt market
Bills of exchange	Short-term debt market
Commercial Paper	Short-term debt market
Treasury bills	Short-term debt market

2. Debt is an obligation by one party to pay a specific amount of money to another party. Equity is the part of something you own. In the securities industry, shares are referred to as equities as they represent ownership in the company.
3. Short-term debt securities have unexpired terms to maturity of less than 12 months while long-term securities have unexpired term to maturity greater than 12 months.

SUGGESTED ANSWERS TO SELF-ASSESSMENT EXERCISE 3

Risk - What level of risk can I tolerate?

Return - What level of return do I want to earn on these funds?

Liquidity - Am I likely to need to liquidate my investment? Will I be able to do this with minimum loss of principal?

Marketability - Will I be able to trade my investment during the five-year period?

Maturity - is the maturity date within my five-year time frame? Taxation - is this investment tax effective?

CHECKLIST

Below is a checklist of main points covered by this topic. Use this checklist to test your learning:

In context of financial markets, a security is either written acknowledgement of a debt along with terms of repayment or proof of ownership.

Debt is an obligation by one part to pay a specific amount of money to another party.

Equity is the part of something which investor owns (*e.g.* share in a company where shareholder is entitled to share in the company's profit and faces possibility of loss in event of poor performance by the company by way of reduction in the market price of the share).

A financial system channels the flow of funds between the various sectors in the economy.

The market is called primary market when funds are raised by an enterprise by issuing fresh securities, resulting in change in its financial position. It is called secondary market when existing securities are traded and their trade does not impact issuing company's financial position.

The short-term debt market or money market is where securities of less than 12 months to maturity are traded.

The long-term debt market is debt market for paper more than 12 months to maturity.

The foreign exchange market provides a market place for buyers and sellers to trade in foreign currency. It is not a 'securities market'.

The trading in the derivatives market is mainly in the form of Forward contracts/Futures, Options/swaps or Exchange Traded Funds (ETFs). Derivative instruments are mainly used as a means of transferring risk.

The insurance products can be used by an investor to cover his risks and/or for investment purposes.

Mutual fund products provide an alternative route to an investor for investing in equity and/or debt market.

A market with a significant number of buyers and sellers is referred to as a 'deep' market and offers the benefit of liquidity. Opposite of a deep market is 'thin' market where there are few buyers and sellers.

Intermediation refers to the activities of financial intermediaries in assisting indirect flow of funds in the financial system.

Disintermediation describes the process of companies arranging their own borrowings and placing their deposits directly in the market, without going through a financial intermediary.

Every security has the following features in varying degrees :

Risk - What is the risk of default?

Return - How much will be earned?

Maturity - How long until the security matures?

Marketability - Can it be sold on a secondary market?

Liquidity - How quickly can it be converted to cash without significant loss of capital?

3 CHAPTER

Participants, Intermediaries & Regulators of the Indian Financial System: Institutional & Non-institutional

ABOUT THIS TOPIC

This topic looks at the financial intermediaries and institutions which form the critical links between savers and users of savings. They are facilitators, engaged in the pooling of funds from a wide range of providers and passing on these funds to a diverse group of borrowers and seekers of capital. In return, they earn a margin (the spread between the rates at which they borrow and lend) or a fee, which is designed to compensate for risk and to earn a profit.

This topic also looks at the functions of the key regulatory and supervisory authorities in the Indian financial system, including:

a. *Reserve Bank of India (RBI)*

b. *Securities and Exchange Board of India (SEBI)*

c. *Insurance Regulatory & Development Authority of India (IRDAI)*

In addition, we examine working of the self-regulatory bodies.

We begin this topic by identifying who the financial intermediaries are and what they do. We also look at the advantages of intermediation as opposed to direct financing. Then we consider the importance of regulation for financial markets and look at the functions and operations of the regulatory authorities in the financial system.

TOPIC OBJECTIVES

At the end of this topic, you should be able to:

- *List the advantages that intermediation brings to the financial system*
- *Distinguish between retail and wholesale financial services*
- *List the major types of financial intermediaries operating within the Indian financial system*
- *Explain how the Indian financial system is regulated*
- *Explain the necessity of regulation of securities business*
- *Describe the role of RBI*
- *Describe the role of SEBI*
- *Describe the role of IRDAI*
- *Explain the role of self-governing bodies, including stock exchanges, in regulating the secondary market for securities.*

1. PARTICIPANTS AND INTERMEDIARIES IN THE FINANCE INDUSTRY

1.1 PARTICIPANTS AND THE FLOW OF FUNDS

Within the financial system, there are numerous market participants who facilitate the flow of funds between the various sectors of the economy. These participants can broadly be classified into borrowers and lenders, capital raisers and investors. These participants interact through the financial markets. To assist them, they generally engage the services of an intermediary or service provider.

All of us participate in the financial system in a manner which we may not easily realize. Look at transactions below to see your role as participant in financial markets :

Transactions which make us participant in financial system

Our saving account with a bank

Credit of our salary into the bank account

Contribution to a superannuation fund

Our credit card transactions

Our home loan payments

Insurance on the House

Ownership of publicly listed shares

Purchase of share through a stock broker

Premium payment for life insurance policy

1.2 WHO IS AN INTERMEDIARY?

Financial intermediaries act as 'middlemen' in the financial system. They facilitate the flow of funds between those with money and those needing money. They pool and package funds from those with surplus capital and pass those funds to those requiring funds for a fee. In the process they assume a number of risks.

Intermediaries however do not match one lender with one borrower, as direct financing does. Intermediaries pool the funds of lenders (*i.e.* those with surplus funds who open deposit accounts) and further lend those funds to a number of borrowers for a fee.

One of the main reasons for the predominance of intermediation in our economy is that the mix of securities offered by businesses and other borrowers, while attractive to the borrower, is often unattractive in terms and conditions to lenders (savers). Financial intermediaries offer 'packaged' securities to investors that are more attractive than original 'lumpy' securities. For example, a small depositor would probably prefer the convenience of a short-term deposit with a bank to a direct investment in a long gestation project by the bank, which is the ultimate investment of the bank. By depositing with the bank, the small depositor has security, a moderate return on the deposit and ready access to cash when desired. The bank bears the risk of default on the project loan, but gets a higher return than the small depositor gets on his deposit with the bank.

1.3 INTERMEDIARIES AND FINANCIAL MARKETS

The financial system is made up of a number of distinct markets, distinguished by the class of transactions and the class of security in which they deal. For example, the derivatives market exists for the trading of futures and options contracts. Financial intermediaries may be specialised in one market, may operate across a number of markets or may be active in all markets. Markets and examples of the intermediaries active in those markets are given in table below :

Financial markets and intermediaries

Market	Examples of intermediaries
Equity and Mutual Fund markets	Stock brokers, fund managers
Long-term debt market	Banks, life insurance companies, superannuation funds, fund managers
Short-term debt market	Banks, fund managers
Derivatives market	Futures Brokers, fund managers
Foreign exchange market	Banks, foreign exchange dealers, fund managers

1.4 ROLE OF INTERMEDIARIES

All the intermediaries, discussed in this topic, perform the same function: acting as a bridge between the borrowers and lenders, providing the channel for the flow of funds between those with money and those needing money. Intermediaries differ in terms of the market(s) in which they operate and the services they provide (wholesale and/or retail). Financial intermediaries range from small specialist institutions to financial conglomerates operating in every area of Indian financial system (*e.g.* banks such as SBI).

Intermediaries exist because of the advantages they provide over direct flow of funds, in terms of bearing risk, providing economies of scale and covering the mismatch between borrowers and lenders. There is evidence of a trend toward large companies bypassing intermediaries and arranging to borrow or lend funds directly with another party. This is known as 'disintermediation'. However, disintermediation is limited to large financially sound companies; and, for all other players in the financial system, use of intermediaries will continue.

The nature of intermediation in the financial system is never constant. The financial system is always changing, often not by choice, but as a result of the regulation to which it is subjected to. International influences are also catalysts for change and will continue to influence the Indian financial system. Intermediaries also initiate change in the financial system through innovation; one need only compare the range of financial services available now with that in previous years. In looking at the intermediaries in the Indian financial system, it is important to consider how they have responded to change to date. This may provide a good indication of the future of that particular intermediary group or segment of the market.

1.4.1 Advantages of financial intermediaries

The cost of intermediation is the fee charged by the intermediary; there must, therefore, be advantages over direct financing or there would be no economic reason for having middlemen in the financial system. These advantages are detailed below :

Risk bearing

The pooling of funds involves the intermediary taking a number of risks. It is the ability of the intermediary to take these risks and the willingness of the borrower to pay a fee for the intermediary's bearing of risk that distinguishes indirect flow of funds (intermediation) from direct flows.

Some of these risks are:

> ***Liquidity risk :*** the risk that the lender would want the money back when it has been on lent to the borrower
>
> ***Credit risk :*** the risk that the borrower will not be able to repay the loan
>
> ***Interest rate risk :*** the risk that interest will move in such a way as to make the transaction unprofitable.

Economies of scale

By operating in volume, intermediaries can achieve economies of scale. Overheads, such as administrative costs and the cost of evaluating potential investments, can be spread over a large number of units, hence reducing costs.

Intermediaries offer specialist skills and knowledge

Intermediaries specialize in a particular business and within their specialty, offer a diverse range of products to meet the needs of borrowers and lenders. For example, fund managers have specialist skills in investing large pools of money, whereas banks have specialist skills in lending money for purpose of working capital.

Covering of mismatch

Intermediaries match the imbalance between borrowers and lenders. Seldom do borrowers' and lenders' needs match exactly in terms of credit risk, maturity dates, interest rate, liquidity, or currency risk. By pooling the funds of lenders, and sometimes pooling the needs of borrowers, intermediaries are able to cover this mismatch.

1.4.2 Disadvantages of financial intermediaries

The main disadvantage is the cost of using an intermediary, which is passed on to both lenders and borrowers through margins and fees. Direct financing is generally less costly because margins do not have to cover the cost structure of an intermediary. Investors must balance this cost with the risk of direct financing. In direct financing, the lender is bearing all the risk, although they may offset this to an extent by taking a charge over the borrower's assets. In indirect financing, risks are spread across a large number of financial assets.

The success of a financial intermediary depends upon its ability to satisfy the needs of borrowers and lenders, while balancing cost and risk.

1.5 INTERMEDIARIES IN THE INDIAN FINANCIAL SYSTEM

We will now examine briefly the major intermediaries in the Indian financial system. Financial market intermediaries can be divided into three main groups :

1. Reserve Bank of India
2. Banks
3. Non-Banks Finance companies, fund managers/Asset Management companies, housing finance companies, investment banks, life insurance companies, stock brokers, superannuation funds,

depository participants, portfolio managers, venture capital funds and collective investment schemes.)

The distinction between the bank and non-bank sector is a legal one. Under the Banking Regulation Act only those institutions licensed under the Act can call themselves a bank. Under the Indian Constitution, the Central Government is empowered to make laws with respect to 'banking, except co-operative banking'.

1.5.1 The Reserve Bank of India

The Reserve Bank of India is India's Central Bank. The RBI is an intermediary in the sense that it acts as banker and agent for the Central Government and provides banking services to State Governments also. For instance, in its capacity as agent for the Central Government, the RBI handles the issue of Government securities and also performs open market operations (sale and purchase) in securities.

RBI is also empowered to provide emergency liquidity support in the event of threats to the stability of the financial system.

RBI holds the country's foreign exchange reserves and manages them along with managing exchange rate of the Rupee by buying and selling foreign currencies in foreign exchange markets.

1.5.2 Banks

These banks include household names such as State Bank of India (SBI) and Punjab National Bank, Bank of India, HDFC Bank and others. They offer a full range of services to both the retail and wholesale sectors.

The banks are promoting themselves as 'one stop shops' for financial services. Rather than just investing in the traditional bank products of a savings account or term deposit, investors can purchase mutual funds, insurance, take out a home loan and other forms of investing, borrowing from one bank.

Banks are India's largest financial institutions. They are regulated by the Banking Regulation Act, which only allows body corporates authorized by the RBI to carry on the business of banking.

A bank can issue cheques in its own name - that is an important distinction between banks and non-banks. Their other activities are very similar; they engage in borrowing and lending and provide a broad range of financial service including:

Current and savings accounts	
Cheque book facility	Housing loan
Overdraft facilities	Leasing
Cash management services	Insurance
Stock broking	Wholesale lending
Foreign exchange	Mutual funds
Personal loans	Money market operations

1.5.3 Investment banks

An investment (or merchant) bank is a non-bank financial intermediary, which specializes in providing financial services to the wholesale market (and more frequently limited services to the higher end of retail market by way of portfolio management services).

A distinguishing feature of these banks is that many of their activities are fee-based for the services rendered, rather than the business of collecting deposits and on lending them.

Financial services provided by investment banks

Investment banks offer a range of wholesale financial services including:

Money market operations - the trading, endorsement and rediscounting commercial bills and negotiable certificate of deposits; underwriting and trading promissory notes; dealing in Government securities; making short term advances to and accepting deposits from customers.

Lending activities - bill acceptance or discount facilities; term loans for large amounts, syndicated loans.

Corporate finance - advising and underwriting of new share issues; the private placement of securities with institutions or major private investors; advising clients on raising funds; and guidance on acquisitions.

Investment management and advice - advice to companies on investment, the short-term money market and funds management.

Equities trading - the buying and selling of securities.

1.5.4 Finance companies

Finance companies developed in the beginning of 1980s as providers of tax oriented solutions by way of leasing. The growth of finance companies in the early years was fuelled by low interest of the banking sector in leasing. Today they can be considered as mini banks focusing on customers not serviced by banks due to procedural norms and winning business by way of fast operational efficiency. Finance companies are more active in areas of loans to small businesses and consumer loans.

1.5.5 Housing finance Companies

Decade of 1970's also saw emergence of first housing company in India *i.e.* HDFC Ltd. Banks were not interested in long-term tenure of housing loans which meant these companies had a free field upto 2000. Emergence of lack of opportunities forced banks to look at this investment avenue. Aggressive marketing, low cost distribution (Using direct sales agent network) and a customer service focus has also contributed to success of these companies.

1.5.6 Fund managers/Asset Management companies

Fund managers invest, manage and monitor the assets of their clients. For example, the person who manages the assets of a particular scheme of a Mutual fund, is called the fund manager of that scheme. The term, "asset management", is used in the financial field to describe people and companies that manage investments on behalf of others. Usually, the Asset Management Companies (AMCs) manage significant Assets in the mutual fund segment. The AMCs also cater to Portfolio Management Services for investors, along with International Advisory Mandates for clients across international markets in asset classes like Debt and Equity. The AMCs endeavor to simplify their investors' journey to meet their financial goals. Portfolio management entails the selection and monitoring of an appropriate mix of investments in a portfolio. The portfolio manager's task is to select the appropriate mix of investments in the asset classes (cash, shares, fixed interest and others) to ensure that the portfolio achieves the maximum return with an acceptable level of risk.

New area of growth have now emerged in shape of investment in venture capital with boom in start-up entities.

1.5.7 Stockbrokers

Stockbrokers act on behalf of investors and issuers of securities by buying and selling those financial assets, which are traded on share markets, particularly equity securities. They also provide a range of financial services in capital raising and investment and corporate financial advice. Stockbrokers fulfil a pivotal role in the financial system through the management of equity raisings, giving companies access to risk capital.

A stock exchange acts as a financial intermediary in raising money for companies by providing a market place where the shares of companies are bought or sold. Similarly debt securities are also traded on the exchange.

1.5.8 Superannuation funds

Superannuation is money saved during your working life, used to fund income needs upon retirement. Superannuation contribution is voluntary in India. These funds are currently invested by the company where you are working or company may decide to enter into a contract with a life insurance company or an asset management company, for the same. The Provident Fund Organisation and various Pension Funds also invest their surplus investible funds, either departmentally or through AMCs.

We are going to see many developments in area of superannuation funds.

1.5.9 Life insurance companies

Life insurance companies command largest amount of asset base after banks. Life Insurance Corporation of India is bigger than the largest bank *i.e.* State Bank of India in terms of assets managed. With opening up of competition and the entry by private sector, this sector is expected to see more growth. Life insurance companies are required to be registered under the Insurance Act. Life insurance companies are required to maintain policyholder assets in a manner defined in regulation.

Life insurance companies operate in longer time horizon of investment as compared to other intermediaries.

1.5.10 Other Intermediaries

Other intermediaries in the finance sector include, depository participants, portfolio managers, venture capital funds and collective investment schemes.

SELF-ASSESSMENT EXERCISE 1

1. Read through the following statements and determine whether they are true or false:
   (*a*) A financial intermediary is a facilitator who channels the flow of funds between those with money and those needing money.
   (*b*) An intermediary serves as an agent between lenders and borrowers; once they are brought together, the lender acquires a direct financial claim on the borrower.
   (*c*) In India, the financial system is based mainly on indirect funds flow.
   (*d*) Financial intermediaries take on a number of risks, including liquidity risk, credit risk and interest risk.
   (*e*) Financial intermediaries are able to match lenders directly with borrowers.
   (*f*) The cost of intermediation is the fee charged by the intermediary through the imposition of interest rates and other charges.
2. 'Financial intermediaries make financial markets more efficient'. What arguments would you put forward in support of this statement?

....

....

....

....

....

....

3. Distinguish between direct dealing and intermediation.

....

....

....

....

....

....

SELF-ASSESSMENT EXERCISE 2

1. As we have seen, financial intermediaries facilitate the flow of funds between those with money and those needing money. They pool and package funds from lenders and on-lend funds to borrowers for a fee. Select a financial intermediary that you have dealt with in the past and answer the following questions:

   (*a*) Is the intermediary a bank or a non-bank?

   ....

   ....

   (*b*) Where does the intermediary operate? (Locally, in one state only, internationally)

   ....

   ....

   (*c*) Does the intermediary offer wholesale financial services, retail financial services, or both?

   ....

   ....

   (*d*) List four examples of service the intermediary provides?

   ....

   ....

   ....

   ....

2. What is meant by underwriting a security?

....

....

....

....

3. Are all financial intermediaries actively engaged in providing financial services to all sectors of the economy?

....

....

....

....

2. TYPES OF FINANCIAL SERVICES

Financial intermediaries are providers of financial services, which fall into two main groups:

Retail financial services: services to individuals and small/medium enterprises

Wholesale financial services: services to large companies and Governments.

In addition to these, the Mutual Funds provide services to both the retail investors and the corporate sector.

Some financial intermediaries are mainly engaged in retail services (*e.g.* Local area banks), while others concentrate on wholesale services (*e.g.* investment banks). Some intermediaries offer both retail and wholesale services (*e.g.* banks which, in addition to retail banking services, offer a range of wholesale financial services, including fund management, share brokerages, equity and debt underwriting, and life and general insurance) Increasingly, however, the distinction between retail and wholesale financial services is becoming less clear, with the emergence of products, which offer retail investors, and borrowers, access to wholesale services (such as mutual funds).

2.1 RETAIL FINANCIAL SERVICES

Retail financial services fall into three main categories:

- Deposit taking
- Lending
- Investment

Deposit taking

A wide range of investment options is available to the retail investor, from savings bank to recurring deposit to liquid mutual funds. Competition between financial intermediaries for the retail investor's wallet is strong. Returns (*e.g.* interest rates paid on these investments are influenced by:

- Interest rates on the wholesale market; however the retail market tends to lag behind changes in the wholesale market. Wholesale rates are in turn influenced by economic conditions.
- The demand for borrowings from financial intermediaries (*i.e.* when demand for retail borrowings is high, financial intermediaries need to attract deposits to fund those loans, and therefore, must offer higher interest rates).

Interest rates are also influenced by the ease of access to those funds which are required by the lender. Funds at call in general pay a lower rate than funds committed for a specific term. This is the case in both the wholesale and retail markets, and relates to the intermediary's role in matching imbalances between borrowers and lenders. From the intermediary's viewpoint, a premium must be paid to the lender in return for obtaining funds for a definite period. A premium in his context is a higher rate to the depositor. The period does not have to be long term; the important factor is that funds are available for a definite period.

The choices available to the retail investors have improved during recent times for a number of reasons:

- Increased competition among life insurance companies
- Increased competition in mutual fund arena
- Emergence of new players in the banking sector

Lending

Retail lending (*i.e.* lending to individuals and small business) takes a number of forms, including:

- Housing loans
- Personal loans
- Credit cards
- Overdrafts
- Term loans
- Hire purchase
- Leasing
- Retail credit
- Educational loans
- Vehicle loans

Services such as overdrafts, leasing and term loans are utilized by both the wholesale and retail markets. The difference between the two markets is the amount borrowed or lent. Financial intermediaries providing this service include banks, co-operative credit unions, chit funds and non-banking finance companies.

The majority of retail sector lending by financial intermediaries is for housing. Once dominated by housing finance companies, the banks have also started marketing these loans aggressively. The educational loans and vehicle loans also form a substantial portion of retail lending. The other major area of retail lending is consumer finance: personal finance commitments which encompass credit cards, hire purchase, personal loans and retail credit.

Investment advice

Investment advice is available from a range of specialists, which includes independent financial advisers, stockbrokers, accountants, solicitors, fund managers, non-banking finance companies, life insurance companies, investment banks and mutual funds.

2.2 WHOLESALE FINANCIAL SERVICES

Wholesale financial services refer to the services provided to large companies and Governments, including State Governments and public sector undertakings. The distinction between the wholesale and retail market is linked to the size of the transaction/business, as well as to the nature of the transaction or service.

The range of services provided overlaps to some degree with those provided to the retail market, with both sectors using services such as:

Overdrafts/Cash credit

Term loans

Leasing

Investment

Services which are generally restricted to the wholesale market include:

Corporate borrowing

Advice on acquisitions

Underwriting new securities (debt and equity)

Foreign exchange dealing

Corporate borrowing

Wholesale borrowing services include the following:

Overdrafts/cash credit

Term loans

Bills of exchange

Project finance

Eurocurrency/other foreign currency loans

Tax oriented financing (*i.e.* leasing)

Debentures

Arrangements/underwriting of equity and debt issues, including promissory notes, corporate bonds, commercial paper, eurobonds, floating rate notes etc.

This list is by no means exhaustive and new borrowing instruments are continually being developed and tailored to the needs of the wholesale market.

The main financial intermediaries providing wholesale borrowing services are banks, finance companies and investment banks, insurance companies, superannuation funds and mutual funds. They have large lending exposures to the Government and increasing corporate lending portfolios.

Advice on mergers and acquisitions

Many companies seek growth by acquiring other companies for inorganic growth. Acquisitions, whether they are by a merger (where the parties have agreed to combine their activities) or a takeover (where the target company may sometimes not wish to be acquired), are complex and involve a number of parties.

Acquisitions are currently administered by Securities and Exchange Board of India (SEBI). Regulations have been enacted to regulate the acquisition process and stock exchange regulations must also be complied with when the acquisition involves a listed company. These regulations are designed to ensure that the directors act in the best interest of shareholders. The basis for an acquisition is the decision to expand, and hence much planning and research must be undertaken to ensure a successful acquisition.

It is usual practice for companies to secure the service of independent advisers in acquisitions. Independent advice is obtained on strategy and tactics for both sides. The independent adviser requires specialist knowledge and experience. Investment banks are the dominant force in providing corporate advice in this area.

Underwriting new securities - Debt and equity

Underwriting is a wholesale service provided by stockbrokers, banks, and investment banks and often by groups of financial intermediaries who will combine to share the risk. Banks and Primary Dealers are the largest underwriters of debt issues, while stockbrokers usually underwrite equity issues.

Underwriting means that if the issuer is not able to sell the entire issue (the purpose of which is to raise funds for the company) to the public or to other institutions, the underwriters will take up the unsold portion of the securities, offered for sale, at the pre-agreed price. Underwriting assures the entity requiring funds that the full amount of money sought will be received. It creates confidence in the securities being issued; the fact that the issue is being underwritten states that the underwriter is confident that at least majority of the securities will be taken up.

Underwriting can be divided into two major areas :

Debt raising - which includes the issue of promissory notes, euro note facilities and the corporate bonds and debentures; and

Equity raising - which includes share issues, rights issues and private placements of shares.

Foreign exchange dealing

All businesses, operating internationally, have a need for foreign exchange dealing services and these services are provided by banks, as well as by the other licensed foreign exchange dealers.

Trade requires foreign currency trading operations due to the need for covering or hedging trade transactions.

Covering trade (hedging)

Foreign exchange risk arises when a contract is written in a currency other than Indian Rupees (IRs) [in US dollars ($US)], and there is a delay between the date the price is agreed and the payment date. Exchange rates will move during the intervening period, altering the amount (in Indian rupees), which will be required to complete the transaction.

For example, an Indian company may have purchased $US 10 million worth of goods from a US company with settlement in three months' time. The goods are priced in US dollars and the Indian company will want to ensure that on settlement, it will pay a certain amount in Indian rupees. Exchange rate movements could significantly alter what the company will pay. If, on contract date, the $US/IRs is 67.80, then to purchase the $US10 million it will cost Rs. 678 million. If the rate moves to $US/IRs 68.50 over the next three months, it will cost Rs. 685 million to purchase $US 10 million.

The role of the financial intermediary in foreign exchange dealing is to pool the risk of adverse exchange movements. The company may now enter into a contract with the financial intermediary to purchase the US dollars three months forward, thus enabling the company to fix the cost in Indian rupees. Although it appears that the intermediary accepts the full risk of adverse exchange rate movements, this may not be the case. The financial intermediary would, in the vast majority of cases, have executed an offsetting position with someone who wished to sell US dollars (ideally) after three months. Foreign exchange dealing is an excellent example of the way in which financial intermediaries are able to mitigate or cover risks by spreading them across a large number of transactions.

2.3 MUTUAL FUNDS

Mutual funds are investment vehicles where the asset manager pools large amounts of money from investors and invests that money in accordance with a stated objective, (*e.g.* equity funds invest in the equity markets). An important element of mutual funds is that the assets of the fund are 'managed' (*i.e.* rarely are securities purchased and held to maturity - rather, securities are traded on market movements, so that, the manager may achieve and hopefully exceed the fund's objectives). Mutual funds are a very popular form of investing and are organized in the form of a trust with investors being the beneficiaries. Mutual funds allow investors to buy a much wider range of investments than they might otherwise be able to purchase individually. Additionally, many mutual funds have systematic investment plans where it is possible to make regular contribution from as little as Rs. 1,000 per month.

There are three main types of investments in mutual funds. Some funds have all of these (multi-sector funds) and others specialize in just one category. The three main categories are:

Cash

Large pools of 'at call' funds, which offer a high rate of return (compared with bank deposits).

Bond Funds

Assets such as Government bonds, corporate bonds and asset-backed securities make up these funds.

Shares/Equities

The funds are invested in the shares of companies, mainly local companies. If you were to buy these shares directly, you would need to own the shares of many companies to reduce the investment risk.

Mutual funds that invest in shares provide the essential volume and mix, as well as the required discipline of professional management. They are an excellent way to own a diversified portfolio.

The time frame for the use of the money, attitude towards investment risk, tax position and need for income/growth are all crucial factors in the selection of investments.

SELF-ASSESSMENT EXERCISE 3

1. Group the following financial services and products under heading retail or wholesale:

Leasing	Overdrafts
Investment advice	Project finance
Credit and debit cards	Bills of exchange
Term loan	Equity raising
Mutual Funds	Eurocurrency loans
Savings account	Advice on acquisitions Underwriting new share issues
Term loan	Foreign exchange dealing

2. (*a*) List ten investment options available to the retail investor.

....

....

....

....

....

....

....

....

(*b*) Identify those investment options, which are securities and those, which are not.

....

....

....

....

....

....

3. REGULATORY CONTROLS IN INDIA

3.1 REGULATION OF THE INDIAN FINANCIAL SYSTEM

3.1.1 Why is regulation necessary?

Public confidence in the soundness of the financial system is essential for growth of any economy. As money is store of value, mismanagement could involve the "Law and Order" issue. If I don't trust the bank I will keep money at home, which in turn would not be available to a borrower who wants to set up a factory for production, which could mean stagnation of economy. Thus investors and lenders need to be confident that companies and financial intermediaries are prudently run and the financial markets are efficient and fair.

All business involves risk. The regulation of financial markets seeks to increase investor confidence by ensuring that investors have all the requisite information they need to make their own informed assessment of the risks involved. Threat of penalty and punishment by the regulators provides a deterrent to fraud by market participants. Existence of safe guards don't obviate responsibility of investor to assess the viability and safety of an investment using the available information.

Fair regulation (image of rule of law) is also important in terms of the perception of India in the international financial system. The safer image of India means access to international debt market and investment by foreign investors.

3.1.2 Drivers of regulatory change in India

Regulatory framework is dynamic. As markets and institutions change, the regulatory role also has to align itself with evolving circumstances. India has made significant gains in regulatory arena since reform process started in 1991. However issue of multiple regulators and gaps in arena of regulated bodies remains. Following factors have driven regulatory change in the Indian market:

- Stock exchange failure in 1992 due to poor controls in forward markets of Government securities.
- Instability in the corporate and financial sectors
- Misuse of "Badla" system
- Overseas experiences of volatility in financial markets
- International agreements (*e.g.* the Basel Agreement on Capital Adequacy levels for banks)
- Increasing problem of money-laundering
- Technological changes - ensuring regulation keeps pace with technological developments in systems and innovation in product and markets
- Globalisation of financial markets has facilitated the flow of funds between countries and increased the need for international co-operation between financial sector regulators
- Failure of collective investment schemes like "Teak plantation schemes", "Goat rearing schemes" etc.

3.2 REGULATORY AUTHORITIES

3.2.1 Reserve Bank of India (RBI)

The RBI is India's Central Bank and is responsible for formulating monetary policy. It has the responsibility for financial system's stability, confidence and efficient performance.

India's Central Bank - the RBI - was established on April 1, 1935 and was nationalized on January 1, 1949. Some of its main objectives are; regulating the issue of bank notes, managing India's foreign exchange reserves, operating India's currency and credit system with a view to securing monetary stability and developing India's financial structure in line with national socio-economic objectives and policies.

The RBI acts as a banker to Central and State Governments, commercial banks, state co-operative banks and some financial institutions. It formulates and administers monetary policy with a view to promoting stability of prices while encouraging higher production through appropriate deployment of credit. The RBI plays an important role in maintaining the exchange value of the Rupee and acts as an agent of the Government in respect of India's membership of IMF. The RBI also performs a variety of developmental and promotional functions. The functions and powers of the RBI are specified in the Reserve Bank of India Act, 1934 and the Banking Regulation Act.

Monetary policy

The RBI has a vital economic and market role in effecting monetary policy for India. A Monetary Policy Committee will decide on policy rates.

Liquidity support

RBI has power to provide liquidity support to financial system *via* its normal domestic market operation or *via* lending directly to a particular institution facing liquidity problems. RBI tries to handle gridlock situation in securities settlement to ensure smooth operations.

Payment system control

RBI by controlling the clearing house for negotiable instruments aims to achieve:

Controlling the risk in the financial system arising from the operation of the payment systems

Promoting the efficiency of payment systems

Promoting the competition in the market for payment services, consistent with the overall stability of the financial system

Supervision of Banking Sector

RBI is the designated regulator for all banking business in the country as per Banking Regulation Act. Its supervisory role of banks includes:

Collecting and analyzing information in relation to prudential matter affecting banks

Evaluating the effectiveness of banks in carrying out these activities

Permission for opening or closing of bank branches

Exposure to priority sector

Exposure to capital market, realty sector and commodity sector as they are identified as sensitive sectors

Ensure capital adequacy ratio adherence

Determination of risk weightings for exposure to various sectors

Authority to conduct inspection of banks

RBI has power to force compulsory merger of weak banks with the strong ones.

Foreign exchange dealers

The RBI oversees the dealers in the foreign exchange market. It authorizes institutions to deal in foreign exchange and sets guidelines with regard to open positions (a measure of exposure to movement in exchange rates) and dealing and management of resources as well as reporting of activities.

Control of Non-Banking Finance Companies

RBI also supervises Non-Banking Finance Companies, with respect to their deposit taking activities. RBI's role is to encourage and promote prudent behaviour by organisation (understand and manage their risks) so as to reduce the likelihood of not being able to meet their obligations to the people who put money with them.

Prudential supervision is, therefore, concerned with how financial institutions go about identifying, measuring and managing the risk in their business. As an example, minimum standards are prescribed for capitalisation and liquidity and limits on the concentration of risk exposures.

3.2.2 Securities and Exchange Board of India (SEBI)

Securities and Exchange Board of India (SEBI) was established with the following objectives:

Conduct of underwriters for issue of capital

Conduct of Foreign Institutional Investors

Conduct of Portfolio Managers

Conduct of managers of Collective Investment Schemes

Conduct of mutual fund industry

Conduct of foreign venture capital investor

Conduct of credit rating agencies

Conduct of Registrar and transfer agents

Conduct of bankers to issue of capital

Conduct of Merchant Bankers

Regulation on issue of sweat equity and employee stock option scheme

Conduct of stock exchanges and stock brokers

Conduct of debenture trustee

Regulation for buy-back of securities and takeover

Regulation on prohibition of fraudulent and unfair trade practice relating to securities market

Exercise of powers under delegation of powers under SCR Act

Regulation of custodian of securities

Guidelines for corporate governance.

Regional Offices handle key operational areas also.

These are:

(a) ***Consumer protection:*** SEBI is responsible for consumer protection issues in relation to financial products and service in relation to capital market.

(b) ***Enforcement:*** As part of its activities SEBI investigates suspected contraventions of the laws for which it has responsibility and may take action where appropriate.

The types of matters SEBI may investigate are wide ranging. They cover matters as:

Insider trading (trading in securities while in possession of information that is not publicly available)

Illegal fund raising (*i.e.* raising money from investors without a required offer document or prospectus)

Fraud or theft by directors of stock broking companies

Issuing false or misleading prospectuses, announcements to the market, takeover documents or financial statement

For consumer protection issues such as misleading and deceptive conduct, SEBI has a number of information gathering powers, including the power to inspect books and records and the power to require a person to attend an examination and to answer questions. Failure to produce documents, destruction of documents, lying to SEBI and not answering questions are all offences under the SEBI Act.

(c) ***Business and Corporate Finance:*** SEBI also covers a range of activities such as licensing (including stock exchange brokers, portfolio managers, asset management companies), takeovers, mergers, fund raising (*e.g. via* prospectuses), disclosure etc.

3.2.3 Insurance Regulatory and Development Authority of India (IRDAI)

IRDAI is an autonomous apex statutory body which regulates and develops the insurance industry in India. The Authority has the power to frame regulations under Section 114A of the Insurance Act, 1938. From 2000 onwards, it has framed various regulations ranging from registration of companies for carrying on insurance business to protection of policyholders' interests. It also licenses insurance brokers and agents. It also formulates required guidelines for solvency margin as well as accounting guidelines for insurance companies. Its role also encompasses parties associated with insurance business such as surveyors and loss assessors. The key objectives of IRDA include promotion of competition, so as to enhance customer satisfaction through increased consumer choice and lower premiums, while ensuring the financial security of the insurance market.

3.3 SELF-REGULATORY BODIES

A self-regulatory organisation, in the financial sector, is an association of the service providers, pertaining to a particular field. This field could be banking, insurance, mutual funds, foreign exchange, micro finance or any other field related to financial sector. It is not necessary that all the players in that particular field should be its members, but, to be effective, it is desirable that a substantial number of them should be associated with it. It is important to note that a self-regulatory organisation does not replace the statutory regulator pertaining to that field, or any of its functions. In fact, a self-regulatory body assists the Regulator in effective implementation of its objectives and, usually, gets formal recognition from the regulator. Recognition by the regulator is subject to fulfilling the criterion laid down by the regulator for this purpose.

An important function of the self-regulatory body is formulating and administering a code of conduct for its members. Other important functions and responsibilities may include a grievance and dispute redressal mechanism for clients, ensuring client protection and education, monitoring compliance by members with the regulatory framework put in place by the regulator, surveillance and monitoring of the related sector, training and awareness programmes for members, etc., and submission of financial data.

Some of the important self-regulatory bodies in the financial sector are;

Indian Banks' Association (IBA)

Foreign Exchange Dealers' Association of India (FEDAI)

Association of Mutual Funds of India (AMFI)

Micro Finance Institutions Network (MFIN)

For a financial planner, the knowledge of the functioning of stock exchanges is very important as he is likely to deal with these, invariably, during the implementation of a client's financial plan. The Securities Regulation and Contract Act governs the operation of stock markets and establishment of exchanges for securities. All stock exchanges including the leading stock exchanges, *i.e.* National Stock Exchange (NSE) and Mumbai Stock Exchange (BSE) are governed by SEBI under this Act. These organisations are classified as self-regulatory bodies. They are required to include certain provisions in their business rules and have duty to assist SEBI in the exercise of its powers.

SEBI is considering more Self-Regulatory Organisations (SROs) in the area of controlling merchant bankers, mutual funds, Registrars and Transfer agents etc. In order for the SRO to effectively execute its responsibilities, it would be required to be structured, organized, managed and controlled such that it retains its independence, while continuing to perform a genuine market development role.

3.3.1 Indian Stock Exchanges

Indian Stock Markets are one of the oldest in Asia. Its history dates back to nearly 200 years.

At the end of the American Civil War, the brokers who thrived out of Civil War in 1874, found a place in a street (now appropriately called as Dalal Street) where they would conveniently assemble and transact business. In 1887, they formally established in Bombay, the "Native Share and Stock Brokers' Association" (which is alternatively known as "The Stock Exchange"). In 1895, the Stock Exchange acquired a premises in the same street and it was inaugurated in 1899. Thus, the Stock Exchange at Bombay was consolidated.

Ahmedabad gained importance next to Bombay with respect to cotton textile industry. After 1880, many mills originated from Ahmedabad and rapidly forged ahead. As new mills were floated, the need for a Stock Exchange at Ahmedabad was realised and in 1894 the brokers formed "The Ahmedabad Share and Stock Brokers' Association".

What the cotton textile industry was to Bombay and Ahmedabad, the jute industry was to Calcutta. Also tea and coal industries were the other major industrial groups in Calcutta. After the Share Mania in 1861-65, in the 1870's there was a sharp boom in jute shares, which was followed by a boom in tea shares in the 1880's and 1890's; and a coal boom between 1904 and 1908. On June 1908, some leading brokers formed "The Calcutta Stock Exchange Association".

In 1935, the stock market activity improved, especially in South India where there was a rapid increase in the number of textile mills and many plantation companies were floated. In 1937, a stock exchange was once again organized in Madras - Madras Stock Exchange Association (Pvt.) Limited. (In 1957 the name was changed to Madras Stock Exchange Limited).

In Delhi two stock exchanges - Delhi Stock and Share Brokers' Association Limited and the Delhi Stocks and Shares Exchange Limited - were floated and later on in June 1947, amalgamated into the Delhi Stock Exchange Association Limited.

Bangalore Stock Exchange Limited was registered in 1957 and recognized in 1963.

During eighties, however, many stock exchanges were established: Cochin Stock Exchange (1980), Uttar Pradesh Stock Exchange Association Limited (at Kanpur, 1982), and Pune Stock Exchange Limited (1982), Ludhiana Stock Exchange Association Limited (1983), Gauhati Stock Exchange Limited (1984), Kanara Stock Exchange Limited (at Mangalore, 1985), Magadh Stock Exchange Association (at Patna, 1986), Jaipur Stock Exchange Limited (1989), Bhubaneswar Stock Exchange Association Limited (1989), Saurashtra Kutch Stock Exchange Limited (at Rajkot, 1989), Vadodara Stock Exchange Limited (at Baroda, 1990) and recently established exchanges - Coimbatore and Meerut. Thus, at present, there are totally twenty-one recognized stock exchanges in India excluding the Over. The Counter Exchange of India Limited (OTCEI) and the National Stock Exchange of India Limited (NSEIL).

National Stock Exchange (NSE)

With the liberalization of the Indian economy, it was imperative to lift the Indian stock market trading system on par with the international standards. The National Stock Exchange was incorporated in 1992 by Industrial Development Bank of India, Industrial Credit and Investment Corporation of India, Industrial Finance Corporation of India, all Insurance Corporations, selected commercial banks and others.

Trading at NSE can be classified under two broad categories:

(*a*) Wholesale debt market and

(*b*) Capital market.

Wholesale debt market operations are similar to money market operations - institutions and corporate bodies enter into high value transactions in financial instruments such as Government securities, treasury bills, public sector unit bonds, commercial paper, certificate of deposit, etc.

Trading at NSE takes place through a fully automated screen-based trading mechanism, which adopts the principle of an order-driven market. Trading members can stay at their offices and execute the trading, since they are linked through a communication network. The prices at which the buyer and seller are willing to transact will appear on the screen. When the prices match, the transaction will be completed, and a confirmation slip will be printed at the office of the trading member.

NSE has several advantages over the traditional trading exchanges. They are as follows:

NSE brings an integrated stock market trading network across the nation.

Investors can trade at the same price from anywhere in the country since inter-market operations are streamlined coupled with the countrywide access to the securities.

Delays in communication, late payments and the malpractice's prevailing in the traditional trading mechanism can be done away with greater operational efficiency and informational transparency in the stock market operations, with the support of total computerized network.

Business and Listing Rules

The rules governing all companies and other securities listed on the Indian stock exchanges are known as the 'Business and Listing Rules'. The business rules govern matters like accounts, audits, client relations, trading and delivery and settlements in case of market participants (Stock brokers). The stock exchanges or SEBI may undertake inspection visits to ensure compliance with the business rules. The listing rules cover the minimum requirements for a company to gain listing and include, among other things, minimum shareholder requirements, profit performance and capital requirements. They also outline requirements to maintain listing and govern a broad range of matters including disclosure of price sensitive information, dividends and announcements.

Stock exchange undertakes extensive monitoring of the market and depending on the nature of any abnormalities detected, either takes action itself and/or refers the matter to SEBI. It is the duty of stock exchanges to notify SEBI of any suspected contraventions of law it detects.

SELF-ASSESSMENT EXERCISE 4

1. Briefly outline the main roles of regulation in the financial system.

   ....

   ....

   ....

2. Name the three regulatory bodies, which regulate the Indian financial system and briefly outline the key regulatory responsibilities that these bodies have.

   ....

   ....

   ....

   ....

SELF-ASSESSMENT EXERCISE 5

1. Name the main regulatory authority currently responsible for supervising each of the following:

Entity	Regulator
Banks	
Superannuation products	
General Insurance Companies	
Stock Brokers	
Mutual Funds	
The market for listed securities	
Life Insurance products	
Foreign exchange dealers	
Money Changers	

SELF-ASSESSMENT EXERCISE 6

What is the purpose of the business rules in Indian Stock Exchanges?

....

....

....

....

....

....

....

....

....

....

....

REVIEW

QUESTIONS

For each of the multiple-choice question, select the best response.

1. Which of the following statements is the most appropriate?
   (*a*) Wholesale financial services are commonly provided by banks, mutual funds and Non-banking financial services
   (*b*) Wholesale financial services are structured and tailored for households and small/medium size enterprises
   (*c*) Retail financial services are largely structured to meet the needs of individuals and small to medium corporations
   (*d*) Retail financial services are largely provided by investment banks, while other banks concentrate on wholesale financial services
2. Which of the following has an intermediary correctly paired with the financial market in which it usually operates?
   (*a*) Investment bank and debt market
   (*b*) Stockbroker and short-term money market
   (*c*) Co-operative bank and international money transfer
   (*d*) Derivative dealer and fixed interest market

   Indicate whether the following statements are true or false
3. Liquid mutual funds have given retail investors access to wholesale interest rates by pooling investors fund.

   True/False
4. Life insurance companies are required to maintain a part of policyholder assets in statutory assets.

   True/False
5. Regulation performs an important role in:
   A. Maintaining confidence
   B. Encouraging investment
   C. Deterring fraud
   D. All of the above

6. Prudential supervision is concerned with:
   A. Regulations imposed on Banks aimed at the protection of depositors, investors and other creditors
   B. Regulations imposed on Banks aimed at the protection of the shareholders
   C. RBI's role in 'guaranteeing' bank deposit
   D. Control over ownership of the bank
7. Which was order of creation of regulation authority?
   A. RBI, SEBI, IRDA
   B. SEBI, RBI, IRDA
   C. IRDA, RBI, SEBI
   D. IRDA, SEBI, RBI

   Indicate whether the following statements are true or false:
8. RBI licenses and prudentially regulates all banks, Insurance Companies and Non-Banking Finance Company

   True/false
9. Prudential supervision by RBI is achieved through controls on banks including amounts of capital held and liquid assets

   True/false

ANSWERS

1. "c"
2. "a"
3. True
4. True
5. D
6. A
7. A
8. False
9. True

IN SUMMARY

In this topic, we have considered the participants, the financial intermediaries and the regulators which operate within the Indian Financial System. We began this topic by identifying the intermediaries and the role they play. We noted that the intermediaries make the financial markets more efficient. We then examined their services both to retail and wholesale clients. We also looked at the new arrangements for regulation and supervision of the financial markets and of financial intermediaries. We examed the importance of regulation and the role and function of the key regulatory authorities: RBI, SEBI and IRDA. Together these institutions ensure that financial intermediaries are prudently run and that securities markets are efficient and fair. Then we looked at self-regulatory organisations and their role in financial industry.

SUGGESTED ANSWERS TO SELF-ASSESSMENT EXERCISE 1

Answer 1

(*a*) True

(*b*) False

(*c*) True

(*d*) True

(*e*) False

(*f*) True

Answer 2 - Three essential components are required in an efficient financial market:

Information about the product being offered, whether it is a savings account or shares in an new company.

Opportunity to sell and to buy at a price.

Assurance that payment will be made on completion of the deal.

Financial intermediaries help to provide this efficiency.

Financial intermediaries can make markets more efficient in a number of ways, including the following:

By achieving economies of scale, financial intermediaries can offer specialist services at the least cost.

Financial intermediaries can channel savings into productive areas and maximize the yield on investment.

To survive in a highly competitive market, financial intermediaries must be innovative in the services they provide and hence able to adapt their services to changes in the economic climate, technology and market preferences.

By accepting risk, financial intermediaries encourage participation in the markets.

Answer 3 - In an advanced economy which uses money as medium of exchange, there are two ways of channelling funds between savers and borrowers:

(*a*) by direct dealing *i.e.* method of transferring funds by a direct meeting between savers and borrowers. This method is efficient for large money transfer only. For small transaction size, transaction cost itself per unit of money will be very high.

(*b*) Through financial intermediation (*i.e.* where financial intermediaries package and pool net savers' funds and then lend those funds to net borrowers for a fee). This is the most often used channel between savers and borrowers in the Indian financial system today.

SUGGESTED ANSWERS TO SELF-ASSESSMENT EXERCISE 2

1. Answers will depend on the selected intermediary
2. A financial intermediary or group of intermediaries will underwrite an issue of securities for an issuer of security. Underwriting means that if the issuer is not able to sell the entire issue (the purpose of which is to raise funds for the company) to the public or to other institutions, the underwriters will take up the unsold portion of the securities, offered for sale, at the pre-agreed price

   The underwriter charges a fee for the service and accepts the financial risk. The advantage to the client (the borrower) is the guarantee that the full amount will be raised.
3. Some financial intermediaries service a number of sectors including the household, corporate and Government sectors. For example banks provide personal loans to the household sector and discount bills of exchange for the corporate sector, and invest certain amount in Government securities.

However not all financial institutions are permitted to service all sectors and some concentrate their efforts on specific sectors. For example, mutual funds are not allowed to undertake lending activities.

SUGGESTED ANSWERS TO SELF-ASSESSMENT EXERCISE 3

Answer 1

Retail	Wholesale
Leasing	Leasing
Overdrafts	Overdrafts
Investment advice	Project finance
Credit and debit cards	Bills of exchange
Term loan	Equity raising
Mutual Funds	Eurocurrency loans
Savings account	Advice on acquisitions
	Underwriting new share issues
	Term loan
	Foreign exchange dealing

You can observe that many services are offered to both wholesale and retail.

Answer 2

Ten investment options available to the retail would include any of the following:

Fixed Deposits

Debentures*

Shares*

Preference Shares*

Convertible Debenture*

Property

Antiques

Gold

Art

Mutual funds*

Derivatives*

*Denotes financial securities

SUGGESTED ANSWERS TO SELF-ASSESSMENT EXERCISE 4

Question one

Maintain public/investor confidence

Promote stability of the financial system

Maintain international confidence

Deter fraudulent behaviour

Protect investors

Question two

(*a*) The Reserve Bank supervises *via* prudential regulations all deposit taking activities as well controls foreign exchange market beside overall stability of financial system and setting monetary policy and payments system.

(*b*) SEBI is responsible for financial market integrity, companies consumer protection in relation to financial products and services, and enforcement of law relating to financial products and services. It also licenses and supervises a number of financial market participants such as security brokers, underwriters, depositories, mutual funds etc.

(*c*) IRDA is responsible for insurance companies in a manner similar to RBI in arena of banking. It licenses all insurance sector related intermediaries and prudentially supervises over them.

SUGGESTED ANSWERS TO SELF-ASSESSMENT EXERCISE 5

Entity	Regulator
Banks	RBI
Superannuation products	IRDA
General Insurance Companies	IRDA
Stock Brokers	SEBI
Mutual Funds	SEBI
The market for listed securities	SEBI
Life Insurance products	IRDA
Foreign exchange dealers	RBI
Money Changers	RBI

SUGGESTED ANSWERS TO SELF-ASSESSMENT EXERCISE 6

Business Rules govern matters like accounts, audits, client relations, trading and delivery and settlements.

CHECKLIST

Below is a checklist of main points covered by this topic. Use this checklist to test your learning.

Financial intermediaries facilitate the flow of funds between people with money and people wanting money.

Financial intermediaries provide a wide range of financial services, and are active in both the primary and secondary market.

Financial intermediaries accept a number of risks, including liquidity risk and credit risk and are compensated for this by spreads between borrowing and lending.

Financial intermediaries make markets more efficient by accepting risk.

Financial intermediaries offer a number of advantages to their clients including:

- Reduced costs
- Specialist skills and knowledge
- Diverse range of products tailored to individual needs
- Safety and convenience

Financial service can be categorised into retail services to individuals and small businesses and wholesale services to large corporations and Governments.

Retail financial services comprise:

- Lending services
- Borrowing services
- Investment advice

Mutual funds provide the retail investor with access to the money market and wholesale market interest rates.

A wide range of avenues is available to the retail borrower, including housing loans, personal loans, leasing, credit cards, hire purchase etc.

Investment advice is available from a variety of sources, including financial advisers, stockbrokers, fund managers and life insurance companies.

The range of wholesale financial services is diverse and includes:

- Corporate borrowing
- Advice on mergers and acquisitions
- Underwriting new securities
- Investment portfolio management
- Foreign exchange dealing

Acquisition may be achieved through a merger (usually friendly) or a takeover (usually less friendly).

Financial intermediaries underwrite the issue of some securities, thus accepting the risk associated with those securities.

Portfolio management entails the selecting and ongoing monitoring of an appropriate mix of investments in a portfolio.

Financial intermediaries are undergoing structural changes, are operating in a more competitive environment and increasingly adopting international practices.

Some large companies are now developing their own in-house trading operations and are also accepting fixed deposits from the public.

This move away from operating through a financial intermediary is called 'disintermediation'.

The stock exchange provides a market place where companies can raise money and investors can invest surplus funds.

Investment banks provide a range of mainly wholesale financial services on a fee for service basis.

Non-banking finance companies provide services to both retail and wholesale clients. They provide consumer finance for a variety of purposes and business finance such as leasing and hire purchase.

Life insurance companies act as financial intermediary, which specializes in channelling funds from the household sector into life insurance and superannuation schemes.

Fund managers invest, manage and monitor the assets of their clients.

Stockbrokers buy and sell securities on behalf of investors.

Superannuation fund is money saved during working life to be used upon retirement.

The Reserve Bank of India (RBI) is the Central Bank. Its role is to oversee the Indian financial system and its stability and to conduct monetary policy so that it operates efficiently in line with Government policies.

RBI is the main regulator for banking system. It has dual control over co-operative banks too.

RBI supervises payment system, NBFC activity besides controlling foreign exchange dealers.

SEBI is responsible for:

- Conduct of underwriters for issue of capital
- Conduct of Foreign Institutional Investors
- Conduct of Portfolio Managers
- Conduct of managers of Collective Investment Schemes
- Conduct of mutual fund industry
- Conduct of foreign venture capital investor
- Conduct of credit rating agencies
- Conduct of Registrar and transfer agents
- Conduct of bankers to issue of capital
- Conduct of Merchant Bankers
- Regulation on issue of sweat equity and employee stock option scheme
- Conduct of stock exchanges and stock brokers
- Conduct of debenture trustee
- Regulation for buy-back of securities and takeover
- Regulation on prohibition of fraudulent and unfair trade practice relating to securities market
- Exercise of powers under delegation of powers under SCR Act
- Regulation of custodian of securities
- Guidelines for corporate governance

IRDA is responsible for:

- Conduct of insurance companies both general and life
- Superannuation and Gratuity Funds
- Implementation of Insurance Act

Protection of interest of policyholders

Conduct of surveyors and loss assessors

Conduct of third party administrator in health care insurance

Regulating maintenance of margin of solvency by insurance companies

Adjudication of disputes between insurers and intermediaries or insurance intermediaries.

NSE operates a screen-based trading in listed securities. Its listing rules govern listed securities, while the business rules govern activities of those authorised to trade on the exchange.

4 CHAPTER

Basics of Financial Planning

ABOUT THIS TOPIC

Financial planning, in its broadest sense, encompasses a wide range of skills and knowledge. It draws much from other disciplines — accounting, risk management, taxation, legal services, investment, economics and small business management to list a few.

Many financial planners are generalists. They bring their skills, knowledge and experience into play as they work with their clients to devise an appropriate financial strategy and translate it into an action plan. When such strategies call for a specialist's skill, these planners have a range of professionals with whom they can work, including the client's existing advisers.

Other financial planners specialise. They might target small businesses or work with retirees. While they have the generalist background, they have further developed their skills and knowledge base in specific areas.

A financial planner should be able to understand his customer and classify his current behaviour and adopt suitable strategies. So, this topic provides insight into investment behaviour at various stages of consumer life cycle. These stages have been studied a number of times and we may find multiple names to describe the stage. This topic provides essential insights into causes for underlying behaviour and exception in case of non-traditional individuals. In the end we have also touched upon normal wealth cycle an individual is expected to go through in his/her working life.

While knowledge and skills are important to financial planners, the key to a successful financial planning practice is the ability to understand clients' needs, attitudes and fears. The most appropriate strategy imaginable will not work if the client will not commit to it.

TOPIC OBJECTIVES

At the end of this topic, you should be able to:

- *Explain why financial planning is needed*
- *Define financial planning*
- *Describe the role of a financial planner.*
- *List the main providers of financial planning services*
- *Compare the different forms of remuneration for financial planning*
- *Outline the responsibilities of financial planners and investment advisers under the relevant legislation*
- *Explain the importance of analysing a client's risk profile.*
- *Identify the customer's life stage*
- *Explain the customer about his needs in relation to his peer group*
- *Explain the customer about reasons for proposed financial plan*
- *Identify the stages of traditional and non-traditional life cycles*
- *Understand the demographic trends underlying the life cycle*
- *Identify the variables that influence financial behaviour*
- *Estimate the income and expense flows over the life cycle*
- *Assess the liquidity needs over the life cycle*
- *Identify the risk preferences by life cycle*
- *The three stages of wealth cycle*

1. INTRODUCTION

Financial planning, as an all-encompassing, centralised programme, is still a relatively new concept. Most individuals have engaged themselves in some form of financial planning. They might have a budget, setting aside an amount from each pay to save for short-term expenditure such as a trip, or a deposit on a longer term 'asset' such as a car or a home. They might have purchased home and contents insurance, taken out a life insurance policy or made a will. All of these form part of a financial plan, but most people lack the skills, knowledge or interest to put all of their financial actions into a formal plan. Until recently, there was little need to do so.

In the past, savings were deposited with a bank or post office. Investments were made in National Savings Certificates (NSC), Public Provident Fund accounts (PPF), property or gold. A small number of people invested in the stock market. Apart from war and depressions, there was overall stability. Interest rates were steady. Families could borrow to build a home and the interest rate would hardly move over the life of the mortgage. Significant social and economic changes began in the late 1980s, when India started deregulating its financial sector. These changes did away with the expectation of stability and changed the financial environment for all. Uncertainty and the rapid pace of change have given rise to the need for a financial planning industry. Investors have started recognising that they stand a better chance of achieving their financial goals if a well-planned and documented process is adopted towards this. NRIs are the prominent users of financial planning as they are keen to see their wealth grow when they return to India. Earlier, the investors were mainly guided by the insurance and real estate agents. With the emergence of registered investment advisers and professional financial planners, the investors are willing to pay fee for the expert advice relating to their overall financial wellbeing.

1.1 FACTORS FOR GROWTH OF FINANCIAL PLANNING SERVICES

Some of the major factors that have influenced the growth of the financial planning services in India, are:

Inflation

The growth of credit

Government need for increased revenue and resources

Regulation and deregulation

Demographic shifts

1.1.1 Inflation

Inflation affects people differently, depending on their circumstances. The high inflation that began in the early 1970s drastically reduced the value of fixed interest portfolios. It took some time for markets to adjust to the sharp rises in inflation. Real yield (*i.e.* the rate of return adjusted for inflation) on interest-bearing investments became very low, especially for longer term assets. When combined with relatively high rates of personal tax, after-tax yields were sometimes negative. The ability of retirees and others dependent on a fixed income, to maintain their standard of living, was severely eroded.

On the other hand, people who owned homes and other properties saw the values of these assets make enormous leaps. The price of land doubled, tripled and then rose even higher. Employees, seeing the value of their pay drop, demanded higher wages. Producers, to cover their high wage bills, increased the prices of their goods and services.

The capital that the investor holds may be yielding lower returns and at the same time high inflation has resulted in negative real returns. This situation also eats into the capital and the savings one has done. On the other hand, life expectancy has increased which brings forth the need for comprehensive retirement planning. Though the inflation and interest rates have shown downward trends from the middle of 2014, the financial planning process is greatly influenced by the estimates of inflation and interest rates.

Reflection

Consider the situation of an elderly couple who own their home. The value of their home has risen significantly, as have their rates, electricity, food, transport and medical costs. Their fixed income stream has not increased.

If they want to increase it, they will have to pay more for it by either using more capital or taking a greater investment risk. What can they do? People need a means to control the impact of inflation on their lives. They need to move beyond simple savings and fixed-interest investments. And they need professional advice on how best to manage their affairs.

You will need to understand the impact of inflation on your clients' investments and lifestyles. Inflation is discussed in detail in Chapter 1: Indian Economic Environment.

1.1.2 The growth of credit

Credit and inflation are linked. When people must pay for all their needs with ready cash, they are limited in their spending. They must save until they can afford something, or they must do without. This leads to a moderation of demand.

Take an example of a couple wanting a house. Because credit is scarce, they first live with their parents and save to buy a block of land. Then they build a small residence, paying for it as they build. Later, they might expand it into a larger home. There is no excess demand for new homes or land, prices remain stable, wages remain stable.

The availability of credit changes things markedly. Rather than a modest residence, the couple saves up a 20% deposit (for margin money on loan) and purchases a fully built home. They want to furnish it fully and perhaps each wants a car. As the demand for credit has increased, interest rates rise, the couple needs to find more money each month to meet their mortgage payments. One person working does not suffice, so both now work. They expect to earn higher wages each year, so they borrow more now, to pay later. The whole fabric of society has changed.

Reflection

What happens when wage growth stops or one partner loses his or her job? People need help in making asset growth work for them. They need to manage their tax liabilities better as inflation and higher wages push them through tax brackets.

You will want to help your clients use credit wisely to maintain a manageable level of debt. The impact of interest rates and easy or tight credit are discussed in Chapter 1: Indian Economic Environment.

1.1.3 Government need for increased revenue

In a similar manner to individuals, governments also feel the impact of inflation in the cost of the goods and services they purchase and the wage spiral that accompanies inflation. They need increasing levels of revenue to pay for their expenditure. And, just like the individual, they have two ways of coming up with more money — spending less or 'earning' more. Governments earn money through taxes. (Whether they are called taxes, tariffs, excises, surcharges, levies or user-pays fees they are still taxes and revenue raises.)

Reflection

Consider the flow-through of an additional one-paisa-per-barrel tax on crude oil. It flows from the refiner, to the dealer, to the pump price, to transport costs, to increases in food prices. Can you explain the effects of tax changes on the economy to your clients?

Governments have two ways of cutting costs. They can cut back on their own expenditure such as staffing and travel, or they can cut back on public works such as building roads, bridges and airports. They can also reduce, or limit, the growth of subsidies by making the qualification criteria stricter, by consolidating and cutting back funding to social welfare agencies, or by making waiting periods longer.

Subsidies are the government's way of providing those in need of assistance with money. In times of economic stress, a large number of people seek such subsidies. Where there is a downturn in the economy, the government's revenue streams (*i.e.* payroll tax, income-tax, corporate tax) are reduced. There is less money available to meet the increasing claims on the government for assistance.

We were, till recently, in an environment of high inflation, both in the Indian economy and the global economy, mainly due to the rise in fuel prices and high primary products prices or food inflation. With a steep decline in the prices of crude oil and metals, since the middle of 2014, there has been a decline in the overall inflation despite food prices remaining high. For the government, high inflation, while increasing the costs of its purchases of goods and services, means that tax revenues will continue to rise.

India has been fortunate to maintain some growth in its economy, even in difficult years. In a low-growth/low inflation environment, governments can no longer expect rapid increase in revenues.

Wage inflation results in an increase in the government's personal tax receipts. While this means that tax revenue will increase, the government also has to pay wages to its employees. Wage increases, therefore, translate into increases in expenditure too.

People were spending less money on goods taxed by excise duty and sales tax, and more money on services, which were untaxed. The government had to look at a wider indirect tax base to maintain its income from indirect tax. Even in terms of contribution to GDP, services account for over 50%. This led to the imposition of tax on services, a few years ago.

Many of the government's outlays are either directly or indirectly indexed to the inflation rate. Revenues, which increase along with asset prices, *e.g.* stamp duty on property sales and share market transactions, are also hit in a low inflationary environment.

1.1.4 Regulation and Deregulation

Any changes, whether major or minor, to the regulatory regime mean additional work (and revenue-generating potential) for financial planners. Existing clients need to know how the changes will affect their finances, and they might need to change product structures. People who previously would not have approached a financial planner recognise that they need help to understand and manage the change.

The media, both the financial press and the popular tabloids, are reporting personal financial news more frequently and in greater depth. This is helping to raise the level of awareness about the management of personal finance. The media might also be creating false expectations and harmful attitudes, which you will have to recognise and combat as you work with your clients.

Two major changes — means testing for eligibility for subsidies, and compulsory superannuation savings — have had an enormous impact on the general public.

Means testing

The government distributes food grains and kerosene at subsidised rates under the public distribution system (PDS). States have their own criteria to determine eligibility for such subsidies. These generally depend on the annual income of the household. The trend is towards making subsidies available to fewer and fewer sections of society - the poorest of the poor. The PDS system itself has its share of anomalies. The government, for political reasons, purchases grains at prices that are higher than the reasonable market rates. These, when released to the market for the eligible poor, are occasionally found to be more costly than better quality grain available off the shelf to all consumers!

Reflection

The service industries that have sprung up around funds management, financial planning and superannuation are extensive. Start with superannuation and consider all of the sub-industries that provide services to superannuation schemes, financial planners and fund managers. There have also been major changes in the regulation of all aspects of the securities industry since 1990s. The trend is towards deregulation. Deregulation is the opposite action to regulation, *i.e.* it is the freeing up of constraints. Corporate scandals and stock market scams are also leading to pressure for regulation.

Regulation (or re-regulation) happens when governments feel that free market forces do not protect investors sufficiently. Deregulation is associated with competitive market forces, which are supposed to drive down prices and increase customer services and available options. Deregulation of financial markets has had a number of effects, both direct and indirect. Directly, it has opened up and expanded a number of markets. Indirectly it has created a greater diversity of fund managers operating in a more competitive environment.

However, the lower fees and increased customer services that were originally expected have not occurred in the banking and finance markets.

While interest rates in the home loan market and the market for top-rated borrowers are definitely lower, other areas within the banking system are charging exorbitantly for simple transactions and credit cards. Banking and finance companies are still charging high interest too.

Reflection

What has been the impact of new entrants into the home loan market? How has regulation affected this market? Why do people still use higher priced banks for home loans?

1.1.5 Demographic shifts

Of all the major economies of the world India has the unique demographic advantage, the advantage of a young population and the growth in these numbers over of the next two decades is expected to support the growth of the economy . This increase in the number and percentage of working population to a large extent will contribute to the savings and spending characteristics of the overall population and the economy.

The government has all along encouraged savings to ensure resources for economic planning and development. This also contributes to enhancement of post-retirement resources for the people to help them maintain their lifestyle and take care of themselves. The efforts from the government has helped push up the gross savings rate over the years.

The clear objective of government initiatives, mainly in long-term funds and schemes, is to raise the level of long-term retirement savings across the entire labour force. With a higher level of personal retirement savings, people should be funding more of their retirement income needs to reduce the burden on the government to provide pension entitlements.

Reflection

What are some of the factors that affect people's ability or willingness to save? Deregulation of the financial system has increased the number and style of products available for clients. Government policy has always been to encourage investments such as those mentioned under section 80 of the Income-tax Act. The planner is expected to help clients arrange their affairs so that they get maximum benefits.

Reflection

To what groups do you belong? Can you identify a target market in which you have a special interest or expertise? What are the features of this group? What special financial planning needs might they have?

SELF ASSESSMENT EXERCISE 1

1. You are discussing a client's need for financial planning. What are the five major economic factors that might influence the client's decision?

   ....

   ....

   ....

   ....

2. List five lifestyle or emotional factors that might influence people to seek assistance from a financial planner.

   ....

   ....

   ....

   ....

2. WHAT IS FINANCIAL PLANNING?

Financial planning is the process whereby an individual moves towards meeting personal and financial goals through the development and implementation of a comprehensive financial plan. While financial planning is seen primarily as a personal process for individuals and couples, it is often integrated into small business planning.

Financial planning is not a static concept. Rather it involves integrating a particular set of circumstances and needs into a continually changing economic environment. It is an ongoing process of relating the client's changing financial position to financial objectives within a constantly changing financial environment. This integration can be best explained by a financial planning model, represented in Figure 1.

FIGURE 1: A FINANCIAL PLANNING MODEL

Investor	Investor Needs		Product Structures	Assets
Investor	To age 45 55 65 Wealth accumulation	Death	Direct investment - Shares	Equity Cash
	Retirement savings		- Property Superannuation	Fixed interest
	Risk management		Property schemes Annuities/pensions	
	Investment income stream		Unit trusts	
	Tax management		Government bonds Corporate bonds	
	Cash flow management		Debentures Investment schemes	
	Estate planning		Risk products *e.g.* life, disability and trauma covers	

Financial planners assess the investor unit's (individual, family, etc.) needs in the light of their general age/lifestyle. A product structure takes the returns generated from assets and puts them into frameworks that provide solutions to the investor needs. For example, if the investor is 60 years of age, all of the need components might be active, but if his age is 45 years, some of the need components, like estate planning, may not be present.

As a financial planner, you will be required to use your specialist knowledge and skills to construct a financial plan, made up of strategies and actions, designed to meet your clients' goals.

These goals might include:

earning a certain level of income

maintaining or increasing the value of assets

saving and investing within a level of risk acceptable to the client

having reasonable levels of liquidity and flexibility

maintaining an adequate level of security through insurance on assets and income earning capacity

reaching financial independence in the future

increasing 'lifestyle' options in the present

maximising the after-tax return within appropriate risk levels

having an appropriate timetable for the purchase of investments, their holding period and subsequent sale

within these goals, emotional and lifestyle requirements will affect financial decisions.

You will need to understand how these interact for individuals and between couples.

2.1 THE IMPORTANCE OF RISK PROFILING

One of the most important factors affecting clients is their ability to withstand risk. The financial planner's role is crucial in determining the risk profile of the client. This is achieved by questioning the client extensively along the following lines:

How concerned are they about having their portfolio keep pace with inflation?

How concerned are they about tax effective investments?

To what extent are they concerned about the capital stability of their investments?

How concerned are they about generating income from their portfolio?

How concerned are they about maximising their estate assets? To what extent do they need assistance in managing their portfolio?

Another factor, which will determine how much risk a client is willing to bear, is the time frame for investment. Past investment purchases might colour clients' attitude to investment if that experience was negative. If funds are required within one to two years, then the risk profile might need to be more conservative as volatility will have a significant effect on the capital value of the portfolio.

The client's level of concern in relation to these issues will assist the planner to establish a risk profile. If the clients were extremely concerned about the capital stability of their investment, a lower risk profile would be appropriate.

Once the correct risk profile has been established, the appropriate asset allocation can be selected to achieve the client's goals.

Reflection

Consider how you achieve an appropriate financial plan for a couple when one person is afraid to take risks (risk-averse) and the other is a moderate risk taker. What if your clients decide to divorce? Can you provide both parties with financial advice?

To recommend actions to your clients, your plan will have to incorporate features of:

- cash flow (budgeting) and financing
- investment planning
- taxation planning
- retirement planning (superannuation and retirement income streams)
- risk management (insurance)
- estate planning (including the use of family trusts)
- business succession planning.

The basic steps in financial planning take you and your clients through a process of defining where your clients are today, where they want to be in the future, and what resources they have to use along the way. You then use your skills and knowledge to map out a beginning — a financial plan. As each year passes, changes to the markets, the regulations, the products and the client will necessitate review and perhaps modification of the plan. As a planner, you will act as a pathfinder. You will need to understand the environment and provide your clients with a clear path to their financial future, removing obstacles and barriers as you go.

2.2 PRE AND POST-RETIREMENT PLANNING

Financial planning should occur both before and after retirement. The strategies and products you recommend at each stage, will be quite different as investors' needs are often different.

Before retirement, clients usually focus on wealth accumulation. Generally, in the accumulation stage, investors can afford to take higher risks.

They have the time to work through peaks and troughs in the investment markets. This does not mean that any particular individual will be more comfortable with a higher level of risk than any other. Each client will have different attitudes to risk, and these attitudes might change over time.

Reflection

Assume your clients are reasonably risk-averse, yet their investment time and financial situation are appropriate for a portfolio with a moderate risk level. What recommendations for risk levels should you make?

After retirement, with no earned income to service regular needs, a client's investment objectives might become largely income-driven. The risk profile (personal attitude to risk) of retirees is usually more conservative as they have little opportunity to rebuild wealth in the event of disaster; however, this might change over time. It is not unusual to find clients in their eighties with 70% or more of their portfolio in equities, and to find them very comfortable with that position.

2.3 USERS OF FINANCIAL PLANNING SERVICES

India has a moderate savings and investment rate. While some people do invest in the share market, the take-up rate of both direct shares and mutual funds is much lower than in the United States, for example, where a significant number of people invest in mutual (managed) funds. However, this is changing in India.

The take-up of mutual funds and financial planning go hand in hand in India. The professional bodies of both fund managers and financial planners are seeking ways to attract more investors to the investment markets through such collective (or pooled) products.

With the rapid increase in the number of people who will need financial planning and the initiatives of fund managers and industry bodies, plus the efforts of individual financial planners, there should be an increasing inflow of funds. There are still many barriers to savings.

While superannuation is seen as a savings mechanism, most people make only the minimum level of personal contributions required. They feel that in doing so, they are providing for their retirement and do not see a need to save outside superannuation. In fact, there are few simple savings products that provide a return significantly over the rate of inflation, over the long term. When taxation is taken into consideration, they might actually offer a negative real rate of return.

While financial planning can be useful to most people throughout their lives, the main categories of financial advice seekers are:

- professionals
- retirees (at regular retirement age or as part of voluntary retirement scheme - VRS)
- retrenched workers
- executives
- small business owners.

Obviously, each of the different groups has a different set of needs and characteristics. It is essential to understand the needs and objectives of different groups and particular clients before drawing on the range of available products to develop an appropriate plan.

You might find that you want to specialise in meeting the needs of one of these groups. You will have to understand their needs and attitudes. Increased use of technology and the ability to access payment systems will help turn the vision of a mobile financial planner described in the next section (3) of this chapter, into a reality. If you have the appropriate skills, experience, financial resources and commitment, the availability of affordable technology means that regulatory and dealer limitations will be the only constraints on what you can do in a financial planning practice.

SELF ASSESSMENT EXERCISE 2

1. Is financial planning a static concept? Why/why not?

....

....

....

....

....

2. The main categories of current users of financial planning are:

   professionals

   retirees

   retrenched workers

   executives

   small business owners.

   Consider a category of possible users outside this group. Why do you think they are reluctant to use financial planning services? How could you focus on this group as a future client base?

   ....

   ....

   ....

   ....

   ....

3. THE ROLE OF A FINANCIAL PLANNER

3.1 THE ROLE OF A FINANCIAL PLANNER

As a financial planner, you will be responsible for designing a financial plan that takes your clients from where they are now to where they want to be in the future, *i.e.* a plan that satisfies their needs and objectives. You will have to:

Analyse their needs and objectives

Match these with appropriate products and services

Work out a financial plan

Implement the plan

Provide ongoing review to ensure the chosen investment strategies continue to match the clients' changing objectives

Modify the investment solutions as required.

Financial planning is divided into several different skill sets. Each skill set has a technical and an intuitive component. You will need to understand the theory behind investing, economics and strategies so that you can reduce that theory to practical plan construction. You can collect data and have your clients take risk tolerance tests, but you will have to interpret that information and make assessments based on your own understanding of how your clients will act and what their attitudes to investing really are. As a financial planner, you will have to be aware of the critical elements that will determine your initial recommendations and that will have a continuing effect on each investment's suitability within the plan.

You will be an implementer, a make-it-happen person. Once your recommendations have been given, you will have to educate or persuade your clients to take action. Obviously, the best financial plans will not benefit your clients unless they are implemented.

Financial planning must be supported by research and training. Specialist organisations often provide these services to the industry.

Trust is considered to be the most valuable asset of a financial planner.

Trust carry with it a significant sense of responsibility. Ethically, it is indicative of a special relationship between individuals which naturally implies confidence and reliance. It also suggests care and concern. It is these associated ideas that underscore the notion of a "fiduciary relationship" which is recognized by Law for mainly any professional relationship that is developed between the Financial Planner and his client.

Paraplanners and financial planners

Internationally, a distinction is drawn between a paraplanner and a financial planner.

'Paraplanner' is a term used to describe a person who researches and prepares financial plans for financial planners, whereas a financial planner deals with clients in planning their finances.

The job description of a paraplanner has a broad possible range. Some paraplanners are involved in the interview process with clients, filling in the data collection forms together with the financial planner. Some dealer groups have a central location where plans are prepared for financial planners in remote locations.

Paraplanning businesses are likely to emerge in India to provide financial plan preparation services to the industry at a relatively small cost. Financial planners can also prepare their own plans; this is normally the case with a small financial planning practice.

The paraplanning profession is an excellent entry point into the financial planning industry. It allows the trainee to gain experience in a backroom ('back office') environment before dealing with clients directly.

3.2 WHO PROVIDES FINANCIAL PLANNING?

In the past, people sought financial advice from the agents who helped them with insurance policies from Life Insurance Corporation (LIC) or mutual fund schemes from Unit Trust of India (UTI). Bank managers were another option, particularly in smaller locations. Despite their best intent, UTI/LIC agents and bank managers were not, and are not, trained to offer advice on a wide range of options. For those who had them, accountants also provided advice. People would also approach professionals in their work environment and discuss ideas with family and friends. In India, financial planners are now beginning to be recognised as a source of financial advice.

There are now many sources for financial advice, including financial consultants who call themselves financial planners. Many of the larger brokerages and distribution houses are creating a financial planning arm. Solicitors, accountants, life agents and life brokers might also provide some level of financial planning advice. Real estate agents might provide contingent financial planning advice, *e.g.* on how to negatively gear into property.

As more people seek investment advice and the number of products available increases, the number of advisers offering financial planning will also increase. The independence of advisers is a major issue. With a large proportion of authorised financial planners working in the big groups, there is both regulatory and investor concern that recommendations are provided with regard to the dealer's product line, not the investor's needs. The manner in which financial planners have been paid, *i.e.* commission from the product providers, has lent itself to criticism that product recommendations were based on the size of the commission rather than suitability for the client. Planner remuneration is discussed at section 3.4. As you would expect, the quality of advice varies considerably, as does the level of client service, research and the range of products available. You would only need to look at the events leading up to investors' recent loss in fly-by-night non-banking finance companies and chit funds to see the effect of poor research and poor advice. A good financial planner should have known that 'high returns' do not equal high levels of security. They should have known that high returns are associated with higher risks.

Reading

For an international perspective on what is meant by good advice, you should read the policy statements in *ASIC Good Advice Handbook.* The information you will need for this subject on regulation and licensing can be found at www.asic.gov.au.

Some of the big players in the financial planning and financial product markets are the life insurance companies and the banks.

Life insurance companies

Life insurance companies are natural investment managers. They collect and invest premium rupees to meet claims and to make a profit. It is a very short step to managing money as an investment manager. In the process known as 'bundling', many products offered by life offices have combined life insurance with an investment component, such as an endowment insurance policy.

Several insurance companies are experimenting with moves away from bundled products to separate investment and insurance products. LIC gains significant business through offering superannuation funds, insurance bonds, annuities and pensions.

Apart from a chain of offices, LIC has a distribution channel in the form of a team of agents spread throughout the country. Most private insurers have distribution companies in their group. Going forward, life companies can consider converting their agency networks into financial planning arms.

Banks

Bank managers have been traditional sources of financial advice. Private banks with a retail focus have fund management and financial planning arms, offering their own line of products and sometimes other fund managers' products as well. They have a natural client base from walk-through bank trade, and referrals from branch managers and loan officers. Other providers of financial planning are listed in Figure 2 and then discussed below.

FIGURE 2: PROVIDERS OF FINANCIAL PLANNING

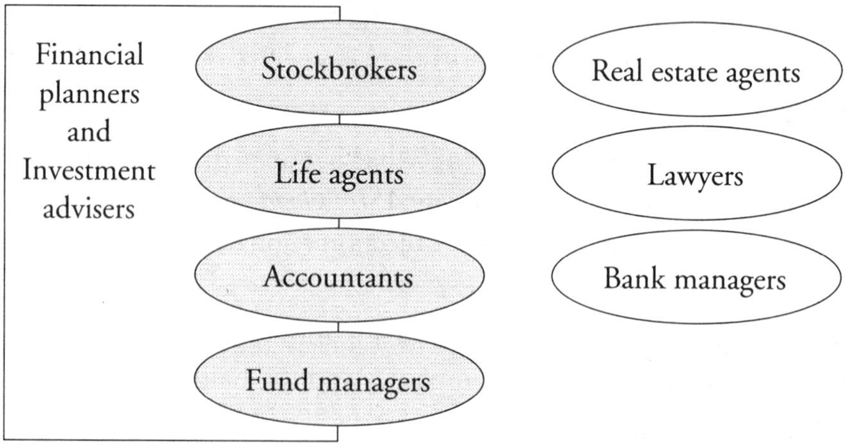

Stockbrokers

Stockbrokers were initially regarded by many people as catering to the wealthy, and offering a limited range of services revolving around securities listed on the stock exchange. Some stockbrokers are beginning to broaden their activities into financial planning, retirement planning, funds management, and financing and advising on unlisted securities. Stockbrokers are governed by the regulations of the Securities and Exchange Board of India and the rules and regulations of the stock exchange with which they are associated. Further, they need to pass the certifying test of the Association of Mutual Funds of India (AMFI), before they can distribute mutual fund schemes.

Trustee companies

In the mutual fund structure, trustee companies have a fiduciary role in protecting the interest (of beneficiary's investors). The actual investment management is handled by asset management companies under the overall monitoring of the trustees.

The Indian Trust Act, 1882 provides for an alternative format for such trusteeship. Instead of trustee companies, individuals can be appointed to the role. Each individual would then be a trustee; collectively they would constitute the Board of Trustees.

Independent financial planners

While as a financial planner you would like to work for a large distribution house or fund management or insurance company, many financial planners have set up their own practices or work within smaller set-ups. You might find that you enjoy providing a personal level of service to your clients and running your own business. Independent financial planners can obtain research and technical information from external sources and software from many different providers. They might also work in conjunction with other professionals, accountants, tax agents and solicitors to form a full service group.

Fund or asset managers

Fund or asset managers develop and offer products that are sold through dedicated agents or distribution houses. The role of financial planners in such distribution arrangements will increase, as the number of such planners increases in the market place.

Asset management companies have been targeting wholesale investors directly, leaving retail investors to the distribution channel. Some fund managers have also begun selling to retail investors directly, for example, through the Internet.

Accountants and solicitors

These people already have specialist skills and clients turn to them for a certain level of financial advice. Accountants, especially, have opportunities to provide a wide range of advice as they are intimately involved in people's finances. The Institute of Chartered Accountants of India, however, does not favour such a role.

Many accountants now run a 'mixed business' - maintaining an independent audit practice, while working under a proper authority with asset management companies and life companies. While these categories of professionals are all able to provide some financial planning advice if it is incidental to their normal activities, there is concern that some might be providing a range of advice beyond their skills and training and well beyond their licensing bounds.

Internationally, even real estate agents provide an element of financial planning advice. In India, such agents are yet to develop the requisite skill sets.

Reflection

Some real estate agents advocate negative gearing into property, implying that the people renting the property will actually be buying the property for the investor. Should they have to hold a proper authority to recommend negative gearing and property investment?

3.3 INCREASING PROFESSIONALISM OF FINANCIAL PLANNERS

Internationally, there has been a concerted effort in recent years to develop a professional standard for financial planners. This change has been brought about by a number of occurrences, including:

- the increased participation of technically competent and ethically minded professionals who are committed to ongoing service and building a reputation to attract referral business
- legislative changes that make financial advisers more accountable for the advice they give
- the operation of professional bodies and industry associations advocating standards of good practice and accountability for breaches of conduct
- better training within the industry (for instance, in Australia, they need to meet ASIC's knowledge and competency requirements, which are included as Appendix 74 in Topic 7)
- closer scrutiny by regulatory bodies of packagers and promoters of financial products and providers of financial planning advice [in Australia, such bodies include the Australian Securities and Investment Commission (ASIC) and the Australian Prudential Regulation Authority (APRA)].

Reflection

What does being a professional mean to you?

Professionalism requires certain standards to be met. Since, in India, the industry is still in its nascent stages, we provide a discussion of the professional organisations at present operating in Australia.

The Securities Institute of Australia has its own set of standards (and code of ethics) to which it expects its members to adhere to. One of the requirements is continuing education. Twenty hours of 'constructed' education is required each year to gain continuing professional development (CPD) points.

Professional organisations

There are a large number of professional organisations that have an interest in the financial services industry. Over 200 such firms, worldwide, are pushing hard to establish International Financial Planning Standards and create a suitable redressal mechanism for investors, as these are also a reflection on the credibility of specific institutions. The Financial Planning industry, in India, is still in the development stage and the statutory regulation for this industry is not yet perfected, though a beginning has been made by SEBI in this direction by issuing regulations for investment advisers, in 2013. However, a few individual firms/institutions are making efforts to set acceptable professional standards, based on the best international practices, standards and legislations. Financial Planning Standards Board (FPSB) India is one such company, based in Mumbai. It is a Professional Standards Setting body for Financial Planners in India. To achieve this objective, FPSB India closely works with the Government, the Regulators, the Industries/Associations, the Corporate, the Media and the General Public. Some entities, that have interest in the industry, have set their own standards and code of professional conduct. Examples of such entities include; the Securities Institute of Australia (SIA), the Australian Stock Exchange (ASX), the Association of Superannuation Funds of Australia (ASFA) and the Financial Planning Association (FPA).Three other groups — the Australian Investment Managers' Association (AIMA), the Investment Funds Association of Australia (IFA) and the Life Investment and Superannuation Association (LISA) — decided they would merge to form one new organisation to represent the retail and wholesale funds management and life insurance industries. The association is called the Investment and Financial Services Association (IFSA) and became operational in January 1998.

In addition, there are consumer groups that lobby to gain increasing information and equity for clients of financial service providers.

Reading

Reading is essential to stay in touch with industry developments. On a minimum, you should expect to:

- read at least one financial daily such as the *Economic Times, Financial Express, Business Standard* or *Hindu Business Line*
- watch a business channel such as CNBC, ET NOW, Zee Business or business programmes on other channels for a daily market round up and corporate news
- read publications read by your target market, *e.g.* if you are targeting lawyers, you should be reading legal magazines.

3.4 REMUNERATION

Changes in the methods of remuneration for financial planners have increased the professional standards of planners.

Based on international experience, planners have been paid in a number of ways:

- Traditionally, planners received a commission (brokerage) from the entry fee paid by investors to the fund managers. Planners did not earn anything unless their clients made investments. This practice led to the belief that planners might have recommended products whose commission was high. It also meant that planners had an incentive to move their clients' money around (churn) in order to get additional commission.
- The introduction of 'trailing commissions', paid to planners over the life of the investment, was an incentive for financial planners to leave investors' money in place, as it provided the planner with a recurrent source of revenue.

Planners are tending to move to a fee-for-service arrangement under which they can:

- charge for work done according to a cost schedule, *i.e.* a written plan for, say, Rs. 5,000
- charge for work on an hourly rate
- charge a rate based on total assets under advice, usually as a percentage of assets, providing an agreed level of service.

Abroad, there is an industry trend towards charging on a fee-for-service basis and rebating all commissions to clients. You might find that your client base will require that you provide a choice of payment methods. Charging fees based on assets under management would require facilitating computer systems. Your principal (the asset management company or life company) will be a clearing house for all fees and commissions. You will want some mechanism to record fees and commissions you earn from servicing your clients. In this way, you will be able to reconcile payments from your principal.

3.5 YOU AND YOUR CLIENT

How you manage your clients is often determined by where you work. Some dealers provide prescribed client service levels, while others will leave the client management almost entirely up to you.

Wherever you work, you will see a divergent group of clients whose attitudes, financial resources, needs and knowledge of financial matters will be different. It will be up to you to develop techniques to draw out clients' objectives, fears and misunderstandings in order to provide them with appropriate advice and a level of service that will keep them as good clients. They might then refer others to you.

Ethics demands that you provide advice that is reasonable and appropriate for your clients' needs and objectives, and all commissions and fees must be disclosed to your clients. Legislation is catching up to ensure adherence to such ethical standards.

3.6 YOU AND YOUR DEALER

Regulation of the financial planning market is discussed in detail in the next section (4) of this chapter. From the beginning, you should be aware of the relationship between yourself, as a financial planner, and the dealer who helps you to provide financial planning advice to the public.

The level of freedom you have in developing your own client base, and your own style, will determine this relationship. Salaried financial planners are like any other employees. The employer establishes the standards, procedures and behaviours.

Agents might have more scope for developing their own targeted client base and their own style with their clients. For agents, certain minimum requirements will be imposed by the dealer. You might also be given sales targets to meet. Within these basic requirements, your target market and to some extent the range of products you offer will be under your control. The dealer who grants you a proper authority is responsible for your actions, omissions and any advice you give. The dealer is under a positive requirement to ensure that you meet regulatory standards, including compliance, customer assessment, continuing education, proper record keeping and standard of financial plans and advice.

It is the dealer's professional indemnity (PI) insurance, against which claims will be made, if a client's complaint is found to be valid and monetary redress is required. The dealer will provide you with formats for plans, and perhaps, to enable you to complete the plans, including ready reckoners, risk-tolerance testing and risk-management assessment packages. Procedures will be outlined in a compliance manual.

You might be required to have your own PI insurance, and it might be wise to do so even if it is not required. The dealer can sue you to recover losses against their PI insurance, if you are at fault.

While the dealer group continues to bear the main regulatory responsibility, the relationship might seem one-sided. There might be changes in the future if the current regulatory regime moves, to a self-regulated model. Under such a model, an association body would take over the regulation of its members. This would mean that the financial planner would bear the full regulatory onus for providing financial advice.

Your relationship with the dealer will be governed by a contract, agency agreement, franchise agreement or some other legal document. You need to ensure that you read and understand this document before signing it. It is in your best interests to understand the relationship between yourself, the dealer and your clients (and perhaps the product fund manager).

Reflection

This triangular arrangement between yourself as a financial planner, your dealer and your client can be an issue for you. The question, 'Who owns the client?' can be easily answered by the stock reply, 'The client does'. However, this answer raises the question,

'What would your attitude be towards client ownership if you worked as a salaried employee of a large dealer group where clients came to you because you worked for the dealer?' How would your attitude change if you spent your time and money attracting clients to your practice as an agent or a franchisee of a dealer?

SELF ASSESSMENT EXERCISE 3

1. Some of the more prominent providers of financial planning advice and its associated products are banks, credit unions, life insurance companies, corporate trustee companies, fund managers, accountants, solicitors and real estate agents. From a client's perspective, what are some of the advantages you have as a financial planner over these providers?

   ....

   ....

   ....

   ....

   ....

2. List some of the developments that have led to a more professional standard for financial planners. Do you consider this increased professionalism has improved your business? Why?

   ....

   ....

   ....

....

....

3. Why do you think so many planners are moving to a fee-for-service arrangement as a basis for remuneration? What is the more traditional way in which financial planners receive their remuneration?

....

....

....

....

....

4. REGULATORY CONTROLS AND PRACTICES FOR FINANCIAL PLANNERS

A key aspect of the regulation of investment businesses is the regulation of people who provide advice or act as intermediaries in the securities markets. These people are known as investment advisers, financial planners (or financial advisers) and securities dealers, and include stock brokers and managers of collective investment schemes.

REGULATION IN INDIA

In India, SEBI is the regulator for financial advisers. It has made a beginning towards regulating the sector by issuing regulations for "investment advisers" vide its circular dated January 21, 2013. The salient features of SEBI regulation are as under:

Registration of advisers: Investment advisers have to compulsorily obtain certificate of registration from SEBI. Detailed guidelines regarding eligibility and exemptions provided, are given in the circular.

General responsibility:

(1) An investment adviser shall act in a fiduciary capacity towards its clients and shall disclose all conflicts of interests as and when they arise.

(2) An investment adviser shall not receive any consideration by way of remuneration or compensation or in any other form from any person

other than the client being advised, in respect of the underlying products or securities for which advice is provided.

(3) An investment adviser shall maintain an arms-length relationship between its activities as an investment adviser and other activities.

(4) An investment adviser which is also engaged in activities other than investment advisory services shall ensure that its investment advisory services are clearly segregated from all its other activities, in the manner as prescribed hereunder.

(5) An investment adviser shall ensure that in case of any conflict of interest of the investment advisory activities with other activities, such conflict of interest shall be disclosed to the client.

(6) An investment adviser shall not divulge any confidential information about its client, which has come to its knowledge, without taking prior permission of its clients, except where such disclosures are required to be made in compliance with any law for the time being in force.

(7) An investment advisor shall not enter into transactions on its own account which is contrary to its advice given to clients for a period of fifteen days from the day of such advice. Provided that during the period of such fifteen days, if the investment adviser is of the opinion that the situation has changed, then it may enter into such a transaction on its own account after giving such revised assessment to the client at least 24 hours in advance of entering into such transaction.

(8) An investment advisor shall follow Know Your Client procedure as specified by the Board from time to time.

(9) An investment adviser shall abide by Code of Conduct as specified in Third Schedule of SEBI circular.

(10) An investment adviser shall not act on its own account, knowingly to sell securities or investment products to or purchase securities or investment product from a client.

(11) In case of change in control of the investment adviser, prior approval from the Board shall be taken.

(12) Investment advisers shall furnish to the Board information and reports as may be specified by the Board from time to time.

(13) It shall be the responsibility of the Investment Adviser to ensure that its representatives and partners, as applicable, comply with the certification and qualification requirements at all times.

Risk profiling: The circular gives details about the information to be collected from the client, assessing the risk a client is willing to take, communicating the risk profile to the client, and updating of risk profile.

Suitability: Investment adviser shall ensure that,-

(*a*) All investments on which investment advice is provided is appropriate to the risk profile of the client;

(*b*) It has a documented process for selecting investments based on client's investment objectives and financial situation;

(*c*) It understands the nature and risks of products or assets selected for clients;

(*d*) It has a reasonable basis for believing that a recommendation or transaction entered into: (i) meets the client's investment objectives; (ii) is such that the client is able to bear any related investment risks consistent with its investment objectives and risk tolerance; (iii) is such that the client has the necessary experience and knowledge to understand the risks involved in the transaction.

(*e*) Whenever a recommendation is given to a client to purchase of a particular complex financial product, such recommendation or advice is based upon a reasonable assessment that the structure and risk reward profile of financial product is consistent with client's experience, knowledge, investment objectives, risk appetite and capacity for absorbing loss.

Disclosures to clients: An investor adviser shall;

(1) disclose to a prospective client, all material information about itself including its business, disciplinary history, the terms and conditions on which it offers advisory services, affiliations with other intermediaries and such other information as is necessary to take an informed decision on whether or not to avail its services.

(2) disclose to its client, any consideration by way of remuneration or compensation or in any other form whatsoever, received or receivable by it or any of its associates or subsidiaries for any distribution or execution services in respect of the products or securities for which the investment advice is provided to the client.

(3) before recommending the services of a stock broker or other intermediary to a client, disclose any consideration by way of remuneration or compensation or in any other form whatsoever, if any, received or receivable by the investment adviser, if the client desires to avail the services of such intermediary.

(4) disclose to the client its holding or position, if any, in the financial products or securities which are subject matter of advice.

(5) disclose to the client any actual or potential conflicts of interest arising from any connection to or association with any issuer of products/securities, including any material information or facts that might compromise its objectivity or independence in the carrying on of investment advisory services.

(6) while making an investment advice, make adequate disclosure to the client of all material facts relating to the key features of the products or securities, particularly, performance track record.

(7) draw the client's attention to the warnings, disclaimers in documents, advertising materials relating to an investment product which it is recommending to the client.

Maintenance of records:

(1) An investment adviser shall maintain the following records,-

- (*a*) Know Your Client records of the client;
- (*b*) Risk profiling and risk assessment of the client;
- (*c*) Suitability assessment of the advice being provided;
- (*d*) Copies of agreements with clients, if any;
- (*e*) Investment advice provided, whether written or oral;
- (*f*) Rationale for arriving at investment advice, duly signed and dated;

(g) A register or record containing list of the clients, the date of advice, nature of the advice, the products/securities in which advice was rendered and fee, if any charged for such advice.

(2) All records shall be maintained either in physical or electronic form and preserved for a minimum period of five years: Provided that where records are required to be duly signed and are maintained in electronic form, such records shall be digitally signed.

(3) An investment adviser shall conduct yearly audit in respect of compliance with these regulations from a member of Institute of Chartered Accountants of India or Institute of Company Secretaries of India.

Appointment of compliance officer:

An investment adviser, which is a body corporate or a partnership firm, shall appoint a compliance officer who shall be responsible for monitoring the compliance by the investment adviser in respect of the requirements of the Act, regulations, notifications, guidelines, instructions issued by the Board.

Redressal of client grievances:

(1) An investment adviser shall redress client grievances promptly.

(2) An investment adviser shall have adequate procedure for expeditious grievance redressal.

(3) Client grievances pertaining to financial products in which investments have been made based on investment advice, shall fall within the purview of the regulator of such financial product.

(4) Any dispute between the investment adviser and his client may be resolved through arbitration or through Ombudsman authorized or appointed for the purpose by any regulatory authority, as applicable.

Segregation of execution services:

Investment advisers which are banks, NBFCs and body corporate providing distribution or execution services to their clients shall keep their investment advisory services segregated from such activities: Provided that such distribution or execution services can only be offered subject to the following:

(*a*) The client shall not be under any obligation to avail the distribution or execution services offered by the investment adviser. (*b*) The investment adviser shall maintain arms length relationship between its activities as investment adviser and distribution or execution services. (*c*) All fees and charges paid to distribution or execution service providers by the client shall be paid directly to the service providers and not through the investment adviser.

Inspection: The circular contains guidelines about inspection of investment adviser's books by SEBI, and his obligations on inspection.

Others: The circular also deals with the action which may be taken by SEBI, in case of default of any of the provisions of the regulation, by the adviser.

CODE OF CONDUCT FOR INVESTMENT ADVISERS

The SEBI circular contains the following code of conduct for the investment advisers.

1. *Honesty and fairness :* An investment adviser shall act honestly, fairly and in the best interests of its clients and in the integrity of the market.
2. *Diligence :* An investment adviser shall act with due skill, care and diligence in the best interests of its clients and shall ensure that its advice is offered after thorough analysis and taking into account available alternatives.
3. *Capabilities :* An investment adviser shall have and employ effectively appropriate resources and procedures which are needed for the efficient performance of its business activities.
4. *Information about clients* : An investment adviser shall seek from its clients, information about their financial situation, investment experience and investment objectives relevant to the services to be provided and maintain confidentiality of such information.
5. *Information to its clients :* An investment adviser shall make adequate disclosures of relevant material information while dealing with its clients.

6. *Fair and reasonable charges :* An investment adviser advising a client may charge fees, subject to any ceiling as may be specified by the Board, if any. The investment adviser shall ensure that fees charged to the clients is fair and reasonable.
7. *Conflicts of interest :* An investment adviser shall try to avoid conflicts of interest as far as possible and when they cannot be avoided, it shall ensure that appropriate disclosures are made to the clients and that the clients are fairly treated.
8. *Compliance :* An investment adviser including its representative(s) shall comply with all regulatory requirements applicable to the conduct of its business activities so as to promote the best interests of clients and the integrity of the market.
9. *Responsibility of senior management :* The senior management of a body corporate which is registered as investment adviser shall bear primary responsibility for ensuring the maintenance of appropriate standards of conduct and adherence to proper procedures by the body corporate.

REGULATION IN AUSTRALIA

Since the financial planning business is in its development stage, in India, regulation is not yet fully developed. It would, therefore, be useful to look at some of the legalities in Australia. The rest of this topic covers the legislation in Australia. These could be pointers to where India might be heading in a few years.

The Corporations Act contains a number of provisions that apply to a financial planner, as they deal in or give advice about securities. The **Australian Securities & Investments Commission** (**ASIC**) is an independent Australian body that acts as Australia's corporate regulator. ASIC's role is to enforce and regulate company and financial services laws to protect Australian consumers, investors and creditors Explanatory statements issued by ASIC, called policy statements, deal with many of these provisions. The main ones are introduced in what follows. (Any reference to a policy statement should be understood to mean one issued by ASIC.) Essentially, policy statements explain how ASIC will interpret and administer the law.

4.1 REASONABLE BASIS FOR RECOMMENDATIONS (SECTION 851)

Section 851 of the Corporations Act (Policy Statement 121) effectively requires that when you make a recommendation about securities to another person who might reasonably be expected to rely upon your advice, you must have a reasonable basis for making that recommendation. There are two main tests for a reasonable basis:

1. The 'know your client' rule. When you make a recommendation on a security, you must ensure that the recommendation is appropriate to your client's investment objectives, financial situation and particular needs (Policy Statement 122: 108-116 and Policy Statement 122: Part V).
2. 'know your product' rule. When you make a recommendation about a security, you must have considered and researched the product and made your recommendation on that basis (Policy Statement 122: 127). You should always keep in mind that a recommendation includes a recommendation to buy, or not to buy, to sell or not to sell, or to hold a security (Policy Statement 122 : 101-107).

If you breach these requirements and your client suffers a loss as a result, you are liable on certain conditions to pay damages to the client.

Not all securities transactions will necessarily be subject to section 851. Some dealers provide 'execution only' services, completing transactions but not providing advice. To be safe, advisers should note this in writing to their client for each transaction for which no advice was given.

4.2 LIMITED ADVICE

Where you conclude that:

the products that you have appropriately researched are not suitable for a client and/or

the client would be best served by products that your licence prohibits you from offering

you should inform the client of this. Tell the client to seek advice from a more suitably licensed person. Where advice is sought for a particular type of security, say a growth oriented superannuation fund, you will not have to conduct research on investments that cannot accept superannuation moneys and are irrelevant to the client's request. You will still have to consider whether the type of investment nominated by the client is appropriate for that client.

4.3 DISCLOSURE REQUIREMENTS

4.3.1 Disclosure of commissions and fees (section 849)

Section 849 of the Corporations Act (Policy Statement 122: 47-68) requires that when you make a recommendation about securities to another person, either in writing or orally, you must disclose full particulars of any commission or fee or any other benefit you or an associate will or might receive in relation to that recommendation. You are also required to disclose any other 'interest' that might reasonably be expected to be capable of influencing you in making the recommendation, such as volume bonuses or trips from the dealer who offers the products you recommend. Fees paid directly by the client (*i.e.* fees for service) are excluded from disclosure.

Where commissions are payable by a third party like a fund manager, the amount and rate of commission for each investment and the circumstances in which it would become payable should also be stated.

You will need to disclose any material interest you might have in a particular public company's shares or in a listed unit trust as well as any relationship with a related product provider you might be recommending. Policy Statement 122: 48-68 sets out ASIC's views on the clear disclosure of an adviser with respect to the obligation in section 849, *i.e.* 'client to be told if adviser's interests might influence recommendation'.

Section 849(6) excludes 'associates' who are not a part of the securities business.

Note, that ASIC considers that representatives must disclose their share of any payment from the client to the licensee.

While the statute notes two types of 'associates' who do not give rise to disclosure obligations, ASIC points out in Policy Statement 122: 169-171 several types that do. These are:

directors and secretaries of the licensee and any related company

any company that is related to you

partners in a securities business

trustees of a trust from which you might benefit

if you are acting as a representative, then your principal

other persons who act together with or under an arrangement with you in relation to making securities recommendations.

Once properly made, a disclosure need not be repeated in subsequent recommendations if :

there is nothing new to add

the client is reasonably believed to be aware of the previous disclosure

its absence does not give the impression that the previously disclosed benefit is no longer applicable.

Materiality

Although the law requires disclosure of all commissions, fees, benefits or advantages, ASIC has implied a materiality test in the statute, and in Policy Statement 122, paragraphs

47-68, the commission explains how advisers are to determine whether a conflict is material in various situations. For example, a promotion by a fund manager under which high-volume sellers enter a draw to win an overseas trip would generally have to be disclosed by an adviser recommending the relevant securities.

If, though, the adviser had no reasonable chance of satisfying the entry requirements, and therefore the promotion was not reasonably likely to influence their recommendation, it need not be disclosed.

Other examples of generally immaterial benefits include free seminars and one-off lunches. Note that virtually any commission payment will be regarded as relevant, and that the general information required in the Advisory Services Guide on rates of commission does not satisfy the disclosure requirement. Particulars must be disclosed that are specific to the actual recommended course of dealing.

Making the disclosure

A disclosure of interests must be a part of each written recommendation, even though it might not differ from the disclosure made to the same client in a previous recommendation (but that previous statement could be incorporated by reference).

Where advice is oral, you need not repeat a previous disclosure if there is no change to the information previously disclosed and if you reasonably expect that the client is fully aware of the previous disclosure (ASIC Policy Statement 122: 80-82 and 87).

To satisfy the statute and ASIC, the interest disclosure must not be buried or obscured, but rather must be obvious and straightforward.

Chinese walls

Some firms maintain Chinese wall arrangements for various legitimate reasons. (This is where different departments within the firm remain separate in order to avoid leakage of information between them.) If, owing to the existence of Chinese walls, an adviser fails to disclose a benefit to the firm because it is not known to that adviser, Corporations Act section 850(2) provides a defense.

Again, if you breach these requirements and your client suffers a loss as a result, you are liable on certain conditions to pay damages to your client and you might also be subject to additional penalties.

Note: Please refer to section 4.10 for an update on disclosure requirements under the financial services reforms.

Reading

Policy Statement 122 provides clarification on sections 849 and 851 of the Corporations Act. Visit ASIC at www.asic.gov.au.

4.3.2 Disclosure of identity

As a representative of a licensed dealer or investment adviser, in all dealings with clients or the public you must disclose that you are acting as a representative and disclose the name of your dealer. In written recommendations about securities, you must include your address(es) and that of your dealer, and the type of licence they hold. (*See* Policy Statement 117:56-77.)

If you have a company, you must be careful about the use of your company's name. The use of a business name is restricted. You should refer to Policy Statement 117 Part III for further information. Generally, your own business name should not be used to create the impression that you are acting as a principal, when you are acting for a dealer group. This limitation might cause conflicts for you if you are also an insurance agent. Insurance agents can run their businesses under a business name. Many do, and have built up a client base under that business name. But you must use your own name as a financial planner. This might mean two sets of business cards and stationery.

4.4 DOCUMENTATION-REGISTER OF INTERESTS IN SECURITIES

Participants in the securities industry, including dealers and their representatives, must keep a register of their interests in securities. This means any securities that you own or control must be accounted for.

4.5 ADVERTISING AND PROJECTIONS ABOUT SECURITIES

The Corporations Act restricts the way you might advertise or promote securities, and the manner of that advertising. It also includes the requirements for making projections on future results and about misleading or deceptive conduct. (*See* Policy Statement 121:62-63.)

You should note that these provisions are not restricted to people who hold a licence or a proper authority. They apply in any situation where a person deals in, or provides advice about, securities. You should be aware that this overview is only an introduction to the requirements of the Corporations Act. Before beginning to offer financial planning advice, you should obtain more detailed information from your dealer or legal adviser. Practice notes and policy statements from ASIC also provide more detailed information, and these can be downloaded from www.asic.gov.au.

4.6 A BRIEF OVERVIEW OF ADVISERS' LIABILITY

Providing investment advice or dealing without a licence is a criminal offence punishable by a fine or 12 months' imprisonment for an individual and a much larger fine for a corporation. In addition, an unlicensed person cannot enforce a contract entered into in that capacity (section 795) and clients have a right to rescind a contract entered into with an unlicensed person (section 798).

Acting as a representative without holding a proper authority is also an offence attracting a fine and/or imprisonment for six months.

Failure by an adviser to disclose conflicts of interest under section 849 is also a criminal offence.

While a breach of the 'know your client' and 'know your product' rule is not a criminal offence, an adviser might be sued by a client for any loss or damage incurred as a result of the breach.

Section 821 prohibits a principal from contracting out of liability for a representative's conduct, but permits principals to take out indemnity insurance or to have an indemnity arrangement with the representative as set out in Topic 2 of this subject.

Advisers are also guilty of an offence and liable to pay compensation to a client where they make false or misleading statements in relation to securities (section 999).

4.7 ASIC FIELD AUDITS

ASIC conducts field visits to the offices of dealers and proper authority holders to review compliance with legislative and regulatory requirements. Dealers are expected to document policies and procedures to be followed by their proper authorities. They are also required to maintain records for compliance audit purposes.

4.8 ASIC LICENSING REVIEW

In 1995, ASIC (then the ASC) undertook a review of its licensing regime to enhance the quality of advice provided to investors. This review recommended:

- enhanced competencies for entry and continuation of licensees (*i.e.* qualifications, experience and management systems)
- increased investor education programmes

an internal complaints resolution mechanism

mandatory professional indemnity insurance cover

provision of a standardized consumer guide on licensee status, services and fees

development of competency standards for representatives

provision of warning statements by media commentators providing non-personalized investment recommendations.

ASIC (then the ASC) has issued a number of policy statements concerning the regulation of investment advisers and securities dealers. Following a review of the regulation of dealers and investment advisers, it issued the *ASIC Good Advice Handbook.*

Reading

This topic cannot provide you with expert legal advice on licensing. For further information on licensing you should contact the ASIC office in your State for a copy of the *ASIC Guide to Securities Industry Licensing.* The ASIC website provides a great deal of information and is regularly updated (www.asic.gov.au).

SELF ASSESSMENT EXERCISE 4

(to be answered on the basis of Australian regulation)

1. After interviewing some clients you conclude that you don't have the appropriate licence to offer them the advice they are seeking. What is your duty?

   ....

   ....

   ....

   ....

   ....

2. List your duties in relation to the disclosure of your commissions and fees.

   ....

....

....

....

....

3. Would disclosure be required if, by selling a particular product, you can be entered in a draw to win a holiday?

....

....

....

....

....

5. THE CONSUMER LIFE CYCLE

If financial change did not occur or could not be predicted, financial planning would not be necessary. The high school student who delivers the "MidDay" (Mumbai-based afternoon newspaper), for example, has little need for financial planning. There are currently 49 houses on the route, and this number may have remained nearly constant for several years. Next year perhaps it will be 50 or may be 47, but there is little that our newspaper deliverer can do to predict this exactly.

In the case of larger corporations, the need for financial planning varies with the amount of change experienced by the business. A small dress shop, for example, must plan for the season, and it also has to make some adjustment for the business cycle. However, unless the small store is on its way to becoming a larger store or a chain of stores, the need for long term financial planning is hardly overwhelming.

For the individual, however, financial planning is imperative. The reason is that changes are not only significant but also highly predictable.

5.1 STAGES OF THE LIFE CYCLE

The life cycle has been found to be a powerful predictor of economic and social behaviour, so much so, that many different categorizations have been made. Expressions such as "empty nester" and "young old" abound in the popular press as well as in scholarly journals.

We can divide the human life cycle into six basic stages, "A" to "F" to which we will assign commonly used, phonetic alphabet non-pejorative names. First is the Alpha ("A") stage which consists of young, single, childless persons who are financially independent from their parents. The second stage is the Bravo ("B") stage in which these persons are married, but still childless.

The Charlie ("C") stage begins with the birth of the first child and continues until the youngest child is of school going age. This is marked as a separate stage due to the fact that family income depends upon whether or not there is a child who is too young to attend school.

The fourth life cycle stage is the Delta ("D") stage in which there are dependent children who are no longer of pre-school age. When the last child has finished his or her schooling and is no longer dependent on the parents, the Echo ("E") stage is entered into. This is the pre-retirement or "empty nest" stage. For those individuals without children, the Echo stage may be said to begin about 10 years before retirement. The Foxtrot ("F") stage is the retirement stage.

5.2 NON-TRADITIONAL LIFE CYCLE STAGES

Not everyone goes through each of the life cycles enumerated above. Some persons choose not to marry, and we will call these persons Perpetual Alphas until they reach the Echo stage, arbitrarily defined as 10 years prior to their planned retirement. Other persons who marry but do not have children are here termed Perpetual Bravos who skip over the Charlie and Delta stages and enter the Echo stage at the same time as their Perpetual Alpha counterparts.

Charlies and Deltas may be single as well as married. To make things more complex, remarriage may cause a Delta or an Echo to suddenly become a Charlie. In our configuration, an 'individual' is always classified at the earliest life cycle group for which he or she is eligible.

5.3 DEMOGRAPHIC TRENDS UNDERLYING THE LIFE CYCLE

Despite the changing world Indian traditional family still consists of a never divorced mother and father living together with their biological children under age 18 (generally higher) constituting a majority of Indian families. However joint or extended family which includes (grandparents or another elderly relative or siblings) is declining slowly.

We may see shift to following redefined family in coming years though they are still exceptions today.

Husband-wife (including blended families from remarriage) Single Parent (usually headed by women) Single person Extended families.

These changes will occur due to bilateral bargaining position of women, enabling them to function economically outside of a marriage. It is due partly to the growing proportion of women with higher education. It is also due to the fact that women are marrying later in life.

Increase in the age of marriage is due to a tendency for young adults to live independently. They feel that living independently helps to develop skills that have traditionally been done by people of the other sex within a marriage. Women learn to fix the plumbing while men learn to cook and sew, thereby diminishing their dependence on a marital relationship. Also delaying the onset of marriage (and probably contributing to the instability of marriage) is a somewhat recent tendency for young adults to live with their parents. This is particularly pronounced among the more affluent since it takes these young people longer to achieve a level of material comfort equivalent to that enjoyed by their parents. Particularly in the constrained housing market, the spacious familial home and parents who grew up in the liberated times are an attractive combination for young people saving to buy a home, start a family, or those trying to end a bad relationship.

Much has been written about the trend towards deferring child-bearing until the parent is older. While this certainly does occur, particularly among fast-track women who build their careers and only have children when the proverbial "biological clock" begins to run down. Since the average women is now predicted to have only 2 children the age of the first child must increase relative to an age when women had many more.

5.4 THE CHANGING WORKFORCE

Life cycle is also related to labour force participation. The traditional concept of a career involved the careful selection of a lifetime career. New "Hire and Fire" culture will force average worker to have three careers in his lifetime. Instead of a linear life plan which involves continuous participation, today's worker has a more cyclic life plan which may involve periodic interruptions for schooling, travel and other such things.

As the labour force participation rates of women continue to increase relative to those of men, the composition and needs of the labour force also changes. It is expected that women will account for major portion of the growth in the work force.

The increase in labour force participation by women is due to at least two factors. First, most middle income families realize that it takes two workers to attain a comfortable existence. Psychological image of staying at home is no longer held in high regard. For many reasons, women want to develop independence and have careers equal to men.

Having two parents employed full time also imposes other problems on the family. For this reason, there is a demand for part-time employment which has still not developed in Indian environment.

Another future trend is towards working at home due to development of telecom infrastructure through the use of computer, fax and modem. Often called "telecommuting," this type of work is generally limited to work that can be done on the personal computer and telephone and that is highly structured.

Many people are beginning to work for themselves. This trend is most pronounced among older workers, often due to organizational downsizing, which is concentrated among the older, higher cost worker.

5.5 VARIABLES THAT INFLUENCE FINANCIAL BEHAVIOUR OVER THE LIFE CYCLE

In general, income patterns over the life cycle vary in the following manner. An individual finishes schooling and begins work at a starting salary (or wages) that reflects the individual's education and skill level but lack of experience. Increases over time depend upon the value of experience in the individual's chosen field. Totally unskilled workers, such as labourers or unskilled production line personnel may find little progression in their compensation over time. Others, whose value is largely based on experience such as doctors, chefs and architects, may see compensation increasing progressively for 10 years or more. After some point, however, no increase in real income should be expected for the duration of the person's working career. This may be in the mid-20's for unskilled workers or the mid-40's for surgeons.

Household income will increase substantially when a single individual enters the Bravo stage merely as a function of definition. The unit of analysis is now a married couple, and since individuals tend to marry others in roughly equivalent socio-economic categories, income should be expected to approximately double during this period. While some Bravos have only a single worker, it is now most common for both individuals to work. Occasionally, one individual continues an education while the other party works, diminishing the disposable income available to the couple. The onset of child-bearing and the Charlie stage is based upon a number of factors. While we have pointed out the impact that fewer children have on the increase in age of a first-time mother, demographics and career choices are also important.

Women with higher education, increased income tends to delay the birth of the first child. In addition, higher earning women also tend to cluster their children more tightly together than do others, presumably because of scale of economy savings in the intrinsic cost of staying home with children or the explicit cost of hiring a nanny or baby sitter to be a surrogate parent though spacing begins to widen as the income of the husband increases. In the Charlie stage, a substantial proportion of families experience at least a temporary decrease in income. While a majority of Charlies now have both parents at work, it is still common in our society for a parent (statistically, most frequently the mother) to either leave the labour force or reduce the number of hours worked for pay in order to be at home with the young child. Therefore, families that follow this more traditional pattern tend to have substantially reduced incomes during the Charlie stage.

In the Delta stage, when the youngest child is in school, most families have both workers engaged in full time work. This means that the incomes of Delta families are often higher than in the Charlie stage.

In the Echo (empty nest or pre-retirement stage), if both parties had been at work in the prior stage, no change in income may be expected. However, when the Foxtrot or retirement stage is reached, income generally drops substantially since pension tends to pay somewhat less than the final earned income. There may, of course, be other sources of income available not only in the Foxtrot stage but also the Delta and Echo stages.

Expense Flows over the Life Cycle

The pattern of expenses over the life cycle, unfortunately, may not correspond to the pattern of income. In the first two life cycle stages, expenses do tend to mirror income. To some extent, as we will see, this reflects a lack of planning on the part of young people. To another extent, this also reflects pressures that are on them to spend almost all of the income that they make.

Much has been written about the rationality of consumers. Year after year we observe families and individuals committing self-destructive acts, such as abusing high-cost credit cards, and some observers have begun to question the rationality of consumer behaviour. This is not a trivial question since consumer rationality underlies much of our economic theory. However, George Katona (1980) posted an "adaptive theory" of consumer behaviour which can accommodate consumer rationality without assuming rational planning on the part of consumers. Katona said that consumers rationally adapt to changing circumstances instead of adhering rigidly to specific rules of behaviour. Such a system may involve mistakes and inefficiencies, but people do tend to learn from them.

Mielauskas (1988) went even further to state that "maturation and history interactively affect consumers' choices." As people pass through the life cycle, their ability to learn from their history changes.

In the Charlie stage, expenditures tend to increase substantially. Children tend to be expensive, but the indirect cost of children may be even higher. At this stage, families often buy a house or move to a larger apartment. In addition, particularly when both individuals remain in the labour force, there is the need for child care which can be expensive. Depending upon location, family situation and child care desired, child care can range from very low (staying with grandma) to hundreds of Rupees per month.

In terms of expenditures, the Delta stage is often divided into two categories. In the early Delta stage, when children have not yet reached college age, expenditures are somewhat higher than they were in the Charlie stage because older children are more costly than younger ones. In the later Delta stage, when the children reach college age, expenditures for many families become astronomical.

In the Echo stage, family expenses generally drop substantially since there are no children at home or in college. The drop in expenses amounts equal to cost of sending the child to college, because the Echo family is not to be free from the basic expenses of supporting the child unless adult child finds a suitable job.

In the Foxtrot stage, expenses may be even lower than the Echo stage, since the individuals no longer have to go to work with the attendant expenses of transportation, parking, clothing and meals.

The mismatch between income and expenses in the typical life cycle may create periods of saving and dissaving. During the Alpha and Bravo stages, most individuals may be expected to just about breakeven. In the Charlie stage, dissaving is most frequent. In the early Delta stage, saving may be expected, but this reverses in the later Delta stage as the children begin attending college.

The Echo stage is the period of greatest saving, as income remains high, expenses are greatly diminished and great incentive exists for the family to put aside money for retirement. Finally, in the Foxtrot stage, families who have accumulated substantial prior resources may dissave slightly while others attempt to live on their incomes.

Savings Behaviours

People save money for a variety of purposes. They may do it actively in order to pay for something in the future (a "commitment") or to build liquidity. Alternatively, they may do it residually during periods when income exceeds habitual expenses. Over the life cycle, the ability to save varies with changing patterns of income and needs. Just as important, however, is the propensity to save which indicates the willingness to put aside funds. As we will see below, this tends to start slowly for many individuals, but increase rapidly, often when savings ability is no longer high.

Liquidity

The need for liquidity is an area which is very life cycle dependent. All individuals need to have a certain amount of liquidity, for a number of reasons. The first is for transactions since, as stated earlier, people are paid periodically and spend almost continuously. A second need for liquidity is based upon the "rainy day" concept. Emergencies can arise and may cause distress to the individual whose financial situation is insufficiently liquid. A third, according to Keynes in his General Theory is for speculation. When assets are perceived to be overpriced, an investor may hold his assets in liquid form, waiting for a market correction and a good time to buy. Within the life cycle, liquidity is dependent upon the diversification of income sources. One reason for maintaining high liquidity is if an individual has only a single income source. In that case, loss of main source of income, generally the job, will cause the stream of income to cease entirely.

Risk Preference

The risk preference of an individual is partly a function of the individual's personality and partly a function of life cycle. It suffices to say at this point that some individuals are willing to take on more risk than others, in search of higher returns. However, no matter what an individual's level of risk preference the amount of risk that he or she is willing to take on depends upon the life cycle.

Willingness to take on risk varies over the life cycle with two important factors. One is the dependence of other individuals upon one's assets, and the second is the time available to recoup funds in the event of a loss.

5.6 STAGE BY STAGE ANALYSIS

In the following section, a detailed analysis will be made of each stage of the life cycle, showing the financial attributes that may be expected. After this, we will look at the financial life cycles of special cases, a perpetual Alpha, a perpetual Bravo and a Dual Income Charlie.

5.6.1 The Alpha Stage

Income/Expenses: Once the Alpha has a job, an entry-level income will begin. Expenses, as we will see, tend to be just about as high as income, leaving the Alpha few surplus funds to save. Why is this so?

There are at least three reasons why Alphas have a tendency to spend nearly all of their incomes. First, very few Alphas have ever done any long range financial planning, which would have demonstrated that this pattern of consumption may be sub-optimal, particularly if the individual plans to marry and have children. Second, virtually all Alphas must bear initial capital outlays, which tend to be quite high. An Alpha who is working at a first job typically lives alone. This means that a flat must be obtained, furnished, and stocked with food. This also requires that a sizable security deposit be paid.

In addition to this, an individual who is expected to show up at work every day often needs a dependable vehicle. This often necessitates the expenditure for a new high speed two wheeler. And, as a last capital investment, a decent wardrobe of clothes must be purchased. All of these so called "capital" expenditures may amount to many thousands of rupees.

In addition to these necessary expenses, there are strong social pressures, which cause Alphas to spend a substantial part of their income. Alphas by definition are unmarried, and biologically there is a somewhat defined window for them to marry and have children. In order to marry, one must find people to date, a pastime, which is not entirely unpleasant but is definitely expensive. As a last consideration, persons who wish to socialize and date may often feel it necessary to spend relatively more money on "marketing" in the form of clothes, furnishings, a car, etc. than would otherwise be the case. Therefore, whether such a high level of expenditure is absolutely necessary is irrelevant to persons at this stage. There are strong pressures from their careers and social activities that cause them to spend nearly all of their incomes.

Ability/Propensity to Save: For reasons given above, the ability of an Alpha to save may be moderate. This is particularly so once the initial capital investments have been made. However, their propensity to save or observed saving behaviour tends to be quite low, as a result of the social pressures upon them.

Housing: In terms of housing status, it is typical of most Alphas, particularly those who are younger, to rent rather than own. Alternatively, Alphas may live with their parents for a period of time, and as a result, expenses would be somewhat lower than if renting.

Credit: The essential credit needs of Alphas tend to be relatively low, concentrated in credit cards and perhaps an automobile loan. In fact, they may be repaying educational loans at this time in their life. It is important to note that their ability to borrow at this stage is also somewhat constrained by their relatively low incomes and lack of accumulated assets.

Life Insurance: The need of Alphas for life insurance is negligible. Since most have no one dependent upon their income, the need to spend money to protect someone does not exist. Exceptions may apply to those who have parents or siblings who are financially dependent upon them or those who have borrowed money based upon the guarantee of a parent.

Liquidity: Since Alphas, by definition, are not married, their dependence upon a single source of income is quite great, increasing their need for liquid assets as a percentage of income. In addition, Alphas generally do not have other sources of income from interest and dividends since they have not yet accumulated substantial financial assets. Compounding this problem, is the fact that Alphas often are subject to the "last hired/first fired" syndrome. Since they are new on the job, any downturn in the business cycle or lay off by the employer may find them out on the street. In addition, Alphas tend to be moved around frequently if they stay with one employer. While they may eventually be reimbursed for this moving, it is generally wise to have a substantial amount of liquidity. As a result of all of these factors, Alphas tend to have liquidity needs that are moderate to high relative to other life cycle groups.

Risk Preference: Alphas, by definition, tend to have no one else dependent upon them financially. For this reason, they are often willing to take on more risk than others. In addition, Alphas look forward to perhaps 40 additional working years to recoup any losses that they might sustain. Therefore, to the extent that Alphas have assets at all, they tend to be willing to take on more risk than other life cycle groups.

Tax Exposure: The tax exposure of Alphas tends to be moderate to high. Alphas have no additional dependants, and, as seen earlier, usually do not live in houses of their own, giving them very few deductions.

Retirement/Estate Planning: In terms of the last two characteristics, retirement planning and estate planning, Alphas have tended in the past to have relatively little interest. They have not often looked into retirement plans since that time is so far off.

Alphas tend to lack concern about estate planning since they generally have no dependants and often few assets that need disposal.

5.6.2 The Bravo Stage

In the Bravo stage a relatively young (*i.e.,* not pre-retirement) married couple has no children. The financial conditions of the typical Bravo are discussed below.

Income/Expenses: Income is relatively high since in most situations both parties are at work. Expenses for the couple have most likely decreased relative to the combined expenses for both as single individuals before marriage. Since they are now presumably sharing living quarters, they pay only once for housing. In addition, there are economies of scale in preparing food for two, and there may be other savings in utilities or perhaps transportation if the parties do not have to commute to work separately by car.

Ability/Propensity to Save: The ability of the Bravo couple to save is quite high. However, the propensity or desire to save may still be low. Why does this occur?

For purposes of simplification, we may divide the Bravo period into early and late Bravo stages. In the early stage, two Alphas marry and see no reason to change their former life style to a drastic extent. If, as Alphas, they like to eat out often, this will not change with the new life cycle stage. If they like to spend money on vacations, sports, or other such things, there is little reason to suspect that these patterns are going to change once the two Alphas have married.

It is only when a change to the Charlie life cycle stage appears imminent, that expenditure behaviour may change. This may occur with a pregnancy or when a couple makes a definite time decision to start a family or purchase a home. At this stage, the couple may begin to save for the expenses of a child, a first house, a larger car and so on. Depending upon decisions the couple has made about whether both parents will continue working or one will stay at home with the child, the expense behaviour of the family may change substantially.

Housing: The housing status of Bravos has been changing in recent years. Traditionally, Bravos rented an apartment or house, and the purchase of a house did not occur until sometime after the birth of the first child. However, with the advent of condominiums and the delays many Bravos plan in having the first child, more and more Bravos began purchasing their first homes in this life cycle stage. This changed during the asset inflation of the mid 1980's when house prices made the purchase of a home unreachable for many. With a decline in both house prices and interest rates in the 90's, this may be changing yet again.

Credit: The credit needs of Bravos are generally not substantial and tend to relate largely to credit cards and automobile loans. Bravos who have purchased a home may have additional expenses connected with that purchase.

Life Insurance: The life insurance needs of the Bravo may be divided into the early and later Bravo stages. In the early stage, two working Bravos have little need for life insurance since each came into the marriage as self-sufficient individuals and presumably can again support themselves. This may vary for the couple who has purchased a home based upon their combined earnings and where each party would want the surviving spouse to continue to live in the same house.

The need for life insurance changes, however, at the time of the first pregnancy. At this point, the couple has obligated itself to a stream of support payments for a dependent individual.

Liquidity: The liquidity needs of Bravos, aside from the immediate pre-Charlie period, tend to be relatively lower than they were for Alphas. This is because both parties presumably are at work, and if one party loses his or her job then there remains a flow of income from the second party.

Risk Preference: The risk preference of the Bravo is generally similar to that of the Alpha. Bravos have no other dependents and a substantial period of time to make up any losses. This also changes as the couple makes the transition into the Charlie stage.

Tax Exposure: Tax exposure of the Bravo was discussed earlier in the housing category. Bravos tend to be in relatively high tax brackets with fairly high incomes and few if any deductions.

Retirement/Estate Planning: The interest of Bravos in retirement planning tends to be quite limited as is their interest in estate planning since the need for both is perceived as being so distant.

5.6.3 The Charlie Stage

Income/Expenses: In the Charlie stage the birth of a child generally costs the young family a great deal, financially. This may be in terms of a decrease in income as a result of a parent being at home, an increase in expenses for child care, or both.

In the typical Charlie stage, it is assumed that either a parent will remain at home until the youngest child is of school age or expenses must be incurred for child care. Here, we will consider the case where a parent stays at home. Later in this chapter we will discuss the financial conditions of a Dual Income Charlie, when both parents remain in the labour force while children are young.

When the income of a breadwinner is lost, income is often drastically cut expenses are up substantially as a result of medical expenses connected with the birth of the child, new furniture, additional food and so on.

Ability/Propensity to Save: Given the combination of increased expenses and decreased income, the ability of Charlies to save has been drastically reduced. In fact, most Charlies find that they are in a period of dissavings. Their propensity to save, however, has perversely become the opposite. They now have strong motivation to save but little ability to do so.

Credit: The credit needs of a Charlie family are often considerable. Depending upon the amount that they were able to save during the Alpha and Bravo stages, they may need a substantial amount of credit in order to maintain a semblance of their previous life-style in the Charlie stage. Many Charlie families need a second car or a larger car. They may need additional furniture and appliances. Available lines of credit such as credit cards and overdraft credit may be used frequently to get through emergency periods.

Life Insurance: The life insurance needs of the family are now substantial. If insurance is seen as the amount of money needed to cover an obligation that was taken on, then the need for life insurance, is greatest at the birth of a child. This is because as children get older, many of the costs necessary to bring them up are paid. As parts of the total obligation are met the amount of insurance may be reduced.

Liquidity: The liquidity needs are now also very substantial. The family is again dependant upon the income of a single worker, and if anything happened to that source of income, the family would be in substantial difficulty. In addition, medical and other emergencies associated with young children create far greater liquidity needs.

Risk Preference: The family's risk preference tends to diminish very substantially in this life cycle period. While there is still time to recoup any losses, the damage of such a loss becomes great due to the increase in the number of dependants. Since the family now literally need all the money that it has, any loss is significant.

Tax Exposure: The tax exposure of the family is now greatly diminished. Income is often reduced, the number of dependents is up and there is often a tax credit available for child's education. In addition, statistics show that most families in the Charlie stage own a home, with the accompanying tax breaks for mortgage interest and property taxes.

Retirement/Estate Planning: In terms of retirement planning, although the family is now older and presumably more interested in retirement, the lack of funds makes this a low priority item. There is a need for estate planning but at this stage it primarily concerns the need for a will. While there may not be substantial assets to pass on, it is important for the parents to have a will to determine the disposition of children in case both parents die. In many places, children in such a situation could become wards of the state or precipitate a battle between relatives if wills have not been made.

5.6.4 The Delta Stage

Income/Expenses: In the Delta stage, both parents are typically back at work since the youngest child is of school going age. Income is higher, nearly as high in real terms as it will ever go. Expenses for the Deltas may be divided into two sections, the early Delta stage and the later Delta stage. The early Delta stage is before the oldest child is in college while the later Delta stage includes college education for the children. Expenses in the early Delta stage are moderate to high, increasing as children become older and costlier.

Ability/Propensity to Save: The savings ability of the Deltas may also be divided into two stages. In the early Delta stage, the increased income is generally greater than the increased expenses, giving the family the opportunity to repay some of the Charlie debts and put aside some money for the education of the children. Once college education begins, however, most Delta families no longer have the ability to save and in fact may be forced to dissave by drawing down previous savings' balances or by taking on debt. The propensity of such a family to save during the early Delta stage tends to be high since they have experienced the necessity for doing so. In the late Delta stage propensity to save is somewhat higher as retirement looms, but ability to save diminishes as expenses mount during the children's college years.

Credit: The credit needs of the family tend to be low in the early Delta stage and substantially greater as children enter college. Some of these credit needs may be borne by the family, while some may be carried by the children through college loans that they sign for themselves.

Life Insurance: The needs of Delta families for life insurance is quite substantial. In real terms it may not be as great as it was the day the last child was born during the Charlie stage, but there are still years of significant obligation to be borne.

Liquidity: The liquidity needs of the Deltas are not as great as in the single earner Charlie stage since there are now likely to be two parties at work. During the later Delta stage, however, when the family has committed most of its income, liquidity may become relatively more important.

Risk Preference: The risk preference of Delta families is generally not very high. There are still dependants, and there are expenses to pay, so the loss of assets may be quite serious. In addition, many Deltas are looking beyond the education of their children to their own retirement. Therefore, they are likely to be more conservative than they might have been at an earlier age.

Tax Exposure: The tax exposure of Deltas tends to be fairly high. Even though there are dependants and most likely a house, the large expenses of college education are not tax deductible. In addition, since Deltas tend to have little credit outstanding in the early stages and have often paid down a large part of a home mortgage, other deductions may not be substantial. Also, two individuals are again in the labour force. Deltas who have accumulated assets may be in the market for investments that offer tax shelter but which do not deplete liquidity needs during the later Delta stage.

Retirement Planning: Deltas tend to be increasingly more interested in retirement planning, since they see this as an approaching reality. Tax sheltered retirement plans such as Public provident fund or insurance company sponsored pension plans (if eligible) have some appeal to Deltas who can afford the loss of liquidity.

Estate Planning: Estate planning, aside from the will, tends not to be a significant priority for most Deltas. Asset accumulation is not yet extremely high, and for most Deltas any estate funds will go to the surviving spouse and dependant children.

5.6.5 The Echo Stage

When last child has left home, or when couples and single individuals without children approach the last decade of their working lives, the Echo stage is reached.

Income/Expenses: Income tends still to be at the high Delta level while expenses have dropped off very substantially. It is worth noting that Echoes have low expenses for a number of reasons. First, they no longer have the expenses of children and their education. Second, Echoes long ago purchased all of their household capital such as furniture, appliances and similar items. While they do buy automobiles, they are not considered to be frequent buyers.

Ability/Propensity to Save: This considerable difference between income and expenses offers a great ability to save; in fact, most families accumulate the majority of their assets during the Echo stage. Part of this accumulation is due to the very high propensity among Echoes to save. The motivation, of course, is retirement which looms ahead.

Housing: Most Echoes remain in their same house as owners. Echoes are still working at the same job and have little desire to move. Some may give up a large house for a smaller one, but many prefer to remain in their familiar homes and accommodate visits from children and grandchildren.

Credit: The credit needs of Echoes tends to be quite low. In fact, they may be repaying funds borrowed during the Delta stage to pay for college education(s). The only real credit need that they might have is for a credit card which is particularly necessary for persons who travel. Since Echoes have spare funds and more time than previously, they may well choose to travel. Furthermore, travel plans may include visits to children who, are now setting up their own households.

Life Insurance: The need of two working Echoes for life insurance; is often quite low since their obligations are largely behind them. In the case of an Echo couple where one is not in the work force, life insurance may be necessary to protect the stream of income that supports the unemployed individual.

Liquidity: The liquidity needs of Echoes are relatively low. This is particularly true when both Echoes are employed and in good health.

Risk Preference: Their risk preference tends to be low to moderate since they can now afford some losses because the funds are not essential for their current support due to the lowering of expenses. But any funds lost in this stage must be made up in a relatively short period of time before retirement.

Tax Exposure: During this stage tax exposure is very high. Income is generally at its highest level. At the same time, deductions for dependant children have stopped, and for those individuals who took on a mortgage many years earlier, interest deductions are quite small.

Retirement Planning: Since this is the last stage before retirement, interest in retirement planning is extremely high. This interest corresponds to the Echo's high ability and propensity to save.

Estate Planning: As the Echos accumulate assets, the need for estate planning becomes much more important. There may be children but they are no longer dependant. In addition, for those Echoes who have accumulated estates in the hundreds of thousands of rupees, there may be concern with minimizing estate taxes.

5.6.6 The Foxtrot Stage

Income: In the Foxtrot stage income most likely is substantially less than in the Echo stage. Sources of income are pensions, annuities purchased earlier and returns on investments.

Expenses: The expenses of the Foxtrots may not have diminished substantially from those in the Echo stage but for most Foxtrots, there is a desire to maintain a standard of living equal to mat of the Echo stage. There may be differences due to the elimination of work related expenses such as the need to maintain two cars and a work oriented

Wardrobe: However, because Foxtrots have more free time, their activity levels may engender even higher expenses.

Ability/Propensity to Save: The ability of Foxtrots to save tends to be quite limited as a result of diminished income. However, the propensity of Foxtrots to save is likely to be as high or higher than it ever was. Retired persons may be thrifty largely because they view their financial independence as being related to assets that they control.

Housing: The housing status of Foxtrots has changed within the last decade as a result of the greater prevalence of condominiums. Some Foxtrots remain in the same house that they have lived in for much of their lives, while others may move to a warmer climate or to a house with less space, less expenses and less maintenance.

Credit: The credit needs of Foxtrots tend to be minimal. Those who remain interested in travelling will continue to need a credit card.

Life Insurance: The life insurance needs of a Foxtrot in most cases is also minimal. This may vary for families that have a single pension paying most of the expenses but in the majority of cases it is possible to elect survivor benefits from the pension. A need for life insurance may arrive in some circumstances as a function of estate planning. If an estate is largely illiquid, as in the case of a family farm, and if it is the desire of the Foxtrot to leave the property intact to a child, life insurance may be needed to provide liquidity for the payment of estate taxes.

Liquidity: The liquidity needs of Foxtrots tend to be extremely high. This is because they tend to have a relatively low cash flow and often run the risk of periods of poor health. A serious medical ailment could require the payment of up to Rs. 50,000 or more before reimbursement is possible from Medicare and other supplemental health carriers.

Risk Preference: Risk preference for Foxtrots tends to be quite low for two reasons: they need their money and there is little time to recoup losses.

Tax Exposure: The tax exposure of Foxtrots tends to be relatively low because of diminished income and income that is not taxable.

Retirement/Estate Planning: Retirement planning is no longer a consideration for the Foxtrot. However, estate planning may continue to occupy a good deal of the attention of the affluent Foxtrots.

Family Life Cycle and Personal Finance

Stage	Alpha	Bravo	Charlie	Delta	Echo	Foxtrot
Budgeting	H	H	H	M	L	L
Income Tax	L	M	M	H	M	M
Risk Management	L	M	H	M	M	L
Debt Management	M	M	H	M	L	L
Investment	L	M	L	H	M	M
Retirement	L	L	L	M	H	H

H = High; M = Medium; L = Low

5.6.7 Non-Traditional Individuals

Although many people go through (or aspire to go through) all six of the life cycle stages, this will not necessarily be the case. Three special cases that we will consider are the Perpetual Alpha, the Perpetual Bravo, and the Dual Income Charlie.

The Perpetual Alpha: The Perpetual Alpha is an individual who either never marries or marries and loses a spouse without having children. In some ways the Perpetual Alpha resembles the Alpha while in other ways the Perpetual Alpha may resemble age cohorts in more traditional life cycle groups.

The income of the Perpetual Alpha is likely to resemble the income pattern of any other individual who remains in the work force. This means that it may increase slightly in early years and then level off to retirement.

The expenses of Perpetual Alphas may be the same as traditional Alphas during the early years. Perpetual Alphas tend to have active life styles, and also tend to accumulate assets and household capital in early years. As the Perpetual Alpha grows older, there is a tendency for expenses to decrease somewhat. This may be the result of "slowing down" or it may be the result of a decreased lack of need to accumulate assets, clothes, cars, or even a house since these have already been acquired. Therefore, the Perpetual Alpha will generally begin saving at a relatively early age and savings will accumulate and grow throughout the Echo stage.

The tax exposure of the Perpetual Alpha is often substantial. Therefore, Perpetual Alphas often have interests in tax sheltered types of investments. Although liquidity needs may be high as a result of a single income, once these needs have been met the Perpetual Alpha may be willing to take on illiquid but tax sheltered investments such as Public provident fund, Insurance company sponsored pension plans and real estate.

The Perpetual Bravo: The Perpetual Bravo is married without children. If anything, the Perpetual Bravo is even better off than the Perpetual Alpha. Just as we have seen that Bravos tend to have lower expenditures than two Alphas, the Perpetual Bravo has the lifelong ability to accumulate at an even faster rate than the comparable Perpetual Alpha due to the dual incomes and shared expenses. Substantial asset accumulation for the

Perpetual Bravo as in the case of the Perpetual Alpha may begin in the thirties. The Perpetual Alphas and Perpetual Bravos form an important segment of the "newly affluent" market.

The Dual Income Charlie: The Dual Income Charlie is a married couple with pre- school children who keep both partners in the work force throughout child-rearing. This stage is referred to here as "non-traditional" only in an historical sense. On fact, a large proportion of Charlies no longer leave the workforce or cut down on the proportion of time worked. Income would be somewhat higher, in real terms, than in the Bravo stage, and substantially higher than in the average Charlie stage. Expenses in the Dual Income Charlie stage are similar to the Charlie stage with the major addition of added child care expenses. The incremental difference between higher income and higher expenses in the Dual Income stage should be a positive one, at least in terms of ability to save. Propensity to save, as in the Charlie stage, is strong.

Credit and life insurance needs should not differ drastically from those for the single income Charlie. Interest in retirement and estate planning should be close to those found in the Charlie stage.

Housing need may differ since, with two incomes, a home or a larger home may be affordable. Need for liquidity should be lower than for Charlies, again due to the two incomes. The risk preference of the Dual Income Charlie may be higher due to the added discretionary funds available with two wage earners.

6. THE WEALTH CYCLE

In his play 'As You Like It', William Shakespeare described the cycle of a man's life as consisting of seven stages. But the cycle of our financial lives, the wealth cycle, consists of only three stages: accumulation, preservation and distribution. These stages may get disturbed by introduction of predictable but not definite "The Inter-Generation Transfer Stage" or in case you get lucky in any manner of "The Sudden Wealth Stage". Generally one uses age as part of the definition for each step in the wealth cycle. By no means is age meant to be the sole determinant of client's station in the cycle. A careful look at all the aspects of any stage may suggest a different position than the one implied by age.

6.1 ACCUMULATION

As the name implies, this is the stage in which client accumulates wealth. Generally between the ages of 25 and 55, we can identify this phase as the time in which client will do the bulk of income producing work, save as much as he can, and implement an investment strategy designed to provide for himself in later years.

The first few years of this phase generally find an individual saving for the down payment on a first home. A wise investor will also begin, as early as possible, to set aside some savings into a retirement plan. The compounding effect of Rs. 20,000 saved annually at 10% interest from age 25 to age 65 will produce a nest egg of nearly one crore rupees. Children's education expenses and, in some cases, reserves for the support of elderly parents are other goals for which one may begin to accumulate assets.

Also during the early years of this stage, life and disability insurance are important protections to own in order to ensure the completion of various plans.

You may tend to be more risk tolerant during this time, willing to assume a greater risk in your investments for a potentially greater growth. The later years of this phase are usually marked by an increase in savings and accumulation. With your largest acquisition expense (your home) behind you, and your income reflecting your highest production years, the last part of this phase may find you catching up for past under-funded saving years.

6.2 PRESERVATION

Most of us enter this phase of the wealth cycle as a result of illness or disability, or upon retirement. Thus the usual ages associated with this stage are 55 through 75 years old. The most common starting ages are, of course, 62 to 65. In absence of social security the retiring population in India is to depend on pension, provident fund, pension and retirement funds and insurance linked pension funds for source of income during retirement. During this stage, you will determine how your estate will operate for you while you are alive.

Most of the preparations will have been accomplished in the prior phase as you worked with your advisors to update your will, establish a living trust, and otherwise plan for your retirement. Now you will want your accumulated wealth to support you for the rest of your life.

You will be much less tolerant of risk during the preservation phase. With your accumulation years behind you, you won't be able to make up for an unwise or risky investment. As for insurance, disability probably will be no longer applicable, and the purpose of life insurance will change at this stage. No longer concerned with providing for unfulfilled goals, life insurance will now serve to protect your assets from estate taxes. Of course, you should be sure that someone else (e.g., a trust) is the owner of the insurance, so that it doesn't compound the problem it is meant to solve.

Finally, although you may possess an estate sizable enough to owe transfer taxes, the risk of a long term illness may forestall you from giving away or otherwise disposing of any large amounts during this stage in the wealth cycle. However, through a carefully designed annual gifting programme you can assist your children and grandchildren through the accumulation phases of their lives.

6.3 DISTRIBUTION

When you reach an understanding that your assets will indeed outlive you, whether because of the amount of those assets, or because of your advanced age or failing health, you are ready to enter the distribution phase of your wealth cycle. At this point, commonly at age 75 or above, you will want to develop and implement a plan that will distribute your assets to the people and organizations you designate to receive.

One principal concern will be to settle one's wealth in life time to avoid family disputes. One can take advantage of abolition of gift tax. During this phase, you may also reorganize some of your assets with a mind to those who will inherit them. You can start a charitable bequest now by establishing a charitable remainder trust.

Factoring uncertain events.

Wealth cycle may get disturbed due to possible but uncertain factors in an individual's life. In any given year, some families will be either above or below their typical or average incomes because of transitory economic factors such as:

- No earnings or part-time earnings while back to college or in training programs.
- Unemployment or business setback.
- Timeout of the work force for family responsibilities or leisure.
- Irregular and fluctuating incomes characteristic of certain occupations and businesses.
- Unusual positive business event so are "lucky breaks".

REVIEW

QUESTIONS

1. Define financial planning.
2. What are the main responsibilities a financial planner has in designing financial plans for a client?
3. Who are the providers of financial planning?
4. Is it essential for an individual to go through all stages (alpha, bravo, charlie, delta, echo & foxtrot)? Discuss some alternate life stages.
5. Explain wealth cycle in brief.

ANSWERS

1. Financial planning is the process whereby an individual moves towards meeting personal and financial goals through the development and implementation of a comprehensive financial plan.
2. Their main responsibilities are to:

   analyse their needs and objectives

   match these with new products and services

   implement the financial plan

   provide ongoing review to ensure the chosen investment strategies continue to match the clients' changing objectives

   modify the investment solutions as required.
3. The providers of financial planning are:

   life insurance companies

   banks

   stockbrokers

   corporate trustee companies

   independent financial planners and dealer groups

   fund and asset managers

   accountants and solicitors.
4. Although many people go through (or aspire to go through) all six of the life cycle stages, this will not necessarily be the case. These exceptions

arise as people may not marry or remarry after a divorce or both partners are working and may decide to not have children.

The Perpetual Alpha: The perpetual Alpha is an individual who either never marries or marries and loses a spouse without having children. Perpetual Alphas tend to have active life styles, and also tend to accumulate assets and household capital in early years. As the Perpetual Alpha grows older, there is a tendency for expenses to decrease somewhat, This may be the result of "slowing down" or it may be the result of a decreased lack of need to accumulate assets, clothes, cars, or even a house since these have been acquired. Therefore, the Perpetual Alpha will generally begin saving at a relatively early age and savings will accumulate and grow throughout the Echo stage.

The Perpetual Bravo: The Perpetual Bravo is married, without children. If anything, the Perpetual Bravo is even better off than the Perpetual Alpha. Just as we have seen that Bravos tend to have lower expenditures than two Alphas, the Perpetual Bravo has the lifelong ability to accumulate at an even faster rate than the comparable Perpetual Alpha due to the dual incomes and shared expenses. Substantial asset accumulation for the Perpetual Bravo as in the case of the Perpetual Alpha may begin in the thirties. The Perpetual Alphas and Perpetual Bravos form an important segment of the "newly affluent" market.

The Dual Income Charlie: The Dual Income Charlie is a married couple with pre-school children who keep both partners in the work force throughout child-rearing. This stage is referred to here as "non-traditional" only in an historical sense. In fact, a large proportion of Charlies no longer leave the work force or cut down on the proportion of time worked. Income would be somewhat higher, in real terms, than in the Bravo stage, and substantially higher than in the average Charlie stage. Expenses in the Dual Income Charlie stage are similar to the Charlie stage with the major addition of added child care expenses. The incremental difference between higher income and higher expenses in the Dual Income stage should be a positive one, at least in terms of ability to save. Propensity to save, as in the Charlie stage, is strong.

5. The wealth cycle, consists of only three stages: accumulation (where networth keeps on increasing), preservation (period in which net worth is nearly maintained as expenses equal income) and distribution (Net worth keeps on declining, as expenses are more than income).

These stages may get disturbed by introduction of predictable but not definite "The Inter-Generation Transfer Stage" or in case you get lucky in any manner of "The Sudden Wealth Stage" by winning a jackpot or discovering new rewarding patent.

IN SUMMARY

This topic has provided an overview of the financial planning process and industry. It covered the major forces that gave rise to the growth of the industry. It discussed the effect that deregulation has had on the industry and the areas of relevance to financial planners and the industry.

It discussed who would use financial planning services and why. It then examined the role of the financial planner, paying particular attention to responsibilities and duties.

It then examined the providers of financial planning and how the types of providers are changing to meet changing needs. In the discussion on who provides financial planning services, it outlined the role that each provider plays, and the efforts made in recent times to increase the professionalism of financial planners. It also presented an overview on the regulation, controls and practices in the financial planning industry in Australia, with a view to showing a possible direction the industry in India could take.

In India, we have gone through a mini baby boom cycle and are now moving towards stabilization of population which would mean increase in elderly households. These household members will live longer and would require increasingly costly medical treatment and care. Combined impacts of increased longevity and fertility decline, would mean increase in elderly households.

At the same time, economic development and growth and increasing preference by ladies towards career development has shown considerable rise in double income families throughout India. This has increased disposable incomes, spending and also surpluses of savings for investment among many families.

This topic discusses the cycle in man's life as it would impact his financial behaviour. We examined the life cycle and attempt to learn how certain financial needs and attributes can be predicted well in advance. In these days when social norms are breaking we may find exception to life cycles. However, for majority individual classification will help the planner. Family life cycle concept is popular as it captures life style, income and expenditure pattern differences brought about by family role traditions.

SUGGESTED ANSWER TO SELF-ASSESSMENT EXERCISE 1

1. Economic factors might include:

   inflation

   growth of credit

   government need for increased revenue

   regulation and deregulation

   demographic shifts.

2. Lifestyle and emotional factors include:

   marriage and divorce

   loss of job

   increased income or windfall gain, *e.g.* inheritance, winnings in competitions like 'Kaun Banega Crorepati'

   birth of children

   purchase of major assets, *e.g.* house/business.

SUGGESTED ANSWER TO SELF-ASSESSMENT EXERCISE 2

1. No. It involves re-evaluating the plan, taking account of changes in circumstances, needs and the economic environment.

2. The answer will be different for each individual but should include a general discussion of why people are reluctant to use financial planning:

   job instability

   debt

   superannuation considered sufficient for retirement planning

   fear of the unknown (*e.g.* uncertainty about fees and commissions)

   lack of trust/knowledge.

SUGGESTED ANSWER TO SELF-ASSESSMENT EXERCISE 3

1. Personal response. A major advantage is that the client should see you as working in the best interests of their financial goals, needs and objectives. The client should perceive you not merely as a 'product pusher' who sells products, but more as a person to manage their financial needs. As a specialist financial planner, advising is your primary focus, but with

other providers financial planning might be just one of many services they offer.

2. Some factors include:

   legislative changes making advisers more accountable

   professional bodies etc. establishing standards and accountability for breaching those standards

   better training

   closer scrutiny by regulatory bodies

   increased participation by competent, ethical people.

3. Clients are seeking fee for service owing to:

   perceived value for money

   greater understanding and disclosure of fee structure

   the manner in which other professionals are remunerated, etc.

The more traditional methods of remuneration were brokerage and trailing commissions.

SUGGESTED ANSWER TO SELF-ASSESSMENT EXERCISE 4

1. You must suggest they seek advice from another adviser with a suitable licence.
2. You must disclose full particulars of any commission, fee, benefit or interest you or an associate will or might receive in relation to the recommendation.
3. Yes, unless there was no reasonable chance of satisfying the entry requirements.

Further Reading

Australian Securities and Investment Commission, 1997, *ASIC Good Advice Handbook* — Investment Advisory Services, Centre for Professional Development; Victoria, Australia. ASIC policy statements can also be viewed on the ASIC website: www.asic.gov.au.

CHECKLIST

Below is a checklist of the main points covered by this topic. Use it to check your learning.

- Inflation, growth of credit, the Government's need for increased revenue, the growth of compulsory superannuation, regulation and deregulation, and demographic shifts are the major forces that are driving the growth of the financial planning industry.
- Financial planning is the process whereby an individual moves towards meeting personal and financial goals through the development and implementation of a comprehensive financial plan.
- Financial planning encompasses a wide range of skills and knowledge drawn from many disciplines such as accounting, risk management, economics and small business management.
- The financial planning process is the design, implementation and regular review of a financial strategy established to achieve the client's objectives.
- Once the plan has been designed and implemented, it is monitored regularly for success, and modified if circumstances change.
- Financial planning should occur both before and after retirement. The strategies and products recommended at each stage should be different, as investors' needs are often different.
- The main users of financial planning services are professionals, retirees, retrenched workers, executives and small business owners.
- Financial planning services are offered by a great variety of organisations. The range of advice available will vary depending on the organisation.
- The traditional boundaries between financial institutions are breaking down and a more comprehensive offering of financial advice, products and services is emerging.
- There has been a concerted effort to develop a professional standard for financial planners. This change has been brought about for a number of reasons.
- There are a large number of professional organisations that have an interest in the financial services industry.

- Advisers can be paid in several ways, but internationally there is an industry trend towards charging on a fee-for-service basis and rebating commissions to clients.
- In Australia, section 851 of the Corporations Act effectively requires that you have a reasonable basis for making a recommendation about securities to another person who might reasonably be expected to rely on your advice. The two tests for having a reasonable basis are the 'know your client' and 'know your product' rules.
- Section 849 of the Corporations Act (Policy Statement 122: 47-68) requires that you must fully disclose full particulars of any commission or fee or any other benefit you or an associate might receive in relation to that recommendation.
- In any dealings with clients or the public, you must, as a representative of a licensed dealer or investment adviser, disclose that you are acting as a representative.
- Impact of life stages on investment.
- Life stages are determined by marriage, age, status of children and working status.
- Family life cycle concept captures lifestyle, income and expenditure pattern differences brought about by family role traditions.
- Demographic patterns will also impact family life cycles.
- Three stages of wealth cycle.

5 CHAPTER

Financial Planning Process

ABOUT THIS TOPIC

This topic contains a discussion of what financial planning process is. Part of this discussion consists of a review of the major events in the evolution of the financial planning profession. The six-step process of financial planning is described in detail, along with the practice standards approved by the CFP Board. This topic also describes the proper content of a comprehensive financial plan. Then the topic addresses one of the most basic concepts of financial planning— financial statements.

TOPIC OBJECTIVES

At the end of this topic, you should be able to:

- *Explain different views of financial planning.*
- *Become familiar with the major events in the evolution of financial planning as a profession.*
- *Describe the steps in the financial planning process.*
- *Identify each of the elements that should be included in a comprehensive financial plan.*
- *Learn the basic concepts underlying the personal financial position statement.*
- *Learn the underlying concepts of the cash flow management, including characteristics of an effective budget* .

1. VARIOUS VIEWS OF FINANCIAL PLANNING

Although financial planning has matured as a discipline and as a profession, disagreement continues among practitioners regarding the exact definition of financial planning. From a conceptual view, the definition of financial planning can concentrate on the breadth of services provided: single purpose, multiple purpose, and comprehensive.

1.1 SINGLE PURPOSE VIEW

Some practitioners take the position that simply evaluating a single financial issue and providing an appropriate financial product or service to address that issue constitutes financial planning. According to this *single purpose* or specialist *view*, all the following individuals could be examples of financial planners:

- a stockbroker who advises a customer to buy shares of common stock of a particular company
- a preparer of income tax returns who suggests that a client establish a retirement plan
- a banker who opens a trust account for the benefit of a customer's handicapped child
- a life insurance agent who sells key person life insurance to the owner of a small business
- a personal finance counsellor who shows a client how to set up and live within a budget

1.2 MULTIPLE PURPOSE VIEW

Other practitioners might argue that none or only some of the preceding persons are really financial planners. These practitioners would claim that real financial planning must embrace more than solving just a single financial problem of a client and must extend beyond the selling of a single financial product or service. Practitioners adhering to the *multiple-purpose view* might emphasize that there are many categories of client financial needs that

Require financial products and services, such as insurance planning, tax planning, investment planning, retirement planning, and estate planning.

From their perspective, true financial planning should deal with at least multiple aspects of one of these categories and, perhaps, some aspects of other categories. According to the multiple-purpose view, the following individuals would probably qualify as financial planners:

- An insurance agent who sells all types of life, health and general insurance
- A tax lawyer who assists clients with their income, estate, and gift tax planning
- A self proclaimed investment adviser
- A life insurance agent who also sells a family of mutual funds to meet both the protection and wealth accumulation needs of clients.

1.3 COMPREHENSIVE VIEW

Still other practitioners would say that financial planning means, and is synonymous with, comprehensive financial planning. According to this *comprehensive view,* financial planning must consider all aspects of the client's financial position, which includes all the client's financial needs and objectives, and must utilize several integrated and coordinated planning strategies for fulfilling those needs and objectives. The two key characteristics of comprehensive financial planning are that it

- Encompasses all the personal and financial situations of clients to the extent that these can be discovered, clarified, and addressed
- Integrates into its methodology all the techniques and expertise utilized in more narrowly focused approaches to client financial problem solving.

Because of the wide range of expertise required to engage in comprehensive financial planning, effective performance commonly requires a team of specialists, although they may not actually be in contact with each other. In addition to contributing expertise in his or her field of specialization, one of the comprehensive planner's tasks is to coordinate the efforts of the team or ensure that the client seeks the services of appropriate specialists. In its purest form, comprehensive financial planning is a service provided by the planner on a fee-only basis. No part of the planner's compensation comes from the sale of financial products, thus helping to ensure complete objectivity in all aspects of the plan. Some team members may be compensated through fees, while others might receive commissions from the sale of products. In reality, a relatively small minority of financial planners operates exclusively as fee-based financial planners. In its less pure but often more practical form, comprehensive financial planning provides the planner with compensation consisting of some combination of fees for service and commissions from the sale of some of the financial products. Again, members of the team of specialists might receive fees or commissions.

Furthermore, in its purest form, comprehensive financial planning is performed for a client in a single planning engagement in which the planner and his or her team of associates creates one plan that addresses all the client's concerns and utilizes all the needed financial strategies. This plan is then updated with the client periodically and modified as appropriate. In its less pure form, comprehensive financial planning is performed incrementally during the course of several engagements with the client. *Example:* The planner in one year might prepare a plan to treat some of the client's tax concerns and insurance planning problems. In another year, the planner's might focus on the client's investment concerns and then dovetail the strategies for dealing with them with the previously developed tax and insurance strategies. In a third engagement, the planner might address the remaining issues in the tax, insurance, and investment planning areas and coordinate all the recommended strategies and previously developed plans. Again, each incremental part, as well as the overall plan, is reviewed periodically and revised as appropriate.

What, then, is financial planning? Can the financial services professional whose focus is on only a single type of financial problem and financial product for clients legitimately be called a financial planner? What if the professional's focus is broader but less than comprehensive? Is the comprehensive approach the only true form of financial planning? The debate goes on among financial services professionals even now.

Moreover, this debate is not merely an exercise in semantics; it becomes intensely practical when questions are raised about such issues as who shall regulate financial planners, who shall set standards for the financial planning profession, what sort of education financial planners should have, or which financial services practitioners may hold themselves out to the public as financial planners.

2. THE EVOLUTION OF FINANCIAL PLANNING AS A PROFESSION

Perhaps the earliest landmark event in the development of financial planning as a profession occurred in 1969 with the formation of the International Association of Financial Planners, later renamed the International Association for Financial Planning (IAFP). The IAFP was a trade association that, among other things, promoted financial planning, conducted educational and training programs for members, sponsored market research about financial planning, and promoted ethical conduct among practitioners.

Several colleges and universities have played an important role in the development of the financial planning profession. In 1972, the College for Financial Planning, which is the educational institution that originally awarded the Certified Financial Planner® (CFP®) professional designation, was formed. (This function was later transferred to another organization, now called the Certified Financial Planner Board of Standards.)

In 1973, holders of the CFP designation formed the Institute of Certified Financial

Planners (ICFP), a membership organization to help build professionalism in the field.

The year 2000 saw the merger of the Institute of Certified Financial Planners and the International Association for Financial Planning, forming the Financial Planning Association (FPA), and the consolidation of the Life Underwriting Training Council with The American College. Recognition has extended internationally as well. In the year 2000, the International Organization for Standardization (ISO), which establishes globally recognized standards in areas ranging from weights and measures to quality management and assurance, voted to develop standards for the personal financial planning service sector based on the certification requirements of the CFP Board. In India, Financial Planning Standards Board (FPSB) India, is licensed for CFP through its affiliate agreement with FPSB Denver, USA.

2.1 FINANCIAL PLANNING AS A PROCESS

Financial planning is a *process* that requires a disciplined methodology. The general model of the financial planning process includes six steps and is valid for both practitioners and self-planning individuals. The CFP Board has also promoted a six-step process that is applicable for practitioners.

Steps in the Financial Planning Process:

2.2 THE GENERAL MODEL

The general model specifies six steps to the financial planning process:

(1) Establishing and defining the client-Planner relationship

(2) Gathering client data, including goals.

(3) Analyzing and evaluating the financial status of the client

(4) Developing and presenting Financial Planning recommendations and/or alternatives

(5) Implementing the Financial Planning recommendations

(6) Monitoring the Financial Planning recommendations.

(Some professionals reverse steps 1 and 2.)

Practitioners and self-planning individuals can apply this process to the full range of goals on a comprehensive basis, but they can also apply it on a narrower basis to a smaller sub-set of goals or even to a single financial goal.

Step 1: Establishing and defining the client-Planner relationship

Few people begin a vacation without having a specific destination in mind. In contrast, millions of people make significant financial decisions without having a specific financial destination.

Goal setting is critical to creating a successful financial plan, but few people actually set clearly defined goals. By leading the client through the goal-setting exercise, the financial professional not only helps to establish reasonable, achievable goals, but also sets the tone for the entire financial planning process.

Clients typically express concern about such topics as retirement income, education funding, premature death, disability, taxation, qualified plan distribution, and a myriad of others. Sometimes clients enumerate specific, prioritized goals, but they are more likely to present a vague list of worries that suggest anxiety and frustration rather than direction. The planner's responsibility is to help the client transform these feelings into goals. Practitioners should query clients to learn what they are trying to accomplish. Usually the response is couched in general terms, such as "Well, we want to have a comfortable standard of living when we retire." At first glance, this seems to be a reasonable goal, but a closer evaluation reveals that this goal is far too vague. When do they want to retire? What is meant by "comfortable"? Do they want to consider inflation? Do they want to retire on "interest only" or draw down their accumulated portfolio over their expected residual lives (here issues of property distribution to children, if any also emerges) ?

Skillful questioning may reveal a more precise goal, such as "We want to retire in 20 years with an after-tax income of Rs. 600,000 per year in current purchasing power, and we want the income to continue as long as we live without eating the principal." Helping the client quantify goals is among the most valuable services a financial practitioner can provide.

Another important service of the practitioner is goal prioritization. Clients usually mention competing goals, such as saving for retirement and saving for education. Practitioners help clients rank these competing goals.

Step 2: Gathering client data, including goals

Because there are many client concerns that a financial planner may need to address, the planner will have to gather considerable information from the client. Defining the client's current situation, determining what the client's desired future situation is and when it is to be achieved, and establishing what the client is willing and able to do in order to get there require information. This information must be accurate, complete, up-to-date, relevant to the client's goals, and well organized. Otherwise, financial plans based on the information will be deficient—perhaps erroneous, inappropriate, inconsistent with the client's other goals, or dangerous to the client's financial well being.

After a client expresses goals, objectives, and concerns, the planner gathers all the information about the client that is relevant to the problem(s) to be solved and/or to the type of plan to be prepared. The more complex the client's situation and the more varied the number of his or her goals, the greater the information-gathering task.

Two broad types of information will need to be gathered: objective and subjective. A few examples of objective (factual) information that might be needed from the client include a list of securities holdings,

An inventory of assets and liabilities,

A description of the present arrangement for distribution of the client's (and spouse's) assets at death,

A list of annual income and expenditures, And a summary of present insurance covers.

Of at least equal importance is the subjective information about the client. The financial planner often will need to gather information about the hopes, fears, values, preferences, attitudes, and non-financial goals of the client (and spouse).

One piece of information worthy of special attention is client risk tolerance. Practitioners must determine the client's (and spouse's) attitude toward risk before making recommendations.

Before the financial planner begins the information-gathering process, he or she should *give* certain information to the client. First, the client should be made aware that he or she would have to invest time, perhaps a significant amount of time, in the information-gathering stage of financial planning. Even though part of the financial planner's responsibility is to avoid consuming the client's time unnecessarily, this commitment of time by the client is essential. The magnitude of the needed time commitment will depend on the scope and complexity of the client's needs and circumstances, but the proper development of even a narrowly focused and fairly uncomplicated plan requires information that only the client can furnish. Second, the client should be made aware that he or she probably will have to provide the planner with some information that is highly confidential, perhaps even sensitive or painful, for the client to reveal. Again, the scope and complexity of the client's needs will influence this matter. The creation of even rather straightforward plans, however, may require clients to disclose such things as their income and spending patterns, their attitudes toward other family members, or their opinions as to the extent of their own financial responsibilities to others. Another pre-requisite for the effective gathering of client information is a systematic approach to the task. Although there are many possible ways to systematize the gathering of information, one way that has been found useful by many financial planners is to use a structured fact finder form. Some fact finders are only a few pages long and ask for basic information, while others are thick booklets that seek very detailed data on each asset and amount. For many client situations, a formal fact finder elicits considerably more information than needed. The sections that should be completed depend on the particular areas of concern to be addressed in each client's financial plan. Obviously, information gathering is far more than asking the client a series of questions or filling out a form. Certainly that is required, but usually information gathering also requires examination and analysis of documents—such as wills, tax returns, and insurance policies—supplied by the client or the client's other financial advisers. It also requires advising, counselling, and listening during face-to-face meetings with the client and spouse. These skills are especially important because the planner needs to help the client and spouse identify and articulate clearly what they really want to accomplish and what risks they are willing to take in order to do so.

Step 3: Analyzing and evaluating the financial status of the client

Once the relevant information about the client has been gathered, organized, and checked for accuracy, consistency, and completeness, the financial planner's next task is to analyze the client's present financial condition. The objective here is to determine where the client is now *in relationship to the goals that were established by the client in step one.* This analysis may reveal certain strengths in the client's present position relative to those goals. For example, the client may be living well within his or her means, and thus resources are available with which to meet some wealth accumulation goals within a reasonable time period. May be the client has a liberal set of health insurance coverage's through his or her employer (like Armed Forces and Government careers), thereby adequately covering the risks associated with serious disability.

Perhaps the client's will has been reviewed recently by his or her lawyer and brought up-to-date to reflect the client's desired estate plan.

More than likely, however, the financial planner's analysis of the client's present financial position will disclose a number of weaknesses or conditions that are hindering achievement of the client's goals. For example, the client may be paying unnecessarily high income taxes or using debt unwisely. The client's portfolio of investments may be inconsistent with his or her risk-taking tolerance. May be the client's business interest is not being used efficiently to achieve his or someone other than the client has overlooked her personal insurance protection goals, or important loss-causing possibilities, such as the client's exposure to huge law suits arising out of the possible negligent use of an automobile.

One conclusion from the planner's analysis may be that the client cannot attain the goals established in step one. For example, the client's resources and investment returns may preclude reaching a specified retirement income goal. In this case, the practitioner helps the client to lower the goal or shows what changes the client must make to achieve the goal. Postponing retirement, saving more money, seeking higher returns, and deciding to deplete principal during retirement are four ways to help achieve the goal. Presented with alternatives, the client can restate the original goal by either lowering it or revising restrictive criteria to make it achievable.

Step 4: Developing and presenting Financial Planning recommendations and/or alternatives

After the information about the client has been analyzed and, if necessary, the objectives to be achieved have been refined, the planner's next job is to devise a realistic plan for bringing the client from his or her present financial position to the attainment of those objectives. Since no two clients are alike, a well-drawn financial plan must be tailored to the individual, with all the planner's recommended strategies designed for each particular client's needs, abilities, and goals. The plan must be the *client's* plan, not the *planner's* plan.

It is unlikely that any individual planner can maintain an up-to-date familiarity with all the strategies that might be appropriate for his or her clients. Based on his or her education and professional specialization, the planner is likely to rely on a limited number of tried and true strategies for treating the most frequently encountered planning problems. When additional expertise is needed, the planner should always consult with an adviser who is a specialist in the field in question to help the planner design the client's overall plan.

Also, there is usually more than one way for a client's financial goals to be achieved. When this is the case, the planner should present alternative strategies for the client to consider and should explain the advantages and disadvantages of each strategy. Strategies that will help achieve multiple objectives should be highlighted.

The financial plan that is developed should be specific. It should detail who is to do what, when, and with what resources. Implicit in plan development is the importance of obtaining client approval. It follows that the plan must not only be reasonable, it must also be acceptable to the client. Usually interaction between practitioner and client continues during plan development, providing constant feedback to increase the likelihood that the client will approve the plan.

Normally, the report describing the plan should be in writing. Since the objective of the financial planning report is to communicate, its format should be such that the client can easily understand and evaluate what is being proposed. Some financial planners take pride in the length of their reports, although lengthy reports are often made up primarily of standardized or "boilerplate" passages. In general, the simpler the report, the easier it will be for the client to understand and adopt. Careful use of graphs, diagrams, and other visual aids in the report can also help in this regard. After the plan has been presented and reviewed with the client, the moment of truth arrives. At this time, the planner must ask the client to approve the plan (or some variation thereof).

As part of this request, the planner must ask the client to allocate money for the plan's implementation. Financial planning does involve *selling*. Even financial planners who are compensated entirely on a fee-for-service basis must *sell* the client on the need to work with the planner to develop and implement a plan.

Step 5: Implementing the Financial Planning recommendations

The mere giving of financial advice, no matter how solid the foundation on which it is based, does not constitute financial planning. A financial plan is useful to the client *only if it is put into action.* Therefore, part of the planner's responsibility is to see that plan implementation is carried out properly according to the schedule agreed upon with the client. Financial plans that are of limited scope and limited complexity may be implemented for the client entirely by the planner. For other plans, however, additional specialized professional expertise will be needed. For example, such legal instruments as wills and trust documents may have to be drawn up, insurance policies may have to be purchased, or investment securities may have to be acquired. Part of the planner's responsibility is to *motivate* and *assist* the client in completing each of the steps necessary for full plan implementation.

Step 6: Monitoring the Financial Planning recommendations

The relationship between the financial planner and the client should be an ongoing one. Therefore, the sixth and final step in the financial planning process is to monitor the client's plan. Normally, the planner meets with the client at least once each year to review the plan, or more frequently if changing circumstances warrant it. The first part of this review process should involve measuring the performance of the implementation vehicles. Second, updates should be obtained concerning changes in the client's personal and financial situation. Third, changes that have occurred in the economic, tax, or financial environment should be reviewed with the client.

If this periodic review of the plan indicates satisfactory performance in light of the client's current objectives and circumstances, no action needs to be taken. However, if performance is not acceptable or if there is a significant change in the client's personal or financial circumstances or objectives, the planner and client should revise the plan to fit the new environment. This revision process should follow the same six steps used to develop the original plan, though the time and effort needed will probably be less than in the original process.

Summary

The financial planning process, described above, is depicted schematically in figure given below. The blocks on the left represent the six steps in the process, while the blocks on the right indicate the main substantive activities that should occur in each step.

FIGURE 1

THE FINANCIAL PLANNING PROCESS: THE GENERAL MODEL

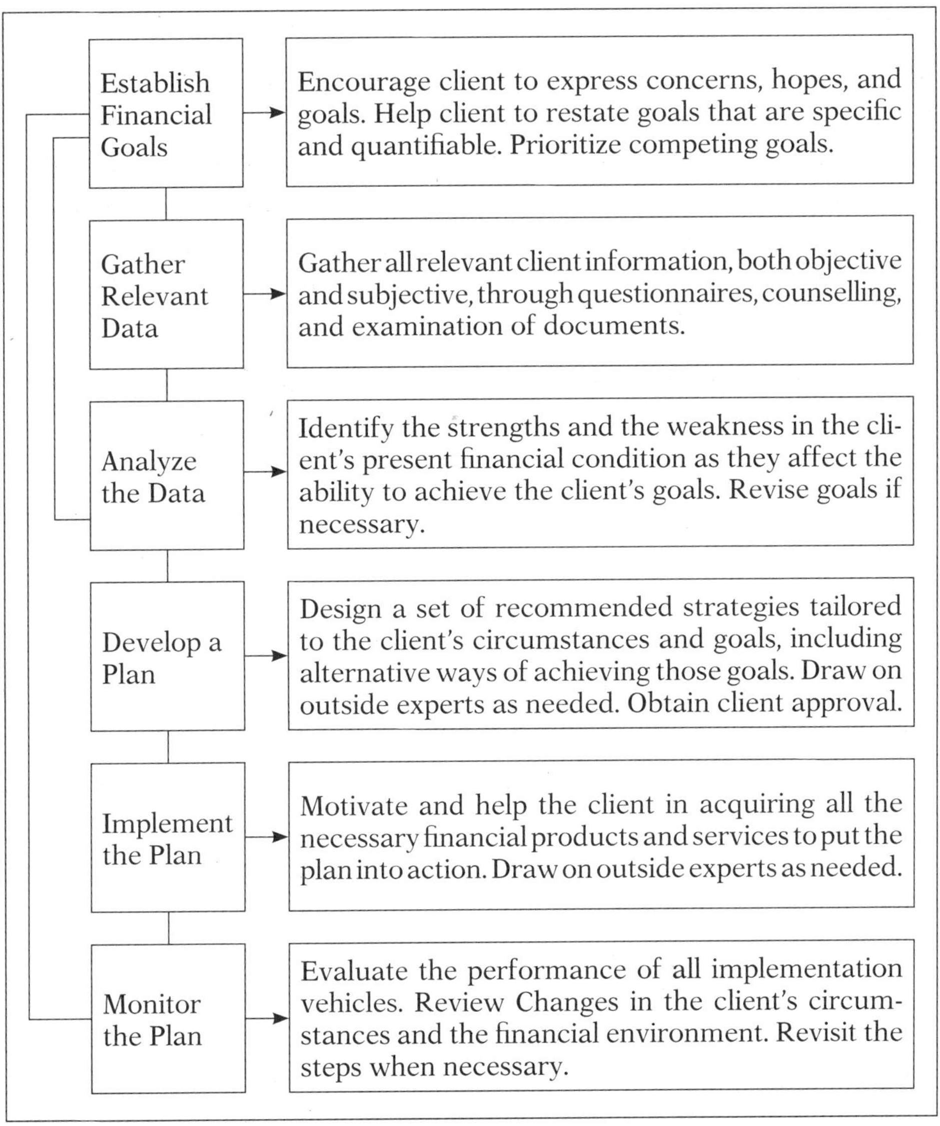

2.3 THE CFP BOARD MODEL

While the six steps in the previous section can be applied by professional planners as well as self-planning lay persons, the Certified Financial Planner Board of Standards has promulgated its own list of six steps that are appropriate for professional financial planners. CFP Board's model, which essentially combines steps 1 and 2 of the general model and inserts a new first step called "Establishing Client-Planner Relationships."

Step 1: Establishing Client-Planner Relationships

The CFP Board asserts that the first step in financial planning involves establishing the working relationship with the client. Planners should explain issues and concepts related to the overall financial planning process as appropriate to the client's situation and needs. They should also explain services provided, the process of planning, and the documentation required. Also included in this step is a clarification of the client and planner's responsibilities.

Step 2: Gathering Client Data and Determining Goals and Expectations

As with the generic model, the data gathering aspect of this step includes obtaining information about the client's financial resources and obligations *via* interview and questionnaire and collecting applicable client records and documents. The planner must also determine the client's time horizons and risk tolerance level. Planners must determine the client's personal and financial goals, needs and priorities, and assess the client's values, attitudes, and expectations.

Step 3: Analyzing and Evaluating the Client's Financial Status

Several categories are involved in analyzing the client's financial status. The general category includes the client's current financial status (such as, assets, liabilities, cash flow, debt management), capital needs, attitudes and expectations, risk tolerance, risk management, and risk exposure. In the special needs category are divorce/remarriage considerations; charitable planning; adult dependent, disabled child, and education needs; terminal illness planning; and closely held business planning. The risk management category includes needs and current coverage for life; disability, health, long-term care; home owners, auto and other liability (for example, umbrella, professional, errors and omissions, directors, and officers); and commercial insurance. The investments category covers analysis and evaluation of current investments and current investment strategies and policies. Evaluation of the tax category involves tax returns, current tax strategies, tax compliance status (such as estimated tax), and current tax liabilities.

In the retirement category, planners should evaluate and analyze current retirement plan tax exposures (for example, assets marked for retirement benefit such as Provident Fund, Gratuity, PPF, Special Insurance Policies) and current retirement strategies.

Planners should evaluate the client's employee benefits, including the benefits available and the client's current participation in those benefits. Finally, the planner should analyze the client's current estate plan, which includes an evaluation of estate planning documents and strategies as well as estate tax exposure.

Step 4: Developing and Presenting the Financial Plan

The planner should develop and prepare a client-specific financial plan tailored to meet the client's goals and objectives, commensurate with client's values, temperament, and risk tolerance. In addition to the client's current financial position, the plan should include the client's projected financial statements under the *status quo* as well as projected statements if the planner's recommendations are followed. Similarly, the planner should include the current status, projections under the *status quo,* and projections if recommendations are followed for the following categories: cash flow, estate tax, capital needs at retirement, capital needs at death, capital needs at disability, special capital needs, income taxes, and employee benefits. The planner should also provide a current asset allocation statement along with strategy recommendations and a statement that assumes that recommendations will be followed. Investments should be summarized and the planner should propose an investment policy statement and additional policy recommendations.

The plan should also include an assessment of risk exposures along with recommendations for insurance and other risk management techniques. Finally, the plan should include a list of prioritized action items.

After developing and preparing the plan, the planner should present the plan to the client and review it with him or her. The planner should collaborate with the client to ensure that the plan meets the goals and objectives of the client and should revise it as appropriate.

Step 5: Implementing the Financial Plan

The planner should assist the client in implementing the recommendations. Often this requires coordinating with other professionals, such as accountants, lawyers, real estate agents, investment advisers, stockbrokers, and insurance agents.

Step 6: Monitoring the Financial Plan

After the plan is implemented, the planner should periodically monitor and evaluate the soundness of recommendations, and review the progress of the plan with the client. The planner should discuss and evaluate changes in the client's personal circumstances such as family births or deaths, illness, divorce, job status, or retirement. Any relevant changes in tax laws and the economic environment should be reviewed and evaluated before the planner makes recommendations to accommodate new or changing circumstances.

SELF-ASSESSMENT EXERCISE 1

1. Describe each of the following views of financial planning:
   a. Single-purpose view
   b. Multiple-purpose view
   c. Comprehensive view

   ....

   ....

   ....

   ....

   ....

   ....

   ....

2. Identify the six steps in the financial planning process, and briefly indicate the kinds of activities involved in each step for both of the following:
   a. General approach to financial planning
   b. CFP Board's guidelines

   ....

   ....

   ....

   ....

   ....

   ....

   ....

   ....

3. GOOD PRACTICES IN FINANCIAL PLANNING

Good Practice Related to Establishing and Defining the Relationship with the Client

Practice 1: Defining the Scope of the Engagement

The scope of the engagement shall be mutually defined by the financial planning practitioner and the client prior to providing any financial planning service.

Prior to providing any financial planning service, a financial planning practitioner and the client should mutually define the scope of the engagement. The process of "mutually- defining" is essential in determining what activities may be necessary to proceed with the client engagement. This can be accomplished by

- identifying the service(s) to be provided;
- disclosing financial planning practitioner's compensation arrangement(s);
- determining the client's and the financial planning practitioner's responsibilities;
- establishing the duration of the engagement; and

- providing any additional information necessary to define or limit the scope.

The scope of the engagement may include one or more financial planning subject areas. It is acceptable to mutually define engagements in which the scope is limited to specific activities. This serves to establish realistic expectations both for the client and the practitioner.

While you may not put scope of the engagement in writing, however it will be advisable to do so to avoid confusion at a later stage.

Good Practice Related to Gathering Client Data

Good Practice 2: Determining a Client's Personal and Financial Goals, Needs and Priorities

The financial planning practitioner and the client prior to making and/or implementing any recommendations shall mutually define a client's personal and financial goals, needs and priorities that are relevant to the scope of the engagement and the service(s) being provided.

Prior to making recommendations to a client, a financial planning practitioner (practitioner) and the client shall mutually define the client's personal and financial goals, needs and priorities. In order to arrive at such a definition, the practitioner will need to explore the client's values, attitudes, expectations, and time horizons as they affect the client's goals, needs and priorities. The process of "mutually-defining" is essential in determining what activities may be necessary to proceed with the client engagement. Personal values and attitudes shape a client's goals and objectives and the priority placed on them. Accordingly, these goals and objectives must be consistent with the client's values and attitudes in order for the client to make the commitment necessary to accomplish them.

Goals and objectives provide focus, purpose, vision, and direction for the financial planning process. It is essential those objectives relative to the scope of the engagement are determined and that they are clear, precise, consistent, and measurable. The role of the practitioner is to facilitate the goal-setting process in order to clarify, with the client, goals and objectives, and, when appropriate, the practitioner must try to assist clients in recognizing the implications of unrealistic goals and objectives.

This practice standard addresses only the tasks of determining a client's personal and financial goals, needs and priorities; assessing a client's values, attitudes and expectations; and determining a client's time horizons. These areas are subjective and the practitioner's interpretation is limited by what the client reveals. A practitioner performing the activity of "gathering client data" should consider together the various good practices applicable to such activity.

Good Practice 3: Obtaining Quantitative Information and Documents

A financial planning practitioner shall obtain sufficient and relevant quantitative information and documents about a client applicable to the scope of the engagement and the services being provided prior to making and/or implementing any recommendations.

Prior to making recommendations to a client and depending upon the type of client engagement and its scope, a financial planning practitioner (practitioner) shall determine what quantitative information and documents are sufficient and relevant.

A practitioner shall obtain sufficient and relevant quantitative information and documents pertaining to the client's financial resources, obligations, and personal situation. This information may be obtained directly from the client or other sources through interview, questionnaire, client records and documents.

A practitioner shall communicate to the client a reliance on the completeness and accuracy of the information provided and that incomplete or inaccurate information will impact conclusions and recommendations.

If a practitioner is unable to obtain sufficient and relevant quantitative information and documents to form a basis for recommendations, the practitioner shall either : (*a*) restrict the scope of the engagement to those matters for which sufficient and relevant information is available; or (*b*) terminate the engagement.

A practitioner shall communicate to the client any limitations on the scope of the engagement, as well as the fact that this limitation could affect the conclusions and recommendations.

Good Practice Relating to Analyzing and Evaluating the Client's Financial Status

Good Practice 4: Analyzing and Evaluating the Client's Information

A financial planning practitioner shall analyze the information to gain an understanding of the client's financial situation and then evaluate to what extent the client's goals, needs and priorities can be met by the client's resources and current course of action.

Prior to making recommendations to a client, it is necessary for the financial planning practitioner to assess the client's financial situation and to determine the likelihood of reaching the stated objectives by continuing present activities.

The practitioner will utilize client specified, mutually agreed upon, and/or other reasonable assumptions. Both personal and economic assumptions must be considered in this step of the process. These assumptions may include, but are not limited to the following: personal assumptions, such as retirement age(s), life expectancy(ies), income needs, risk factors, time horizon, and special needs; and economic assumptions, such as: inflation rates, tax rates, and investment returns.

Analysis and evaluation are critical to the financial planning process. These activities form the foundation for determining strengths and weaknesses of the client's financial situation and current course of action. These activities may also identify other issues that should be addressed. As a result, it may be appropriate to amend the scope of the engagement and/or to obtain additional information

Good Practice Relating to Developing and Presenting Financial Planning Presentations

Good Practice 5: Identifying and Evaluating Financial Planning Alternative(s)

A financial planning practitioner shall consider sufficient and relevant alternatives to the client's current course of action in an effort to reasonably achieve the client's goals, needs and priorities.

After analyzing the client's current situation and prior to developing and presenting the recommendation(s), the financial planning practitioner shall identify alternative actions. The practitioner shall evaluate the effectiveness of such actions in reasonably achieving the client's goals, needs and priorities.

This evaluation may involve, but is not limited to, considering multiple assumptions, conducting research, or consulting with other professionals. This process may result in a single alternative, multiple alternatives, or no alternative to the client's current course of action.

In considering alternative actions, the practitioner also must recognize and, as appropriate, take into account his or her legal and/or regulatory limitations and level of competency in properly addressing each of the client's financial planning issues.

More than one alternative may reasonably achieve the client's goals, needs, and priorities. Alternatives identified by the practitioner may differ from those of other practitioners or advisors, illustrating the subjective nature of exercising professional judgment.

Good Practice 6: Developing the Financial Planning Recommendation(s)

A financial planning practitioner shall develop the recommendation(s) based on the selected alternative(s) and the current course of action in an effort to reasonably achieve the client's goals, needs and priorities.

After identifying and evaluating the alternative(s) and the client's current course of action, the practitioner shall develop the recommendation(s) expected to reasonably achieve the client's goals, needs and priorities. A recommendation may be an independent action or a combination of actions that may need to be implemented collectively.

The recommendation(s) shall be consistent with, and will be directly affected by, the following:

- a mutually defined scope of the engagement;
- a mutually defined client goals, needs and priorities;
- quantitative data provided by the client;
- personal and economic assumptions;
- the practitioner's analysis and evaluation of client's current situation; and
- alternative(s) selected by the practitioner.

A recommendation may be to continue the current course of action. If a change is recommended, it may be specific and/or detailed or provide a general direction. In some instances, it may be necessary for the practitioner to recommend that the client modify a goal.

The recommendations developed by the practitioner may differ from those of other practitioners or advisors yet each may reasonably achieve the client's goals, needs and priorities.

Good Practice 7: Presenting the Financial Planning Recommendation(s)

A financial planning practitioner shall communicate the recommendation(s) in a manner and to an extent reasonably necessary to assist the client in making an informed decision.

When presenting a recommendation, the practitioner shall make a reasonable effort to assist the client in understanding the client's current situation, the recommendation itself, and its impact on the ability to achieve. The client's goals, needs and priorities. In doing so, the practitioner shall avoid presenting the practitioner's opinion as fact.

The practitioner shall communicate the factors critical to the client's understanding of the recommendations. These factors may include but are not limited to the following material:

personal and economic assumptions;

interdependence of recommendations;

advantages and disadvantages;

risks; and/or

time sensitivity.

The practitioner should indicate that even though the recommendations may achieve the client's goals, needs and priorities, changes in personal and economic conditions could alter the intended outcome. Changes may include, but are not limited to: legislative, family status, career, investment performance and/or health.

If there are conflicts of interest that have not been previously disclosed, such conflicts and how they may impact the recommendations should be addressed at this time.

Presenting recommendations provides the practitioner an opportunity to further assess whether the recommendations meet client expectations, whether the client is willing to act on the recommendations, and whether modifications are necessary.

Good Practice Relating to Implementing the Financial Planning Recommendations

Good Practice 8: Agreeing on Implementation Responsibilities

A financial planning practitioner and the client shall mutually agree on the implementation responsibilities consistent with the scope of the engagement.

The client is responsible for accepting or rejecting recommendations and for retaining and/or delegating implementation responsibilities. The financial planning practitioner and the client shall mutually agree on the services, if any, to be provided by the practitioner. The scope of the engagement, as originally defined, may need to be modified.

The practitioner's responsibilities may include, but are not limited to the following:

- identifying activities necessary for implementation;
- determining division of activities between the practitioner and the client;
- referring to other professionals;
- coordinating with other professionals;
- sharing of information as authorized; and
- selecting and securing products and/or services.

If there are conflicts of interest, sources of compensation or material relationships with other professionals or advisors that have not been previously disclosed, such conflicts, sources or relationships must be disclosed at this time.

When referring the client to other professionals or advisors, the financial planning practitioner shall indicate the basis for the referral.

If the practitioner is engaged by the client to provide only implementation activities, the scope of the engagement shall be mutually defined, orally or in writing.

This scope may include such matters as the extent to which the practitioner will rely on information, analysis of recommendations provided by others.

Good Practice 9: Selecting Products and Services for Implementation

A financial planning practitioner shall select appropriate products and services that are consistent with the client's goals, needs and priorities.

A financial planning practitioner will use professional judgment in selecting the products and services that are in the client's interest. Professional judgment incorporates both qualitative and quantitative information. A financial planning practitioner shall reasonably investigate and evaluate products or services that address the client's needs. The financial planning practitioner shall have a reasonable basis for believing that the products or services selected are suitable for the client. Products and services selected by the practitioner may differ from those selected by other practitioners or advisors. Alternative products or services may be suitable for the client and could reasonably achieve the client's goals, needs and priorities, illustrating the subjective nature of exercising professional judgment.

The practitioner must make all disclosures required to comply with applicable regulations.

Good Practice Standard Relating to Monitoring the Financial Planning Recommendations

Good Practice 10: Defining Monitoring Responsibilities

The financial planning practitioner and client shall mutually define monitoring responsibilities.

The purpose of this standard is to clarify the extent of the practitioner's role in the monitoring process. The practitioner and the client may have different perceptions about monitoring responsibilities. When monitoring is included in the scope of the engagement, the financial planning practitioner shall identify which monitoring activities may be appropriate. The practitioner shall make a reasonable effort to define and communicate which monitoring activities the practitioner is able and willing to provide.

The practitioner and client shall mutually agree on the extent, frequency and duration of the monitoring activities, if any, to be provided by the practitioner. The scope of the engagement, as originally defined, may need to be modified.

Monitoring responsibilities may include but are not limited to:

- Identifying changes in conditions that would impact existing recommendations.
- Obtaining information from the client to determine changes in personal circumstances.
- Reviewing work done by other professionals or providers.
- Reviewing the client's progress toward financial goals.

The monitoring process may reveal the need to reinitiate any or all of the steps of the financial planning process.

4. CONTENT OF A COMPREHENSIVE FINANCIAL PLAN

As noted earlier, comprehensive financial planning is only one type of financial planning. In practice, it is the least frequently encountered type for most planners for several reasons. First, not many clients are willing to invest as much of their own time in the undertaking as comprehensive financial planning requires. Second, usually only affluent clients are willing and able to pay for all the time of the planner and his or her staff that is needed in developing a comprehensive financial plan. Third, not many clients can easily deal with the totality of their financial goals, capabilities, and difficulties all at one time. Instead, most prefer to concentrate on only one or a few related issues at a time. (As has been mentioned, however, even clients in the last group can have a comprehensive plan developed and implemented for them in incremental stages.)

For those cases in which the planner is called upon to prepare a comprehensive financial plan for a client, whether entirely in one engagement or incrementally over a period of years, what should the plan contain? Clearly, comprehensive financial planning is such an ambitious and complex undertaking that it must cover numerous elements. For quality of service and protection from law suits, financial planning practitioners need guidelines to make certain that their plans are truly comprehensive.

Likewise, consumers need assurance that a planner will be able to provide a well- rounded, comprehensive plan that spans all aspects of his or her financial situation.

Each group benefits from the existence of a set of standards by which a comprehensive financial plan can be judged. Both the Certified Financial Planner Board of Standards and the Registry of Financial Planning Practitioners, which was an arm of the former International Association for Financial Planning, have published such guidelines.

Elements of a Comprehensive Financial Plan: General Guidelines

Over a decade ago, the Registry of Financial Planning Professionals developed the following guidelines for comprehensive financial plans. They represent the first formal, written presentation of a set of standards for practitioners to follow. Although the Registry no longer exists, the guidelines are still valid.

4.1 OVERVIEW OF PLAN ELEMENTS

A comprehensive financial plan should contain an analysis of all pertinent factors relating to the client. While order and style of presentation may vary, the plan should include, but not necessarily be limited to, the following elements:

1. Personal data
2. Client goals and objectives
3. Identification of issues and problems
4. Assumptions
5. Balance sheet/net worth
6. Cash-flow management
7. Income-tax
8. Risk management/insurance
9. Investments
10. Financial independence, retirement planning, education, and other special needs
11. Estate planning

12. Recommendations
13. Implementation.

When developing a comprehensive financial plan, the planner is responsible for all of the elements of the plan, from data gathering through analysis and presentation to the client. Those elements of the plan that the planner does not personally perform remain the responsibility of the planner to coordinate. When technical areas (such as legal and insurance services) are not personally performed by the planner, the financial plan or supplement should include supporting documentation that these areas have been or will be coordinated by the planner. Analysis of each element of the plan should consist of a review of pertinent facts, a consideration of the advantages and/or disadvantages of the current situation, and a determination of what, if any, further action is required. The plan should include a summary statement providing the planner's comments on the analysis, and his or her recommendations, where appropriate, for each element of the plan.

4.2 GUIDELINES FOR A COMPREHENSIVE FINANCIAL PLAN

Personal Data

1. Should include relevant personal and family data for parties covered under the plan.

   Should include, but not be limited to, name, address, social security number, birth date and other relevant data.

Client's Goals and Objectives

2. A reiteration of the client's stated goals and objectives, indicating their priority and including a timeframe where applicable.

   The statement of goals and objectives will form the basic framework for the development of the financial plan.

   The client's goals and objectives should be expressed in as specific and precise language as possible. For example, a statement of a goal should read "Retire at age 62 in present home and maintain a current standard of living" rather than "A comfortable retirement."

Identification of Issues and Problems

3. A plan must address relevant issues and problems identified by the client, the planner and/or other advisers.

    List personal and financial issues and problems that affect the client such as major illness, education costs, taxes, etc. While the client may be aware of many, if not all, of the issues, the planner may discover other areas that are or could develop into problems.

    These issues and problems, when combined with the client's goals and objectives, will complete the framework and direction for the financial plan. Since style and order are not the primary consideration, the analysis of recommendation section(s) of the plan may be more appropriate for identifying issues and problems.

Assumptions

4. Identify and state material assumptions used in the plan's preparation.

    Assumptions should include, but not be limited to, inflation, investment growth rate, mortality, etc.

Balance Sheet/Net Worth

5. A presentation and analysis to include, but not be limited to, a schedule listing assets and liabilities with a calculation of net worth and itemized schedules of liabilities and assets to be included as appropriate.

    In addition to the schedules, footnotes should be included as appropriate.

Cash Flow Management

6. Statements and analysis to include, but not be limited to, a statement of the client's sources and uses of funds for the current year and for all relevant years, indicating net cash flow, as well as a separate income statement, where appropriate.

    Sources—earned income, investment income, and sale proceeds, gifts, etc.

Uses—living expenses, debt service, acquisition of assets, taxes paid, etc.

Net cash flow—both positive and negative.

Income-tax

7. An income-tax statement and analysis to include, but not be limited to, the income taxes for the current year and for all relevant years covered in the plan.

   Projections should show the nature of the income and deductions in sufficient detail to permit calculation of the tax liability. The analysis should identify the marginal tax rate for each year and any special situations such as alternative minimum tax, passive loss limitations, etc., that affect the client's tax liability.

   The financial plan should include footnotes to let the client know which taxes if any, have not been addressed.

Risk Management/Insurance

8. A. An analysis of a client's financial exposure relative to mortality, morbidity, liability and property, including business as appropriate.

   Mortality—survivor income and capital needs analysis.

   Morbidity—impact of loss of health.

   Liability—legal exposure.

   Property—loss of value.

   Business—loss due to business involvement.

   B. Listing and analysis of current policies and problems to include, but not be limited to, life, disability, medical, business, property/casualty and liability.

   Analysis of existing coverage and/or risk exposure in relationship to the client's needs, goals and objectives.

   If any area of insurance is not within the competency range of the financial planner, the planner has the responsibility to coordinate with other professionals and document such coordination in the financial plan. Documentation of the above areas can include the insurance professional's summary, if completed, or the professional's name and time frame when such review will be completed.

Investments

9. A listing of the current investment portfolio and an analysis or discussion of the liquidity, diversification and investment risk exposure of the portfolio. In addition, the suitability of the investments in relationship to the client's needs, goals and objectives should be addressed, to include, but not be limited to, risk tolerance, risk management of investments, suitability, liquidity, diversification and personal management efforts :
    - Risk tolerance—addresses the client's willingness to accept investment risk.
    - Risk management—analysis of client's exposure relative to loss of invested capital.
    - Suitability—appropriateness of the investment for the client.
    - Liquidity—the availability of assets that can be converted into cash at acceptable costs.
    - Diversification—appropriate mix of assets to meet the client's needs, goals and objectives.
    - Personal management efforts—the degree to which the client wants to manage and is capable of managing his or her assets.

Financial Independence, Retirement Planning, Education and Other Special Needs

10. An analysis of the capital needed at some future time to provide for financial independence, retirement, education, or other special needs. The analysis should include a projection of resources expected to be available to meet these needs at that time :
    - In achieving the above, inflation, growth of assets and company benefits should be considered where applicable.
    - Special sections of the above topics may require a separate heading in the financial plan. For example, company benefits may require an analysis of types available, pre-and post-tax

contributions needed, tax treatment of plans and investment of benefit plan assets.

Estate Planning

11. Identification of assets that can be included in the client's estate and an analysis of the control, disposition and taxation of those assets :
    - Control—authority to manage or direct the use of assets by means of title, trusteeship, power of attorney, etc.
    - Disposition—transfer of ownership by will, trust, beneficiary designation or operation of the law.
    - Taxation—taxation of the client's estate and the income-tax and estate tax consequences to the beneficiaries.

12. Recommendations

- Written recommendations that relate to goals and objectives as well as financial issues and problems.
- Written recommendations should specifically address the client's goals and objectives and all issues and problems identified in the plan, as well as a determination of the actions necessary to compensate for any shortfalls. Recommendations should be clearly identified and stated. They should not be conveyed by implication or inference.

Implementation

13. A prioritized list of actions required implementing the recommendations, indicating responsible parties, action required and timing :
    - Implementation should include a schedule reflecting actions to be taken as well as priority, dates and responsible parties.

Beginning a Dialogue on Ethics

Ethics is a topic that should be implicit in any discussion of financial planning and the role of the financial planner. It is appropriate that we address a question that many planners have asked: "Is the highly ethical financial planner financially rewarded for being ethical?" The answer is that she or he may be, but there is no guarantee. There are examples to the contrary, just as there are some illustrations of the shady planner reaping significant financial gains. Disciplined ethical conduct, by itself, does not guarantee financial success.

Perhaps the question should be addressed from a different perspective. Do clients want to do business with someone who really understands financial planning but who has questionable morals? Do clients want to do business with someone whose integrity is unassailable but whose financial planning skills are marginal? The answer to both questions is no.

The skilled financial planner, who is client-centered and ethically well disciplined, clearly has the attributes that clients desire and deserve. Again, ethical practice provides no guarantees of financial success. It is clear, however, that clients want to do business with financial planners who have earned their trust and are technically competent.

Code of Ethics :

FPSB India adopted the Code of Ethics to establish the highest principles and standards. These Principles are general statements expressing the ethical and professional are expected to display in their professional activities

Code of Ethic 1 – Client First

Place the client's interests first

Placing the client's interests first is a hallmark of professionalism, requiring the Financial Planning professional to act honestly and not place personal gain or advantage before the client's interests.

Code of Ethic 2 - Integrity

Provide professional services with integrity

Integrity requires honesty and candor in all professional matters. Financial Planning professionals are placed in positions of trust by clients, and the ultimate source of that trust is the Financial Planning professional's personal integrity. Allowance can be made for legitimate differences of opinion, but integrity cannot co-exist with deceit or subordination of one's principles. Integrity requires the Financial Planning professional to observe both the letter and the spirit of the Code of Ethics.

Code of Ethic 3 - Objectivity

Provide professional services objectively

Objectivity requires intellectual honesty and impartiality. Regardless of the services delivered or the capacity in which a Financial Planning professional functions, objectivity requires Financial Planning professionals to ensure the integrity of their work, manage conflicts and exercise sound professional judgment.

Code of Ethic 4 - Fairness

Be fair and reasonable in all professional relationships. Disclose and manage conflicts of interest

Fairness requires providing clients what they are due, owed or should expect from a professional relationship, and includes honesty and disclosure of material conflicts of interest. It involves managing one's own feelings, prejudices and desires to achieve a proper balance of interests. Fairness is treating others in the same manner that you would want to be treated.

Code of Ethic 5 – Professionalism

Act in a manner that demonstrates exemplary professional conduct

Professionalism requires behaving with dignity and showing respect and courtesy to clients, fellow professionals, and others in business-related activities, and complying with appropriate rules, regulations and professional requirements. Professionalism requires the Financial Planning professional, individually and in co-operation with peers, to enhance and maintain the profession's public image and its ability to serve the public interest.

Code of Ethic 6 - Competence

Maintain the abilities, skills and knowledge necessary to provide professional services competently

Competence requires attaining and maintaining an adequate level of abilities, skills and knowledge in the provision of professional services. Competence also includes the wisdom to recognize one's own limitations and when consultation with other professionals is appropriate or referral to other professionals necessary. Competence requires the Financial Planning professional to make a continuing commitment to learning and professional improvement.

Code of Ethic 7 - Confidentiality

Protect the confidentiality of all client information

Confidentiality requires client information to be protected and maintained in such a manner that allows access only to those who are authorized. A relationship of trust and confidence with the client can only be built on the understanding that the client's information will not be disclosed inappropriately.

Code of Ethic 8 - Diligence

Provide professional services diligently

Diligence requires fulfilling professional commitments in a timely and thorough manner, and taking due care in planning, supervising and delivering professional services.

PREPARING FINANCIAL STATEMENTS

The preparation of organized financial information is an important but often ignored aspect of personal financial planning. Like businesses, individuals must often prepare financial information for external use. Banks and other lending institutions rarely make loans to individuals without first analyzing their current financial position and future ability to repay the loan. However, the primary use of financial information in personal financial planning is for internal purposes.

Financial analysis, planning, and control are important planning techniques, whether conducted by the individual alone or by the individual assisted by a professional. The focus of this appendix is on financial statements useful for such internal purposes. It is difficult, if not impossible, to identify financial objectives and formulate strategies for their achievement without knowing a client's current financial situation and resources. In addition, the ongoing analysis of personal financial information is crucial in monitoring whether financial objectives are being achieved. Two primary pieces of client information used by planners are the current financial position (represented by the *financial position statement,* or *balance sheet)* and the cash-flow status (represented by the *cash-flow statement).* Before each is discussed in greater detail, a few general comments introduce this topic.

While it is common to see personal financial statements that have been prepared only at the end of a calendar or fiscal year, both the timing and frequency of financial statements often vary. When a lending institution needs personal financial information for loan purposes, it usually requires that the information be prepared as on the date of the loan application. Similarly, a financial planner needs financial information at the time the planning process begins and at the time of each subsequent review of a client's financial plans. If reviews take place every 6 months, it is necessary to update personal financial statements at these intervals. In other words, personal financial statements are not prepared at arbitrary times, but rather when the information is needed for the financial planning process.

The financial position and cash-flow status relate to what has occurred in the past. For financial planning, it is necessary to prepare *proforma* (or projected) balance sheets and cash-flow statements. These proformas illustrate future financial statements if certain activities are implemented under specified assumptions. Finally, actual financial statements can be compared with past projections to see if the client's financial plan was realized.

Financial position statement

The financial position statement shows an individual's (or family's) wealth at a specified time and reflects the results of the individual's past financial activities. It contains three basic classifications— assets, liabilities, and net worth—that make up the basic accounting equation:

ASSETS = LIABILITIES + NET WORTH

Financial planners can choose from many different formats for the financial position statement since there is no standard. Usually, statements group the items that make up assets and liabilities into sub-classifications that better enable the planner to analyze the components of the client's total financial situation and to evaluate the mix of assets in relation to the client's objectives.

Assets

Assets are items the client owns. It is immaterial whether the item was purchased for cash, financed by borrowing, or received as a gift or inheritance. Items that the client possesses but does not own, such as rented apartments or leased automobiles, are not shown as assets.

It is common practice for personal financial position statements to show assets at their current fair market values. These values may vary considerably from the original purchase prices. In contrast, business financial statements must list many assets on the basis of adjusted historical costs, net of depreciation.

At a minimum, assets should be sub-divided into two categories: financial assets and personal (or non-financial) assets. Many statement formats include other categories such as use assets, non-use assets, personal assets, investment assets, and retirement assets, among others.

Liabilities are the debts of the client. For example, the statement might show sub-totals for short- term liabilities (due in one year or less), intermediate-term liabilities (due in one to 5 years), and long-term liabilities (due in more than 5 years). In theory, the liabilities section of the financial position statement should show all liabilities as of the date of the statement—even if the client has not received a formal bill. This process may require the client to make estimates for such items as taxes due, utility charges owed, and credit card obligations. In practice, clients and planners often ignore relatively small accruals for unaudited statements.

Net Worth

Net worth measures the client's wealth or equity on the date of the financial position statement. It is calculated by restating the basic accounting equation as follows:

NET WORTH = TOTAL ASSETS - TOTAL LIABILITIES

In other words, net worth is what remains if all the client's assets are sold at their fair market values and all debts are paid. If a client has a negative net worth, the client is considered to be bankrupt. However, such clients can avoid formal bankruptcy proceedings if cash flow is sufficient to service all financial obligations.

By itself, net worth reveals little about the nature of the assets or liabilities. A client with considerable net worth may have all his or her assets tied up in non-income-producing assets, such as homes, automobiles, and other personal possessions. Conversely, a client with a modest net worth may hold most assets in the form of financial assets that may be generating income, capital appreciation, or both. Further, it is possible for a client to have a positive cash balance with a negative net worth or to have a zero cash balance with a very high net worth. The key to understanding net worth is to recognize that it is simply a residual—the difference between total assets and total liabilities.

A client's net worth may increase or decrease during a period of time. Other things being equal, a client's net worth will increase as a result of any one of the following:

- appreciation in the value of assets
- addition to assets through retaining income
- addition of assets through gifts or inheritances
- decrease in liabilities through forgiveness.

The following are examples of actions that have no effect on net worth:

- paying off a debt. The cash account declines by the same amount that the liability declines, leaving the difference between total assets and total liabilities unchanged.
- buying an asset with cash. Total assets remain unchanged because cash declines by the same amount that the other asset category increases. However, commissions and other transaction costs cause net worth to decline because the cash that pays these costs is not reflected in the value of the purchased asset.

The Format of the Financial Position Statement

Obviously, any financial statement should be in a format that is understandable, and uniformity is desirable. However, the actual format is really secondary to the quality of the information. It should be noted that the format of a financial position statement (and a cash-flow statement) is often determined by the software system used by the financial planner for analyzing data and producing reports.

Financial position statements have traditionally been presented in two columns—one containing assets, the other containing liabilities and net worth. The term *balance sheet is* derived from the fact that these two sides must balance according to the accounting equation (total assets = total liabilities+net worth).

It is now more common in personal financial planning to present financial position statements in a single column format. The major advantage of the single column format is that it facilitates the preparation of proforma financial position statements and the comparison of consecutive statements over time.

Cash-flow Management

Cash-flow management is one of the most basic tools in financial planning. Ironically, practitioners frequently find that clients resist the management process more than any other technique even though it is critical to reaching a goal. Communicating the importance of cash-flow management and talking the client through the process are among the practitioner's greatest services.

Although the well-heeled client sometimes considers cash-flow management as an activity for the less fortunate, the advantages cut across income levels. Cash-flow management is always beneficial and is especially useful when the client needs to accomplish any of the following objectives:

- measure periodic progress toward the achievement of specific goals
    - (*a*) within a defined time frame and
    - (*b*) within the confines of limited resources.
- monitor especially complex elements of economic activity
- provide guidelines for evaluating the economic performance of elements constituting the client's cash flow
- communicate a planning strategy to those affected by the budget
- provide incentive (goals) for the performance of individuals involved control household expenses
- achieve desired wealth accumulation/savings goals, such as retirement or children's education
- monitor the performance of a specific investment, such as a securities portfolio, rental property, or a closely held business
- reposition assets to improve the likelihood of accomplishing goals.

What is Cash-Flow Management?

Cash-flow management is essentially a euphemism for the budget planning and control process. Financial planners adopted the change in terminology partly because cash-flow management is more inclusive than budgeting. More importantly, the word *budget* carries negative connotations for many clients, making them less likely to participate in the process. Cash-flow management consists of three basic components: cash-flow analysis, cash flow planning, and budgeting. In practice, many planners mix aspects of each of the three and consider them as a single process.

Cash-Flow Analysis

Cash-flow analysis, or revenue and expense analysis, is the process of gathering data concerning the client's cash-flow situation, presenting the data in an organized format (the cash-flow statement), and identifying strengths, weaknesses, and important patterns. Cash-flow analysis is the starting point for the client and the financial counseling team to develop objectives. It also reveals inefficient, ineffective, or unusual utilization of resources, highlights alternative courses of action, motivates the client, and makes family members aware of the need to conserve resources.

Cash-Flow Planning

Cash flow planning involves identifying courses of action that will help optimize *net discretionary cashflow.* Net discretionary cash flow is defined as the difference between income and expenses. Positive cash flow is available for any use, whether for consumption, investment, or gifting.

However, in most financial planning situations, the primary benefit of net discretionary cash flow is to provide a source of investible funds. Note that the goal is to optimize rather than to maximize. Maximizing net discretionary cash flow means to make it as large as possible. Pursuit of this goal suggests increasing income in any way possible. Presumably this mandate includes working longer hours, finding a second job, or seeking employment for the non-earning spouse. On the expense side, maximization implies having a less expensive home and automobile, quitting the club, and discontinuing vacations and eating out. Clearly these approaches represent changes in lifestyle and standard of living, not to mention family relationships. In contrast, optimization means seeking the best, not necessarily the largest, net discretionary income.

Optimal net discretionary income implies a balance between investing for the future and maintaining and/or improving the current lifestyle. While the distinction between maximizing and optimizing may seem arcane, the difference is important not only in substance, but also in style. Optimization holds greater appeal to clients because it puts wealth accumulation in perspective. It also gives clients greater control since they ultimately decide their own funds allocation according to their own personal preferences. Cash flow planning is interwoven through almost all aspects of personal financial planning. At the extreme, each of the following is a factor or a tool in cash flow planning:

- income tax planning
- investment planning
- insurance planning
- estate planning
- retirement planning
- employee benefits
- saving/investment vehicles.

Some practitioners believe that cash flow planning includes each of the six steps in financial planning in a sort of microcosm of the larger process. Some even view cash management as the framework within which other planning functions are employed. The more common approach is simply to use cash flow planning as an extension of cash-flow analysis in an iterative process that involves other planning areas. For example, cashflow analysis reveals opportunities for increasing net discretionary income by addressing income and expense factors. Cash flow planning then considers what to do with the increase in discretionary net income. The result may include an insurance or investment alternative that represents a financial commitment. Typically, the commitment raises expenses, thus lowering net discretionary income calculated in the cash-flow analysis. Based on this new level, the client may consider another alternative for the remaining net discretionary income.

Budgeting

Budgeting is the process of creating and following an explicit plan for spending and investing the resources available to the client. In simplest terms, the process works *via* the establishment of a working budget model followed by a comparison of actual and expected results. By constantly monitoring the budget, the practitioner and client can recognize problems as they occur and even anticipate problems. Budgeting provides both a means of financial self-evaluation and a guideline to measure actual performance.

Budgeting does have some disadvantages, however. For example, many individuals have a psychological aversion to the record keeping required and may not maintain sufficient information for the budget to be useful. Obviously, to the extent the data utilized are inaccurate, the conclusions drawn from the budget may be misleading. For some clients, a rote dependence on budgeting numbers inhibits creativity, stifles risk taking, and encourages mechanical thinking. Such clients may forfeit investment opportunities or fail to minimize losses.

Here are some guidelines for establishing a budget:

- Make the budget flexible enough to deal with emergencies, unexpected opportunities, or other unforeseen circumstances.
- Keep the budget period long enough to utilize an investment strategy and a workable series of investment procedures—typically one calendar year.
- Make the budget simple and brief.
- Follow the form and content of the budget consistently.
- Eliminate extraneous information.
- Estimate especially with insignificant items.
- Tailor the budget to specific goals and objectives.
- Remember that a budget is also a guideline against which actual result is to be measured. Unexpected results should be analyzed: they may be the norm and deserve to be incorporated in a revised budget.
- Pinpoint, in advance, variables that may influence the amounts of income and expenditures. Income items include expected annual raises and increases or decreases in interest or dividend rates. Expenditures include costs, changing tastes or preferences, or changes in family circumstances.

Creating the Cash-Flow Statement and Budget

Budgeting requires looking to the future, but for most clients the best place to start is the past. The basic sources of budget information are personal financial statements, prior years' tax returns, cancelled checks, and projections of income and expenditures for the target period. Once initial estimates have been made, they must be adjusted in light of special circumstances or considerations. Usually, practitioners use a cash-flow worksheet in assembling the data and input the data in a computer program to create the cash-flow statement.

A family budget should project income and expenditures for any planning period that is convenient or appropriate for a specific purpose. Most planners budget for 12 months at a time, usually coinciding with a calendar year. Generally, the budget is calculated on a month-by-month basis since some cash flows occur only in specific months. It is often appropriate to budget for longer periods of time, such as a 4-year period of college education. However, for long-range budgeting, keep in mind that the budget's accuracy decreases as the length of the period covered increases. Constructing a cash-flow statement or a cash budget is largely a mechanical process involving very specific steps. Although some clients present unusual situations, the majority fit into the following framework.

STEP 1—Estimate the Family's Annual Income

Identify fixed amounts of income expected from each of the following:

- salary
- bonus
- self-employment
- real estate
- dividends—closely held corporations
- dividends—publicly traded corporations
- interest—savings accounts
- interest—taxable bonds
- interest—tax-free bonds
- trust income

- other fixed-payment income
- variable sources of income.

The client's income can be affected by salary increases, bonuses, dividend or interest-rate changes, proceeds from the sale of stocks or other assets, inheritances, and many other events.

If a family experiences an irregular income flow or extreme variations of income, two income estimates should be developed. One estimate should be based on the lowest amount of income that might be received, while the other should be based on a higher but still reasonable estimated figure.

STEP 2—Develop Estimates for Both Fixed and Discretionary Expenses

Annual expenditures can be classified as either fixed or discretionary. However, "fixed" applies only in the short run and can often be changed without imposing a radical shift in the client's lifestyle. Even the most fixed of all expenditures, housing, can be changed if necessary.

Discretionary expenditures, by definition, can be prevented or timed through proper budgeting so that sufficient income is available. Cancelled checks and charge account receipts serve as a good basis for developing the following expenditure estimates:

- fixed expenses
    - Housing (mortgage or rental payments)
    - Utilities
    - Food, groceries, and so on
    - Clothing and cleaning
    - Income taxes
    - Property taxes
    - Transportation
    - Medical
    - Debt repayments
    - Household supplies and maintenance
    - Life and disability insurance

  - Property and liability insurance
  - Current school expenses.
- discretionary expenses
  - Vacations, travel, and so on
  - Gifts and contributions
  - Household furnishings
  - Education fund
  - Savings
  - Investments
  - Other.

Note that a client's expenditures can vary as a result of increased costs of living, unexpected business expenses, financial catastrophes (such as uninsured theft or fire losses), changes in tastes or preferences, and large scale expenses (such as college or retirement).

STEP 3—Determine the Excess or Shortfall of Income within the Budget Period

Subtracting total expenses from total income reveals the client's net cash flow. Discretionary expenses already include listings for savings, investments, and an education fund. If projected net cash flow is positive, the client can allocate even more to these categories (although most clients are more adept at finding ways to spend the money).

Individuals, like businesses, commonly project some months with positive net income and others with negative. In practice, cash or cash equivalent balances simply grow in positive months and shrink in negative months.

STEP 4—Consider Available Methods of Increasing Income or Decreasing Expenses

If net cash flow is negative, either income must increase or expenses must decrease. This is bad news for the client, but it is better to recognize the situation early. Clients should be realistic in identifying categories for revision—blind optimism is counterproductive. Practitioners should encourage clients to avoid lowering the savings, investment, and education planning figures, unless there is no alternative.

STEP 5—Calculate Income and Expenses as a Percentage of the Total to Determine a Better Allocation of Resources

Many clients benefit from a comparison of their spending patterns to those of the general population. However, practitioners must recognize that the ratios can vary dramatically according to age, income, family structure, geography, and other factors.

As noted earlier, an organized cash-flow planning approach is useful in evaluating the potential of major adjustments in cash flows and portfolio characteristics.

Other Considerations

Families who experience difficulty in predicting income or who have highly variable cash outflows should consider two budgets—one based on the lowest income and highest expenditures expected (worst-case budget), and the second based on the client's reasonable expectations of income and expenses (average-case budget).

In some cases, it also makes sense to prepare a budget based on the highest possible income and lowest possible expenditures (best-case budget). This third alternative budget is often used to ascertain whether the cost of "hoped for" expenditure, such as a new car, is within reach if everything falls into place.

Another conservative approach is to base the budget on only fixed and certain income. Limiting expenditures to this conservative estimate ensures that fixed and expected costs will be covered. Any excess income can then be used for investment or discretionary spending, or placed in a *contingency fund.*

Budgeting should allocate cash reserves for such contingencies as—

(*a*) Liquidity needs,

(*b*) Emergencies,

(*c*) Scheduled expenditures, and

(*d*) Investment opportunities.

These cash reserves should be invested according to the speed at which they will be needed. In other words, funds should be placed in investments suitable for the needs to be satisfied. Short-term reserves to meet liquidity needs—day-to-day transactions— should be placed in an interest-bearing checking account. Clients should maintain balances that are large enough to qualify for payment of interest and, if available, waiver-of-service fees. However, they should not allow excessive amounts to accumulate in the checking account since the interest rate is very low. The optimal size depends on numerous factors, such as monthly cash flow, timing of receipts and payments, and the client's comfort level. Practitioners often advise retaining intermediate reserves equal to 3 to 6 months of expenses in a money market account as an emergency fund.

Some families, rather than building emergency funds, have lines of credit through various banks or credit cards. This enables them to invest any excess income, or use it to increase their standard of living. There are two drawbacks to using this technique. First, the interest charged on credit-card borrowing is usually high. Second, the client must have sufficient income to repay the loan. If the emergency is a case like a lost job, for example, payment becomes problematic.

REVIEW

QUESTIONS

1. Describe the three major categories in a personal financial statement.
2. List the ways in which net worth can grow.
3. List client objectives that indicate that cash-flow management would be especially useful.
4. List guidelines to follow when establishing a budget.
5. List the steps in constructing a cash budget.

True/False Questions

1. According to the single-purpose view of financial planning, a life insurance agent who sells key employee life insurance to the owner of a small business might properly be called a financial planner.
2. A financial plan developed for a high-income client is unacceptable unless it includes an analysis of the client's cash-flow position.
3. Effective performance of comprehensive financial planning requires the planner to develop and implement all aspects of the plan for the client.
4. In its "purest" form, comprehensive financial planning is done with the planner's entire compensation consisting of commissions from the sale of financial products.
5. Once a client has expressed an interest in having a financial plan developed, the first step in the process specified by the CFP Board is for the planner to analyze the client's present financial position.
6. Data gathering in the financial planning process typically entails more than asking the client a series of questions in order to fill out a form.
7. One result of analyzing the strengths and weaknesses of a client's present financial position may be the need for the planner to work with the client to revise the client's goals and objectives.
8. Part of a financial planner's responsibility is to motivate and assist the client in completing all of the steps necessary for full plan implementation.
9. The general guidelines for a comprehensive financial plan prescribe both the elements to be included in a plan and the order in which they should be presented.

10. The planner's assumptions concerning inflation should be specifically stated in a comprehensive financial plan.
11. Recommendations in a comprehensive financial plan should be conveyed only by implication or inference rather than being directly identified and stated.
12. According to the basic accounting equation, it is impossible for cash to exceed networth.
13. The need for cash flow management is restricted to individuals in the lower and middle income groups.
14. The goal of cash flow planning is to maximize net discretionary cash flow.
15. For some clients, the budgeting process stifles risk-taking.
16. Very short-term cash reserves should be placed in a money market account.

Answer 1

A. Assets

B. Liabilities

C. Networth.

ANSWERS

Answer 2

a. Appreciation in the value of assets

b. Addition to assets through retaining income

c. Addition of assets through gifts or inheritances

d. Decrease in liabilities someone forgiving claim.

Answer 3

A. Measure periodic progress toward the achievement of specific goals (1) within a defined time frame and (2) within the confines of limited resources

B. Monitor especially complex elements of economic activity

C. Provide guidelines for evaluating the economic performance of elements constituting the client's cash flow

D. Communicate a planning strategy to those affected by the budget

E. Provide incentive (goals) for the performance of individuals involved

F. Control household expenses

G. Achieve desired wealth accumulation/savings goals, such as retirement or children's education

H. Monitor the performance of a specific investment, such as a securities portfolio, rental property, or a closely held business

I. Reposition assets to improve the likelihood of accomplishing goals.

Answer 4

a. Make the budget flexible enough to deal with emergencies, unexpected opportunities, or other unforeseen circumstances

b. Keep the budget period long enough to utilize an investment strategy and a workable series of investment procedures—typically one calendar year

c. Make the budget simple and brief

d. Follow the form and content of the budget consistently

e. Eliminate extraneous information

f. Estimate especially with insignificant items

g. Tailor the budget to specific goals and objectives

h. Remember that a budget is also a guideline against which actual results are to be measured.

Unexpected results should be analyzed—they may be the norm and deserve to be incorporated in a revised budget

i. Pinpoint, in advance, variables that may influence the amounts of income and expenditures.

Income items include expected annual raises and increases or decreases in interest or dividend rates. Expenditures include costs, changing tastes, or preferences, or changes in family circumstances.

Answer 5

Step 1—*Estimate the family's annual income*

Step 2—*Develop estimates for both fixed and discretionary expenses*

Step 3—*Determine the excess or shortfall of income within the budget period*

Step 4—*Consider available methods of increasing income or decreasing expenses*

Step 5—*Calculate income and expenses as a percentage of the total to determine a better* allocation of resources.

True/False Questions

1. True
2. False. A plan that does not include an analysis of a client's cash flow position may be an acceptable one. Such a plan, is not, however, a comprehensive plan.
3. False. The wide range of expertise needed to develop and implement a comprehensive financial plan typically requires a team of specialists.
4. False. In its "purest" form comprehensive financial planning is done entirely on a fee for service basis with no compensation to the planner in the form of commission.
5. False. In the general approach to financial planning, the first step is to set goals. In the CFP Board's approach, the first step is to establish client planner relationships.
6. True.
7. True.
8. True.
9. False. The guidelines do not prescribe the order in which the elements of a comprehensive financial plan should be presented.
10. True.
11. False. Recommendations should be clearly identified and stated rather than conveyed by implication or inference.
12. False. The basic accounting equation (Assets= Liabilities +Networth) does not mention cash.

In addition, consider that even someone with a negative networth is likely to have some cash.

13. False. The need for cash flow management affects all income levels. Wealthy individuals often have objectives that indicate the need for a budget.

14. False. The goal of cash flow planning is to optimize net discretionary cash flow. This difference in approach allows clients to consider constraints relating to life style and value systems.
15. True.
16. False. Very short term cash reserves are intended to meet day to day expenses and should be placed in a easy to draw account.

IN SUMMARY

This topic has provided an overview of the financial planning process and the industry. It discussed evolution of financial planning industry. It discussed multiple views about financial planning as well as general and CFP Board model.

We also discussed good financial practices and identified elements, which should be, included in a comprehensive financial plan.

Appendix discussed how to prepare the financial statements.

SUGGESTED ANSWERS TO SELF-ASSESSMENT EXERCISE 1

Question 1

a. single-purpose view—the belief that simply evaluating a single financial issue and providing an appropriate financial product or service to address that issue constitutes financial planning.

b. multiple-purpose view—the belief that financial planning involves at least multiple aspects of one of the following categories and, perhaps, some aspects of other categories: insurance planning, tax planning, investment planning, retirement planning, and estate planning.

c. comprehensive view—the belief that financial planning must consider all aspects of the client's financial position, which includes all the client's financial needs and objectives, and must utilize several integrated and coordinated planning strategies for fulfilling those needs and objectives.

Question 2

a. General approach to financial planning

Establish financial goals

Gather relevant data

Analyze the data

Develop a plan for achieving goals

Implement the plan

Monitor the plan.

b. CFP Board's guidelines

Establish client-planner relationships

Gather client data and determine goals and expectations

Analyze and evaluate the client's financial status

Develop and present the financial plan

Implement the financial plan

Monitor the financial plan.

CHECKLIST

Below is a checklist of main points covered by this topic. Use this checklist to test your learning.

- Financial planning is the process whereby an individual moves towards meeting personal and financial goals through the development and implementation of a comprehensive financial plan.
- Financial planning encompasses a wide range of skills and knowledge drawn from many disciplines such as accounting, risk management, economics and management.
- The financial planning involves design, implementation and regular review of a financial strategy established to achieve the client's objectives.
- Once the plan has been designed and implemented, it is monitored regularly for success, and modified, if circumstances change.
- Financial planning can be done at any age. The strategies and products recommended would be different, as investors needs change with the age.
- Understanding of good practices in financial planning.
- How to prepare financial statements including cash flow and budgeting concepts.

6 CHAPTER

Recommending Financial Planning Strategies to Investors

ABOUT THIS TOPIC

This topic explains how financial planning function is related to the investment advisory function, seeking to serve as a guide to practical implementation of financial planning principles. As a financial planner, you would have studied the investor's situation in terms of his life cycle or wealth cycle stage. Before you converted your understanding into an investment plan for the client, you need to advise him on some basic financial planning strategies that succeed, using the basic planning tool that helps you convert the financial plan into a concrete investment goal. The first step in the financial planning process and the basic tool needed to translate financial plans into action is what is known as Asset Allocation. This topic outlines some basic planning strategies and the use of Asset Allocation. The financial planner has to review all investment options available to investors. This topic discusses the financial products available to investors in India and compares their investment potential relative to mutual funds.

TOPIC OBJECTIVES

At the end of this topic, you should be able to explain and understand:

- The power of compounding

- Implication of various strategies to maximize returns on investment asset allocation
- How right allocation is bedrock of long term investment.
- Various asset allocation principles
- Benjamin Graham's 50/50 balance asset allocation principle
- Strategic asset allocation
- Difference between fixed and flexible asset allocation
- Importance of tactical allocation Various investment product categories
- Evaluation by current performance
- Advantage of investing directly into mutual funds
- Mutual funds - panacea for a lay investor?

1. FINANCIAL PLANNING STRATEGIES - INVESTING FOR THE LONG TERM

1.1 POWER OF COMPOUNDING

Investing is a lifetime activity, not an *ad hoc* process. A planner needs to avoid the temptation of giving *ad hoc* investment recommendations, which may be the flavour of the season. You need to encourage the investor to have a long-term plan, suited to his age and financial needs.

Why should one invest for the long-term? Quite simply, to benefit from the power of compounding the returns,, on the investment, and to accumulate a large capital at the end of the long-term. If you invest a hundred rupees in a bank deposit that pays interest at 12% per year which you simply keep withdrawing, you will still have your capital at rupees hundred ten years from now. On the other hand, if you keep your hundred rupees deposit and keep reinvesting the 12% interest (no tax to be paid on this amount is underlying assumption) each year, your capital would have grown more than threefold to Rs. 311 at the end of ten years. Or to Rs. 965 at the end of twenty years!

This is the first principle of financial planning: invest for the long term and let your money grow on a compounded basis. The more frequent the compounding, the greater the growth in capital. Six-monthly compounding of the same 100 rupees after ten years will result in capital of Rs. 321, instead of Rs. 311 with annual compounding.

In the mutual fund industry, most funds offer what is called the 'growth' option, meaning reinvestment of dividends. They have the same power of compounding as a compound interest deposit, unlike the other option whereby the investor receives the dividends. As no dividend is declared there is no liability to pay tax in that particular year. Investors need to know the effect of compounding. All of us need fixed income at some stage in our lives, to a smaller or greater extent. But, what an investor earns over his immediate needs, he ought to invest and compound. With open-end schemes, even in the debt category, it is now possible to benefit from compounding by choosing the growth option, and withdrawing the capital in parts as required. Keep the Compound Interest Tables with you as ready references and let the investors see the power of compounding.

1.2 CHOOSE A STRATEGY TO MAXIMISE RETURNS ON INVESTMENT

There are different ways of investing. One strategy may suit one type of investor, and another will be appropriate for another type. Let us see what the different strategies are.

(a) **Buy-and-Hold** is the most common strategy. Whether you hold many shares or many mutual funds, the principle is the same: do not fall in love with your holdings. Track your investments, discard the non-performers and keep the good- performers. Holding on to losing investments means losing the power of compounding. Long-term investing does not mean buy and hold without adjusting the portfolio to sort out winners from losers.

(b) **Rupee Cost Averaging:** Investment is a matter of discipline. Advise investors to invest regularly. If you invest the same amount every month or at regular intervals, you will average out the cost of your purchase, with per unit price being 'always' less than if you make irregular investments in trying to guess the highs or lows of the markets.

Let us see an example. If a fund's NAV stands at Rs. 110 today, and you invest Rs. 1000, you will buy 9.09 units. Next month, if NAV is 120, Rs. 1000 will buy 8.33 units, and the third time if NAV stands at 130 you will buy 7.69 units. On an average, the price per unit for 25.11 units you now hold will be Rs. 119.4, Rs. 10.6 less than if you were to buy the units today. On the other hand, if the NAVs keep falling from 110 to 100 and 90, you will have bought more units-30.2 at an average price per unit of Rs. 99.3. You always win.

There is one limitation of the rupee cost averaging method. It does not tell the investor exactly when to buy or sell a fund, or to switch from losing to winning funds. However, as compared to lump-sum investing, the investor still gains.

A variant of this disciplined strategy is Value Averaging. The investor keeps the target value of his investment constant by investing the amount by which the investment value has come down, or by cashing the increased value of his investment, or by doing nothing, if the value is unchanged.

(c) **Jacobs' Recommendation of a Combined Approach:** You can, of course, combine the rupee-cost and value averaging strategies. To accomplish this, Jacobs recommends using an aggressive growth fund and a money market mutual fund (MMMF) of the same family. Place Rs. 1000 in an MMMF every month. Set a target value for the aggressive equity fund. Later, if the value of the equity fund has declined, transfer 1000 from the MMMF to the equity fund. If the equity fund value has increased by 1000, do nothing. If the value has risen by 2000, transfer 1000 from the equity fund to the MMMF book the profit.

Active Switching: Using switching method to actively move in and out of different schemes of the same fund complex is the most effective strategy to maximise profits in theory. It will work if you get your market timing right all the time, which is a big assumption.

1.3 CHOOSE THE RIGHT FINANCIAL PLANNING STRATEGIES

The following are some key concepts that clients should be recommended to follow:

(*a*) When to Invest and When to Cash Out

In terms of when to invest, clients should invest when they have the money because that gives their money more time to grow, whether in equity or fixed income markets.

The question of when to cash-out needs considerably more thought and skill. Some pointers are provided below:

- If the client is holding individual shares or fixed income securities, he has to learn to be very active and sell out as soon as the price rises beyond reason, or when fundamentals start to deteriorate. A 'buy and hold' strategy rarely works in the case of individual securities
- In the case of mutual funds, clients could consider redeeming in the following circumstances
- When their goals have arrived and clients need the money for the purpose for which they had been investing

- If the market overall appears 'overvalued' in terms of fundamentals and historic valuations.

A 'buy and hold' strategy works well in a good mutual fund if the client is willing to wait out a full market cycle, because fund managers do the buying and selling based on their research and analysis, and are likely to perform well, given enough time.

In this regard, keep in mind that it is you as a financial planner who has to advise the client to exit or enter an asset class.

(*b*) **Start Planning and Investing Early**

People who save or invest small amounts of money early often, tend to do better than those who wait until later in life. Similarly, by developing good financial planning habits early in life, such as saving, budgeting, regularly investing and periodically reviewing finances, a person will be better prepared to meet changes in his/her life and to handle emergencies. This is a basic fact that you should tell your clients - Don't delay financial planning'.

(*c*) **Have Realistic Expectations**

Financial planning is a common sense approach to managing one's finances to reach one's life goals. It cannot change a person's situation overnight; it is a lifelong process. Every client needs to realize that events beyond anybody's control such as inflation or changes in the stock markets or interest rates will affect their financial planning results. For example, in 1996, Indian investors could expect bank and corporate deposit interest rates of 14% and above. Now, in the second decade of the new millennium, depositors can expect interest rates of around 7 to 9% at a maximum. With regard to equity investments, a return premium of 4% to 5% over the yields of fixed income securities can be expected over time. While markets will have their surges and crashes, the mean for the markets and for a well- managed equity fund is likely to revert over time to a level of around 13% to 15% compounded annually. Therefore, if the client's financial goals are to be achieved, the return expectations from their investments should be realistic.

(*d*) Invest Regularly

Even if the client does not have a lump-sum readily available, he can use his future surpluses to invest on a regular basis. Investment strategies such as rupee cost averaging, double rupee cost averaging, and value cost averaging can bring down the average cost of investments, and have been known to harness the power of compounding to deliver superior results over time.

2. ASSET ALLOCATION - THE STRATEGIC TOOL

So far we have discussed two principles of financial planning: using a long-term investing approach to benefit from the effect of compounding and following the right strategy to maximise the return on investment. With that, we have answered two questions - how long to go on investing and how much to invest. The third question is where to invest, or which kind of assets to invest in. This question brings in the third principle of financial planning - Allocation of Investment Assets. Here, we look at the approach suggested by Bogle.

2.1 ASSET ALLOCATION PRINCIPLES

Asset allocation means determining the percentage of your investments to be held in various asset classes, like equities, bonds and money market/cash instruments. It has been observed that over 94% of returns on a managed portfolio comes from the right levels of asset allocation between stocks and bonds/cash. So any financial planning for an investor must determine a suitable asset allocation plan.

2.2 BENJAMIN GRAHAM'S 50/50 BALANCE

Bogle starts with the fundamental asset allocation advice given by one of the stalwarts of investment planning, Benjamin Graham, who advocates 50/50 split between equities and bonds, the common sense approach to start with. When value of equities goes up, balance can be restored by liquidating part of the equity portfolio, and *vice versa*. This is the basic defensive or conservative investment approach. Benefits include not being drawn into investing more and more into equities in rising markets. Both the gains and losses will be limited. But it is good to get about half the returns of a rising market and to avoid the full losses of a falling market.

50/50 Portfolio of Mutual Funds

Graham's approach can be translated into reality by holding different kinds of portfolios of funds. Bogle suggests the following combinations:

1.	A Basic Managed Portfolio	— 50% in diversified equity 'Value' Funds
		25% in a Government Securities Fund
		25% in High Grade Corporate Bond Funds
2.	A Basic Indexed Portfolio	— 50% in Total Stock Market/Index Fund
		50% in Total Bond Market Portfolio
3.	A Simple Managed Portfolio	— 85% in a Balanced 60/40 Fund
		15% in medium term Bond Fund
4.	A Complex Managed Portfolio	— 20% in diversified equity fund
		20% in aggressive growth funds
		10% in specialty funds
		30% in long-term bond funds
		20% in short-term bond fund
5.	A Readymade Portfolio	— Single Index Fund with 60/40 equity/ bond holdings

2.3 STRATEGIC ASSET ALLOCATION

Graham's 50/50 is the basic asset allocation. Bogle recommends adjusting the percentages for each group of investors after taking account of their age, financial circumstances and objectives. He classifies investors in terms of their lifecycle phases. During the Accumulation Phase, an investor would be building assets by periodic investments of capital and reinvestment of all dividends received. During the Distribution Phase, he will stop adding assets and start receiving dividends as income. Considered in conjunction with the investor's age, he recommends the following strategic allocations:

Older Investors in Distribution Phase	:	50/50
(equity/debt) Younger Investors in Distribution Phase	:	60/40
Older Investors in Accumulation Phase	:	70/30
Younger Investors in Accumulation Phase	:	80/20

In other words, younger investors can be more aggressive and let the magic of compounding work for them, while older investors take a more conservative approach. Similarly, investors in the Accumulation Phase can take greater risk than those who need income and are in their Distribution Phase.

Bogle gives a nice rule of thumb for asset allocation: debt portion of an investor's portfolio should be equal to his age. So let a 30-year-old investor make 70/30-asset allocation, and at age 50 let him balance it out. And so on.

2.4 FIXED VS FLEXIBLE ASSET ALLOCATION

Once a strategic asset allocation has been decided, should it be re-balanced periodically to benefit from market movements and as investors' circumstances, returns obtained or, time horizon, change?

A fixed ratio of asset allocation means that balance is maintained by liquidating a part of the position in the asset class with higher return and reinvesting in the other asset with lower return. This is not what investors normally do. They tend to increase their equity position when equity prices tend to climb up and vice versa. But, this approach is more disciplined and lets him book profits in rising markets and increase holdings in falling markets.

A flexible ratio of asset allocation means not doing any re-balancing and letting the profits run. As stocks and bonds will give different returns over time, the initial asset allocation will change, generally in favour of equity portion as its return would be higher than bond portion. The distribution-oriented investor will find his initial ratio change in favour of equities much more than the accumulation-oriented investor. As an example:

Rs. 200 invested equally in Stocks and Bonds, with returns being	10% & 7%
at the end of 10 years, for accumulating investor, will result in	57/43 ratio
at the end of 20 years	63/37 ratio
but for the distribution-receiving investor, 10 years will see	66/34 ratio
and 20 years will see	79/21 ratio.

Can you work out how? Note that the investor who takes out the income from debt funds without reinvesting, stands to automatically increase his equity part of the portfolio much more significantly than the accumulating investor, since his debt capital remains fixed.

Which option will likely give better returns? If stocks continue to return more than bonds, then a fixed ratio is better than variable ratio. If bond returns are close to equity market returns, then the variable ratio may work better. The answer depends upon whether one can really forecast the future. It is logical to assume that stocks will give higher returns than bonds, so fixed ratio approach to asset allocation is better at least in bull markets.

2.5 TACTICAL ASSET ALLOCATION

Despite the difficulty of forecasting, people do it. Fund managers themselves change their asset allocation percentages in the light of their views on the future movements in asset prices. They seek extra returns by taking bets on relative valuations of different assets. For example, you may invest in the-small-company more than the-large-company shares, or prefer value stocks over growth stocks. Further, you may change the equity/ debt mix itself in favour of where you expect greater returns. These tactical changes in asset allocation within the overall percentage holding or in the strategic ratio itself may yield extra returns, if the bet is right. But, clearly, there is no guarantee. In Indian financial markets of the new millennium, what would you expect? Lower interest rates and higher stock prices? If that is your view, what tactical adjustment would you make to your investor's basic/ strategic asset allocation? Can you work it out using the Bogle approach?

Investors certainly look for the best returns on different options. However, to determine which option is better, the comparison should also be made in terms of other benefits that the investor ought to look for in any investment. Besides returns, other potential benefits of any investment also include the safety of the capital, the risk or the stability of returns, the liquidity or access to the funds when needed, and the convenience with which the investment can be managed.

2.6 INCREASED RETURN WITHOUT INCREASED RISK

The above discussion assumes that you cannot expect increased returns without increased risks. But, Bogle points out at least one important way in which mutual fund investing can offer higher returns, which come without higher risk level. This is the issue of costs of investing. A fund that earns a higher return than another can still give lower net returns, if its expense ratio or loads are higher. If the first fund's higher return is on a riskier portfolio, the investor gets a higher risk and a lower overall return. Choose a fund that holds a lesser-risk portfolio and has lower expense-impact on amounts distributed to investors. A fund that holds higher risk assets will have a risk premium built into its return. But, its costs can act as a penalty for investors. While doing the investment planning for your investor, remember to either hold the similar funds in terms of both risk level of the portfolio and the fund costs, or choose the right risk level for the investor and then the fund with less "cost penalty".

3. COMPARISON OF PRODUCTS

Investors tend to constantly compare one form of investment with another. However, such comparisons ought to be done carefully, comparing only options that are comparable.

Until 1980s, Indian investors had bank deposits as virtually the only investment option. The only mutual fund scheme, UTI's US 64 Scheme, was perceived by investors and managed as a fixed return investment, as safe as banks, and paying out comparable though slightly higher dividends. Later, the investors were introduced to direct investing on the stock markets including direct purchases of capital market securities in the primary markets. This form of high-risk investment was not perceived as such because of the under-pricing of primary share issues due to guidelines of Controller of Capital Issues. Only after the crises of 1992 and the introduction of free market pricing of shares, the virtual guarantee of secondary market prices being higher than issue prices ended. Faced with the risks of direct investing, the investors are now turning to indirect investing through mutual funds that provide the benefits of professional management and lower risk through diversification.

Comparison by Nature of Investment and by Performance

There are two kinds of comparisons possible among different investment options. First, one must compare the options by the nature of the investments - their characteristics, benefits and risks. From this comparison will emerge certain types of investment which may be considered superior to other types. Next, one needs to look at the specifics of each investment option in terms of its current performance and its suitability for the investor in the light of the investor's specific situation (taxability, age, etc.). From this comparison at a given point of time will emerge the options considered superior to others for a given investor.

3.1 COMPARISON BY NATURE OF INVESTMENT

Investors certainly look for the best returns on different options. However, to determine which option is better, the comparison should also be made in terms of other benefits that the investor ought to look for in any investment. Besides returns, other potential benefits of any investment also include the safety of the capital, the risk or the stability of returns, the liquidity or access to the funds when needed, and the convenience with which the investment can be managed.

The table below compares the investment options discussed in the previous section under the broad heads *viz.* return, safety, volatility, liquidity and convenience.

	Return	Safety	Volatility	Liquidity	Convenience
Equity	High	Low	High	High or Low	Moderate
FI Bonds	Moderate	High	Moderate	Moderate	High
Corporate Debentures	Moderate	Moderate	Moderate	Low	Low
Company Fixed Deposits	Moderate	Low	Low	Low	Moderate
Bank Deposits	Low	High	Low	High	High
PPF	Moderate	High	Low	Moderate	High
Life Insurance	Low	High	Low	Low	Moderate
Gold	Moderate	High	Moderate	Moderate	Low
Real Estate	High	Moderate	High	Low	Low
Mutual Funds	High	High	Moderate	High	High

Although the table provides a qualitative evaluation of various financial products, the comparison serves as a useful guide towards determining the best option.

It is clear from the above that equity investing, in general, has good potential in terms of return, liquidity and convenience. Individual stocks can give varied performance, one stock being more liquid than another or one stock giving lower return than another. For this reason, equity investing is more risky and is not ideal for every individual investor. It is recommended only for investors who are willing to and who have the capacity to bear the inherent risk.

Bonds, issued by institutions, are an attractive option, particularly now with the liquidity that accompanies their listing on stock exchanges. Bonds are a stable option in terms of fixed returns, and are recommended for the risk-averse investor. However, bonds can lose value when interest rates go up. Bonds are also subject to credit risk or risk of default by the borrower. In case of corporate bonds, the risk must be assessed in terms of the strength of the borrower, as indicated by the credit rating assigned to the bonds. In the absence of credit rating, it is extremely difficult for the investor to decide on the quality of the bonds or debentures. The secondary market in corporate bonds in India is also very thin, leading to lack of liquidity for the investors who wish to sell.

Company fixed deposits fall short on several counts and are recommended only if the issuing company and the deposits on offer are rated high by credit rating agencies.

The major advantage of bank deposits, relative to other products, is the liquidity they offer. Banks are usually willing to give loans against fixed deposits at a nominal charge over the interest rate applicable to the deposits. Deposit rates offered by banks vary as per the interest rate scenario in the economy. Bank deposits score high on safety, as the return of capital is guaranteed to the depositor by the bank. However, the financial soundness of the bank is important. PPF combines stability with a respectable return. Its tax-exempt status makes it an attractive mechanism for the small investor to build his savings portfolio. However, the lock in period involved in PPF means that the investor loses out in terms of liquidity, particularly during the early years of the scheme. Being a government supported investment, PPF scores very high on safety, compared even to bank deposits.

Insurance has become another contender as investment vehicle due to opening of insurance market in India. In today's scenario, the opportunity cost in terms of return is too high for insurance to be compared on even terms with the other options. Its liquidity is also extremely low, though safety is considered high.

3.2 COMPARISON BY CURRENT PERFORMANCE

Besides the inherent advantages of investing through mutual funds, the tax advantages have helped create interest in mutual funds. Dividends distributed by mutual funds are exempt from tax in the hands of the investor.

Comparisons among different investment options are not valid for all time as the financial markets are now deregulated and dynamic, causing frequent changes in comparative returns from time to time. Each year, the mutual funds and other options may give different returns. For example, when the banks increase or reduce the deposit interest rates, the mutual funds performance may look better or worse. If the government changes the PPF interest rate, again there will be an impact on the comparative status of different options. Similarly, the individual taxpayer's situation may change, whereby he may pay higher or lower tax on his income. That will make a difference in his after- tax return on different options. That is why, it is recommended that the specific comparisons of different investment options be made at a given point of time, using the then prevalent return data.

3.3 DIRECT EQUITY INVESTMENT VERSUS MUTUAL FUND INVESTING

As mentioned earlier, investors have the option to invest directly in equities through the stock market instead of investing through mutual funds. However, a practical evaluation reveals that mutual funds are indeed a more recommended option for the individual investor. Here is a comparison between the two options:

- Identifying stocks that have growth potential is a difficult process involving detailed research and monitoring of the market. Mutual funds specialise in this area and possess the requisite resources to carry out research and continuous market monitoring. This is clearly beyond the capability of most individual investors.

- Another critical element towards successful equity investing is diversification. A diversified portfolio serves to minimise risk by ensuring that a downtrend in some securities/sectors is offset by an upswing in the others. Clearly, diversification requires substantial investment that may be beyond the means of most individual investors. Mutual funds pool the resources of many investors and thus have the funds necessary to build a diversified portfolio, and by investing even a small amount in a mutual fund, an investor can, through his proportionate share, reap the benefit of diversification.
- Mutual funds specialise in the business of investment management, and therefore employ professional management for carrying out their activities. Professional management ensures that the best investment avenues are tapped with the aid of comprehensive information and detailed research. It also ensures that expenses are kept under tight control and market opportunities are fully utilised. An investor who opts for direct equity investing may lose out on these benefits.
- Mutual funds focus their investment activities based on investment objectives such as income, growth or tax savings. An investor can choose a fund that has investment objectives in line with his objectives. Therefore, funds provide the investor with a vehicle to attain his objectives in a planned manner.
- Mutual funds offer liquidity through listing on stock exchanges (for closed-end funds) and repurchase options (for open-end funds). In case of direct equity investing, several stocks are often not traded for long periods. While some closed- end funds may not be traded frequently, they are nevertheless more liquid than many stocks. In any case, all funds provide one of the two avenues for liquidity.
- Direct equity investing involves a high level of transaction costs per rupee invested in the form of brokerage, commissions, stamp duty, etc. While mutual funds charge a management fee, they succeed in keeping transaction costs under control because of the economies of scale they enjoy.

- In terms of convenience, mutual funds score over direct equity investing. Funds serve investors not only through their investor services networks, but also through associates such as banks and other distributors. Many funds allow investors the flexibility to switch between schemes within a family of funds. They also offer facilities such as cheque writing and accumulation plans. These benefits are not matched by direct equity investing. It is clear that investing through mutual funds is far superior to direct investing except perhaps for the investor who has a truly large portfolio and the time, knowledge and resources required for direct investing.

3.4 BANK DEPOSITS VS DEBT FUNDS

It needs to be understood that bank deposits cater to a segment of the investor class that looks for safety and accepts a relatively lower return. Equity funds cannot clearly be compared with the bank deposits, as investors can expect higher returns from equity funds only at the risk of losing part of the capital also. Given the risks, Indian investors are currently investing heavily in debt funds. However, before a bank depositor considers shifting his funds to debt funds, he should compare the two in a meaningful manner.

A bank deposit is guaranteed by the bank for repayment of principal and interest. Any risks associated with investment of the investors' funds have to be borne by the bank. The depositor has a contractual commitment from the bank to pay. A mutual fund, on the other hand, invests at the risk of the investor. Hence, there is no contractual guarantee for repayment of principal or interest to the investor.

The bank depositor does not directly hold the bank portfolio of investments, as he does in case of a fund. The investor needs to assess the risk in terms of the credit rating of the bank, which provides an indication of the financial soundness of the bank. In case of investments in debt funds, however, only a few debt funds in India are rated by a Credit Rating Agency. Where a fund rating is available, it is a useful guide for the investor to know the risk level of the fund. In all other cases of unrated funds, the investor has to assess the risk on the portfolio held by the fund. The investor needs to know whether the fund invests in high quality assets or lower rated debt. Unlike in case of bank deposits, therefore, the investor needs to know his own investment objective and risk appetite before investing in a debt fund. The expected returns will be commensurate with the level of risk assumed by the fund.

It can be seen that the bank deposits are not totally free from risk, while generally giving lower returns. A conservative debt fund can give higher returns than a bank deposit, even if there is no contractual guarantee, as in a deposit. An investor, seeking higher returns from the capital market securities, while still investing small amounts, and a portfolio that matches his objective and risk appetite, is well advised to consider part of his investment in debt funds.

The Investor Perspective: Funds vs. Other Products

	Investment Objective	Risk Tolerance	Investment Horizon
Equity	Capital Appreciation	High	Long Term
FI Bonds	Income	Low	Medium to Long Term
Corporate Debentures	Income	H-M-Low	M-L Term
Company Fixed Deposits	Income	H-M Low same	Medium
Bank Deposits	Income	Generally Low	Flexible
			All Terms
PPF	Income	Low	Long Term
Life Insurance	Risk Cover	Low	Long Term
Gold	Inflation Hedge	Low	Long Term
Real Estate	Inflation Hedge	Low	Long Term
Mutual Funds	Capital Growth	H-M-Low	Flexible
Mutual Funds	Income	H-M-Low	All Terms

The comparison above highlights the flexibility offered by mutual funds from the investors' perspective. An investor can choose from a wide variety of funds to suit his risk tolerance, investment horizon and investment objective. Bank deposits offer similar flexibility in investment horizon and risk level, but only a fixed income. An investor looking for capital growth has to consider mutual funds, both equity and debt. Direct equity investment offers the capital growth potential, but at high risk and without the benefit of diversification and professional management offered by mutual funds. Gold and real estate are attractive only in high inflation economies. Other options are largely for the risk-averse, income-oriented investor. Mutual funds present the widest choice to the investors.

3.5 MUTUAL FUNDS - THE BEST INVESTMENT OPTION?

From the comparative analysis provided above, it emerges that each investment alternative has its strengths and weaknesses. Some options seek to achieve superior returns (e.g. equity), but with correspondingly higher risk. Others provide safety (such as PPF), but at the expense of liquidity and growth. Options, such as bank deposits, offer safety and liquidity, but at the cost of return. Mutual funds seek to combine the advantages of investing in each of these alternatives, while dispensing with the shortcomings. Clearly, it is in the investor's interest to focus his investment on mutual funds.

However, a note of caution is in order. While the mutual funds are one of the best options for the individual small investor, there are many mutual funds already available for the investor to choose from. It must be realised that the performance of different funds varies from time to time. Also, the Indian mutual fund sector has been in an evolving phase over the past five years during which time several investors have encountered some poorly performing funds, while others have been fortunate to be with good performers. Besides, evaluation of fund performance is meaningful when a fund has access to an array of investment products in the market. Currently, in India, there are limited investment opportunities available to mutual funds, and their track record must be studied in this context. Therefore, the Indian investors have moved over to mutual funds in a gradual process. But, there is little doubt that mutual funds will increasingly attract the small investors as compared to other intermediaries such as banks and insurance companies.

REVIEW

QUESTIONS

Pick the best possible answer from the multiple choices given:

1. The strategy advisable for an investor to maximize investment return in the long run is:
   (*a*) Buy and hold on to investment for a long time
   (*b*) Liquidate poorly performing investments from time to time
   (*c*) Concentrate investments in one sector
   (*d*) Switch from poor performers to good performers
2. A criticism of rupee cost averaging is:
   (*a*) Investment is for the same amount at regular intervals
   (*b*) Over a period of time, average per share price will be more than guessing the highs and lows
   (*c*) It does not tell you when to buy, sell or switch from one scheme to another
   (*d*) Rupee cost averaging has no serious shortcoming
3. If you maintain a flexible ratio of asset allocation, would you
   (*a*) Rebalance the Debt/Equity allocation periodically?
   (*b*) Rebalance the Debt/Equity allocation frequently?
   (*c*) Generally avoid portfolio rebalancing?
   (*d*) Keep fixed percentages of equity and debt investments at all times?
4. Direct investment in stock markets can be a better option over investing through mutual funds, if:
   (*a*) The investor wants better returns than those offered by mutual funds
   (*b*) The investor has large capital, knowledge and resources for research
   (*c*) The investor has identified a bullish phase in the stock market
   (*d*) The investor wants to invest for the long term

5. An investor in need of regular income should not select:
   (*a*) A bank deposit
   (*b*) A debt fund
   (*c*) An equity growth fund
   (*d*) Public Provident fund

ANSWERS

1. d 2. c
3. c 4. b
5. c

IN SUMMARY

This topic started with harnessing the power of compounding and discussed advantages of various investment strategies like "Buy and Hold", "Rupee cost averaging" and Jacob's recommendation of a combined approach. Later we discussed importance of asset allocation and discussed famous Benjamin Graham's 50/50 balance. Topic also discussed alternate asset allocation strategies like strategic asset allocation, fixed and flexible asset allocation as well as tactical asset allocation.

In this topic, also discussed was the available financial products in India to various investors and compared their investment potential relative to mutual funds.

CHECKLIST

Below is a checklist of main points covered by this topic. Use this checklist to test your learning :

- Compounding is an important tool for long term investing
- Buy and hold is the common mistake done by the investors.
- Rupee cost averaging does not guide the investor about choice of a fund. However, it is still better than lump-sum investing.
- In value averaging the target value of investment is kept constant.
- One needs to start planning and investing at an early age.
- One needs to have realistic expectations.

- Investment should be done on regular basis.
- Asset allocation means determining the percentages of investment in multiple asset classes.
- Strategic asset allocation adjusts for stage of wealth and life cycle.
- A fixed ratio of asset allocation means that balance is maintained by liquidating a part of the position in the asset class with higher return and reinvesting in the other asset with lower return.
- A flexible ratio of asset allocation means not doing any rebalancing at all.
- Mutual funds have multiple benefits over investing directly in equity.
- Cost of fund management is an important factor in determining net returns.

7 CHAPTER

Towards a Financial Plan

ABOUT THIS TOPIC

A balance of priorities — a case study

Sanjeev and Sanjana Gupta filled out an information request form at a recent 'Money Show'. They have been offered a 'free' one-hour meeting with a financial planner (you). They have made an appointment to see you in a few days' time. What do you already know about them?

While you know very little, you have two important clues: they already feel a need to obtain more information regarding investment (they attended the Money Show); and they probably have some current issues as they want to see a financial adviser.

This topic brings together the elements of creating a financial plan. You should take note of Appendix 7.2, which lists the elements to be included.

As a financial adviser you have to identify your client's financial goals, develop solutions to complex financial problems, identify priorities, provide recommendations and satisfy conflicts of interest. You need to implement the plan with the outcome, sometimes decades away. You need to communicate with your client and deal with concerns, questions and, perhaps, complaints, years into the future.

How do you accomplish all this?

A written financial plan is the solution used by professional financial advisers and planners. A financial plan provides a permanent record, not only of the decisions that were made but also of the environment in which those decisions were made. It provides a benchmark for you to review with your clients the success of your recommendations, and a tool to help you adjust the program strategies as the financial environment and your client's needs change.

As you prepare plans, the initial stages of working with your clients can be very challenging. Your clients might not understand the benefits you bring to the financial planning process. They might have questions about your motives and reservations about giving you the information you need to construct a financial plan.

In this topic, we deal with a specific case study in order to illustrate the steps involved in developing a financial plan. This will bring together skills you have developed from the other topics.

Although each client will have differing needs, this case study is used to explain the basic issues involved in the financial planning process.

As we progress, keep in mind these points:

- *There will not be a single 'right' financial plan because a plan reflects many decisions and compromises to help customers achieve their goals.*
- *Sometimes these goals are not solely about profit. The customer might want a plan that is simple and be willing to forgo some investment benefits to achieve this. In other cases the client might be reluctant to transfer investment assets to a spouse on a lower tax rate.*
- *As a result of these decisions and compromises, clients might not always get what you would see as the 'ideal' plan. Your goal is to develop a financial plan that meets your client's needs, not your own. However, you should note in the plan areas you feel need to be included,* e.g. *income splitting, even if the clients don't want to proceed.*
- *Regulatory and compliance requirements need to be integral to the initial financial planning process and not an afterthought or an 'add-on'.*
- *While normally providing a long-term focus, a plan must be sufficiently flexible to accommodate the changing needs of clients and be modified as their needs and the investment environment change.*

- *Ongoing monitoring and review help keep the financial plan on track and remind the client that the planner is actively working for them.*

Topic objectives

At the end of this topic, you should be able to:

- *Explain the process of introducing a financial adviser to a client, including the use of a financial services guide*
- *Identify the information a financial adviser must receive from clients, if they are to complete an effective financial plan*
- *Describe some of the obstacles that must be overcome when gathering the information necessary to complete a financial plan*
- *List the steps, that must be followed, to develop an investment and insurance strategy for a client*
- *Explain the process used to match products to customer goals*
- *Explain the key points to be considered, when constructing an investment portfolio*
- *Examine a portfolio and assess its suitability for a particular client*
- *Outline the steps to present a financial plan to a client*
- *Outline the requirements to disclose fees, commissions or any other interests the adviser or dealer might have in making the recommendation*
- *Describe the process to deal with the natural concerns, a client has, when implementing a financial plan*
- *Explain the need for ongoing monitoring of a financial plan*
- *Determine the expectations of a client, to ensure they are met in any review process*
- *Apply the financial planning process to a specific scenario*
- *Understand the knowledge requirements a financial adviser must satisfy.*

1. WORKING WITH CLIENTS

1.1 THE CLIENT INTRODUCTION

As a financial planner we would like to know what our client expects from us. The initial interview is an opportunity to get to know the client, build the relationship and inspire the confidence. Confidence carries with it a sense of safety and security.

Financial advisers meet their customers in many different ways. Some of the more common ways are:

- a referral from an existing client
- a referral from other professionals such as accountants or solicitors
- From another part of their organization, *e.g.* a bank might refer clients to their financial services subsidiary
- Through telemarketing or mail campaigns.

Regardless of how the customer is introduced to the adviser it is important that the customer understands the basis on which financial advice is being given. There are many ways of communicating this information. For instance, the Australian Securities and Investments Commission (ASIC) require the use of the Financial Services Guide (FSG) (formerly called the Advisory Services Guide). In the absence of an appropriate Indian reference point, let us review the information sharing requirements in Australia.

1.2 THE FINANCIAL SERVICES GUIDE (FSG)

Before providing financial services, licensees and authorized representatives are supposed to give their retail clients a financial services guide containing key information about the type of services being offered. This guide must be given to the client before financial services are provided and must be in printed or electronic form.

Required information

A financial services guide, given by a *licensee* (who is the providing entity), must contain specific information, including the following:

- the licensee's name and contact details
- special instructions about how the client might provide instructions

- the kinds of financial services offered
- for whom the licensee acts, when providing financial services
- the remuneration, commission and benefits received by the licensee, from a related body corporate, a director or employee of the licensee or related body corporate, an associate of any of these and any other prescribed person
- any associations or relationships between the licensee and the issuer of the financial product that might reasonably be expected to influence the licensee in providing financial services
- information about the dispute resolution system.

The content requirements of a guide given by an *authorised representative* are similar to those set out above but are expanded to require information about the licensee(s) who have authorised the representative and information about the employer of the representative (if relevant).

Disclosure statements to the prospective clients

The financial planners and their Agencies can make a standard disclosure statement for all their clients. A licensee or representative will be required to give a retail client, who is given personal advice, a statement of advice. Generally, if the statement is not the means of providing the advice, the statement must be given when, or as soon as practicable, after the advice is given. If the statement is not given when the advice is provided, the client must generally be informed orally of:

- any commission, fee, benefit or advantage that will be received by the adviser in connection with the advice
- any other interests of the adviser or an associate and any associations or relationships between the adviser (or an associate) and a product issuer that might reasonably be capable of influencing the advice
- if the advice includes a recommendation to replace existing financial products, details of any charges the client will incur in replacing the business and any other consequences of the client replacing the business.

The content requirements of a statement of advice given by a licensee and authorised representative are prescribed too. (The statement of advice was previously known as a customer advice record (CAR)).

Reasonable basis for advice

A licensee or authorised representative cannot give advice to a retail client unless:

Reasonable consideration and investigation

1. they determine the relevant personal circumstances in relation to giving the advice and make reasonable inquiries concerning those personal circumstances
2. having regard to information obtained from the client concerning those personal circumstances, they give reasonable consideration to the subject matter of the advice and conduct reasonable investigation
3. the advice is appropriate to the client, having regard to that consideration and investigation.

Reflection

If you were seeking financial advice what questions would you ask concerning:

- the person who was proposing to give you financial advice (the adviser)
- the organisation who employed the adviser
- the process that you were going to complete?

How would you normally find out this information, and would you be comfortable asking these questions?

In the past many customers only found out important information about their adviser well after their plans were implemented or when problems arose.

The requirement for an advisory services guide (now called the financial services guide) was introduced by the Australian Securities and Investments Commission to ensure clients received sufficient information to help them make an informed judgment about the capabilities of the financial service they were about to receive and to answer many of the common questions that clients asked.

Case Study — Your introduction

After greeting Sanjeev and Sanjana you have introduced yourself using the Financial Services Guide. This allowed you to clearly explain the process you would be following in the interview. It also helped them understand that the interview today was at no cost but, if you identified any areas you believed you could help them with, you would construct a written plan. The cost of this plan would depend on the issues identified at your meeting, but you would be able to give them an outline of these costs at the end of the interview.

Sanjana wanted to know if they were expected to make a decision today about investing but you assured her that the only decision they needed to make was whether to proceed with the development of a financial plan.

2. GATHERING INITIAL INFORMATION FROM THE CLIENT

2.1 DATA COLLECTION

Gathering client information can be one of the most challenging parts of the financial planning process. This is because many clients come to interviews poorly prepared.

If a data collection sheet is not sent to the client before the interview, it is important to introduce the need for full information to be disclosed so that a comprehensive plan, that addresses all needs, is produced.

The tables in this section include examples of the type of information needed by the financial adviser. In the case study, we have used information about Sanjeev and Sanjana Gupta, who filled out an information request at a Money Show.

The information below was collected using a data sheet, sent to the client, and also from further information gathered at the first interview.

When gathering client information, most financial advisers use a document called a "client profile", a "fact find" or "needs analysis". The purpose of this document is to help the customer by ensuring that the financial adviser has sufficient information to identify whether he can assist the client or not. This information falls into the following categories:

Personal information

Personal information includes a client's name, date of birth, address, marital status, spouse's details, number of dependant(s), place of birth, employer, contact details and who advises them on financial and legal matters.

This information should help an adviser identify issues, such as the possible need for insurance to provide income for a non-working spouse on the death of the income earner.

TABLE I

PERSONAL INFORMATION — SANJEEV AND SANJANA GUPTA

	Sanjeev	*Sanjana*
Name	*Sanjeev Gupta*	*Sanjana Gupta*
Home address	15, M Karve Road Churchgate, Mumbai	15, M Karve Road Churchgate, Mumbai
Date of birth	24 June 1971 (45)	9 April 1974(42)
Marital status	2nd Marriage	1st Marriage
Place of birth	Mumbai	Delhi
Smoker	No	No
Employer	ABC Computers	XYZ Tutorials
Job title	Head - Software Devt.	Solicitor
Address	Arcadia	Industry House
Location	Nariman Point	Churchgate
Telephone	Ph: 12345678	Ph: 23456789
Commenced	July 2007	December 2003
Date of expected retirement	2026(55)	2026(52)
Dependants	2 children from first marriage aged 8 and 14,1 child with Sanjana	1 child aged 4
Accountant	RSM & Co.	None (always done own)
Insurance Co.	New India - car, home and contents LIC-term life	None
Solicitor	Palkhivala (divorce)	Self
Real estate agent	None	None

Case Study — Initial issues

The above information seems innocent enough. Yet, it tells you something more about the Guptas.

Identifiable issues

From this early set of data, what issues can be identified, that you should consider, when developing a plan?

- While they are a married couple, Sanjeev has two children from an earlier marriage. There might be residual financial issues (such as child support) and there might be income flow concerns and a need for a discretionary trust.
- The job descriptions for both Sanjeev and Sanjana indicate senior positions with executive salaries. If this is the case, taxation might be an issue and salary restructuring options (with consent of employer) might be available.
- Sanjeev's two children from his first marriage are both likely to go on to tertiary studies, so he will continue to incur expenses for them for some years to come. Education could be a continuing cost for a further 15 years or more.

Estate planning details

At this point, we are trying to identify if the client has considered their estate planning needs. The information, we collect, would be as follows:

Do they have a will? When was it last updated? Are the beneficiaries current? Table 2 provides some answers.

TABLE 2

ESTATE PLANNING DETAILS

	Sanjeev	*Sanjana*
Wills:		
Do you have a will?	Yes	No
When was it drawn?	2009	-
When was it last reviewed?	N/A	-
Who are the main beneficiaries?	Wife and children	-

	Sanjeev	*Sanjana*
Wills:		
If you have eligible funds in the super-annuation environment, has your partner been nominated as beneficiary?	Yes, Sanjana	Yes
Bequests:		
Have you made provisions for any bequests?	Children	-
Inheritance:		
Do you anticipate receiving an inheritance in ten years?	No	No the next
Enduring power of attorney:		
Has a power been granted to any person?	No	No

New marriage Invalidates a will.

Sanjeev believes that he has a will. As you will remember, depending on the religion, a new marriage could invalidate a will (Sanjeev drew up his will in 2009 and was remarried in 2011).

You would have expected Sanjana to have a will as she is a solicitor. As is often the case, a practitioner often neglects to take the same care with their own affairs as they would with those of their clients.

Special estate planning issues

Identifiable issues

Sanjeev and Sanjana have special estate planning issues as there are two 'families' involved. Although Sanjana is a solicitor, it would be best to have a legal specialist in estate planning work with them to put their legal affairs in order. Some of the issues that will need to be addressed are:

- Potential for first wife to claim against estate
- Equitable treatment of all children
- Sanjana's wishes regarding her estate and her child.

Case study - Estate planning issues

Sanjeev and Sanjana have been meaning to update their wills for some time. An outdated will could be a significant problem, given that Sanjeev has children from a previous marriage. If he died without a current will, these children could challenge the distribution of assets.

Assets

List all assets the clients own and who owns what. It is useful to identify when the items were purchased (to know any capital gains liability) as well as when, if ever, the client plans to dispose of the assets.

Advisers would also identify the amount of income derived from the asset and the client's expectation of the reliability of that income. For example, will the investment income continue and has the income varied in the past years?

When discussing financial assets, insurance, investments and superannuation, the adviser will also identify how the client decided to buy these investments. This is valuable information because it gives the adviser clues to the client's experience in making investment decisions and the process they follow when considering these matters.

TABLE 3

ASSET DETAILS — SANJEEV AND SANJANA GUPTA

Category	Description	Owner	Balance/ value	Liability	Equity	Income
Property	Home	Joint	28,00,000	12,00,000	16,00,000	—
Savings	Cheque	Joint	30,000			Nil
Category	Description	Owner	Balance/ value	Liability	Equity	Income
	Term deposit	Joint	15,00,000			75,000
	Savings — CMT	Joint	3,50,000			15,000
Superannuation	Employer	Sanjeev	6,00,000			—
	Employer	Sanjana	14,50,000			—
	Rollover	Sanjeev	18,00,000			—
Personal	Car	Sanjeev	2,40,000	1,10,000	1,30,000	—
	Car	Sanjana	1, 85,000	70,000	1,15,000	—
	Home contents	Joint	5,00,000			—
Total			94,55,000	13,80,000	18,45,000	90,000

Case Study — Identifiable issues

Identifiable issues

We see from Table 3 that excluding preserved superannuation, the only investment assets Sanjana and Sanjeev own are in non-growth, income producing assets.

Liabilities/Expenditure

This should include any money owed by the client to banks or other financial institutions, including housing loans, balances, personal loans and credit card debt, the rate of interest charged, whether the interest is tax deductible, any tax liabilities and any repayment goals the client has (*e.g.* repay the housing loan early).

Also included, under this heading, is the client's cost of living and how much they spend on essential and non-essential items. Do they have a surplus that could be directed towards a savings plan?

Sometimes, it can be very difficult for the financial adviser to gather expenditure details because many clients do not have a budget or any record of their expenditure.

TABLE 4: LIABILITY/EXPENSE DETAILS

Category	Description	Owner	Balance/ Value	Liability	Monthly payment
Mortgage @8%	Home	Joint	2,800,000	1,200,000	13,690
Loans*	Car	Sanjeev	240,000	110,000	4,800
	Car	Sanjana	185,000	70,000	3,750
	Credit card	Joint	120,000	200,000	6,750
Insurance policies	Term life	Sanjeev	2,500,000		600
	Private health	Joint			2,500
Variables	Food/clothing	Joint			9,000
	Utilities Rates	Joint			1,500
	Car	Joint			1,500

Category	Description	Owner	Balance/ Value	Liability	Monthly payment
	Childcare	Combined			5,000
	Maintenance/	Joint			9,000
	Child support	Sanjeev			18,800
	Lifestyle	Joint			9,000
Total			5,845,000	1,500,000	85,890

*Monthly payments on the mortgage and loans total Rs.28,990. Interest on all of the above loans is not tax deductible, whereas the interest earned is taxed.

Reflection

Identifiable issues

If you were seeking financial advice, would you be able to provide the adviser with a budget?

What financial opportunities can be revealed by constructing and following a regular budget?

Income

State any earned income, the source of that income and the relative certainty of that income continuing. For example is it a regular fortnightly income, paid by an employee or, is it dependent upon the client finding contracting work? How secure is the position?

Also include any unearned income from investments or other sources.

TABLE 5

INCOME DETAIL

Salary plus Interest		Personal Super contribution	Tax	Net income after tax and super	Employer Super contribution
Sanjeev	9,90,000	36,000	1,95,170	7,58,830	1,04,760
Ranjana	8,85,000	-----	1,69,130	7,15,870	1,21,000
Total				**14,74,700**	

Identifiable issues

Including investment income, Table 5 tells us the couple's total monthly net income is Rs. 1,22,890 while their monthly expenses are Rs. 85,890.

Putting these figures into a budget draft, we get the picture set out in Table 6:

TABLE 6

TWELVE-MONTH BUDGET

	Apr	May	Jun	July	Aug	Sept	Oct	Nov	Dec	Jan	Feb	Mar
Balance	37,000	74,000	111,000	148,000	85,000	222,000	259,000	296,000	333,000	370,000	407,000	444,000
Mortgage	13,690	13,690	13,690	13,690	13,690	13,690	13,690	13,690	13,690	13,690	13,690	13,690
Cars	8,550	8,550	8,550	8,550	8,550	8,550	8,550	8,550	8,550	8,550	8,550	8,550
Credit	6,750	6,750	6,750	6,750	6,750	6,750	6,750	6,750	6,750	6,750	6,750	6,750
Insurance	600	600	600	600	600	600	600	600	600	600	600	600
Health	2,500	2,500	2,500	2,500	2,500	2,500	2,500	2,500	2,500	2,500	2,500	2,500
Food etc.	9,000	9,000	9,000	9,000	9,000	9,000	9,000	9,000	9,000	9,000	9,000	9,000
Utilities	1,500	1,500	1,500	1,500	1,500	1,500	1,500	1.500	1,500	1,500	1,500	1,500
Rates	1,500	1,500	1,500	1,500	1,500	1,500	1,500	1,500	1,500	1,500	1,500	1,500
Trans	5,000	5,000	5,000	5,000	5,000	5,000	5,000	5,000	5,000	5,000	5,000	5,000
Child-care	9,000	9,000	9,000	9,000	9,000	9,000	9,000	9,000	9,000	9,000	9,000	9,000
Mainte-nance	18,800	18,800	18,800	18,800	18,800	18,800	18,800	18,800	18,800	18,800	18,800	18,800
Life-style	9,000	9,000	9,000	9,000	9,000	9,000	9,000	9,000	9,000	9,000	9,000	9,000
Total	85,890	85,890	85,890	85,890	85,890	85,890	85,890	85,890	85,890	85,890	85,890	85,890
Income	122,890	122,890	122,890	122,890	122,890	122,890	122,890	122,890	122,890	122,890	122,890	122,890
Balance	74,000	111,000	148,000	185,000	222,000	259,000	296,000	333,000	370,000	407,000	444,000	481,000

Their savings ability is Rs. 37,000 per month, plus mortgage payments of Rs. 13,690 per month, car payments of Rs. 8,550 per month and credit payments of Rs. 6,750.

Sanjana and Sanjeev have been married for several years, yet they still do not have a professional accountant who could assess their joint tax situation. Opportunities to minimise their total tax position could have been missed.

3. ADDITIONAL INFORMATION

The information collected so far allows us to develop an overview of the clients' current financial situation. However, this is only a small part of the information we need. A financial adviser also needs to understand what the clients want to achieve and how they have planned to achieve these goals.

3.1 FINANCIAL GOALS

Some questions to ask would be: How satisfied are the clients with their current financial situation? What personal goals do they have that could be achieved through financial planning? How important are those goals (*i.e.* what would they be prepared to sacrifice to achieve them)?

Determining financial goals can be difficult because:

some clients might think they don't have any

a client might be so preoccupied with current issues that they do not consider long-term problems

most people are not used to talking seriously about their plans and goals for the future.

Reflection

What financial goals do you have? Have you a clear plan to help you achieve your goals? Do you have any process in place to check if you are on track?

When clients claim they don't have any financial goals or plans, focus on their, superannuation savings or housing loan. Both are plans to help them achieve specific goals. Are there other things they would like to achieve? When clients don't indicate a purpose for their investments, ask them what their plans are for the use of these funds. This will often lead to a discussion on goals.

The client's financial goals are the single most important piece of information a financial adviser needs to develop an appropriate financial plan. Until the client's goals are understood the adviser will not know what their client is trying to achieve.

Once the financial goals have been identified, the financial adviser can explore any issues that have arisen during the discussion.

Case study — Identifying goals

During Sanjeev and Sanjana's interview, you would need to get answers to the following questions:

- Why are they seeking advice at this time?
- What are their retirement plans?

- What do they expect from the financial planning process?
- What financial goals do they want to achieve in the short-term (<1 year), medium term (1-5 years) and long-term (5-15 years)?
- What are their lifestyle goals and current issues?

Need for an overall plan

You would also need to advise them that an overall plan would include:

- appropriate insurance
- cash-flow management to meet current and ongoing commitments
- a saving plan to fund early retirement
- tax planning
- estate planning.

Sanjeev and Sanjana discussed their reasons for consulting a financial adviser. Their main issue was that while both were earning a good salary, they did not seem to be managing their money well. They wanted to become more financially secure, accumulate wealth and manage their money more effectively. They felt that they were not achieving a lifestyle in line with their resources and were concerned that they would not have the funds for the retirement lifestyle they wanted.

Both had spent considerable time getting an education after which they went directly into the work force. They expect their youngest child to be at high school when they retire. They want to ensure that they can meet financial commitments and still fulfil their 'retirement', dream. Both are avid nature photographers and want to be in a financial position to freely indulge in their passion (hopefully for remuneration) but without dependence on their hobby to earn income.

3.2 ASSESSING RISK TOLERANCE

Risk tolerance test

A major source of quantitative data, which will help you to make judgments about your client's financial possibilities, is a risk tolerance 'test', which assesses your client's attitudes toward investment risk. Many financial planning software packages or hardcopy data collection forms include some assessment of the client's attitude towards risk.

You must get this right as the client's risk tolerance will influence your recommendations. In any later dispute, you must be able to prove that you accurately assessed your client's risk tolerance and matched your recommendations to it. Without this assessment and match, your client might be able to effectively sue you for negligence.

You should expect a result that categorizes clients as:

Categories of clients

Conservative	highly risk averse
Moderately conservative	risk averse
Moderate	risk neutral
Aggressive	risk tolerant
Very aggressive	risk seeker

This range is indicative only. Some would disagree with the categories and there is considerable overlap. Many investors would want a combination of some of the products suitable to different categories, or they might want to consider the lower risk products in other categories.

While testing your client's risk tolerance provides you with valuable tools for understanding your client when developing your recommendations, you should understand that you are required to act on what you learn and, include their tolerance levels in your plan.

Assessment of a client's risk profile is an inexact science. Different methods are used by different dealer groups. Some involve a detailed set of questions while others are very limited. While some provide a numerical value representing the client's risk profile, others provide a descriptive summary of the personalities involved.

Diagnostic questionnaire

Diagnostic questionnaires range from questions with a choice of answers to complex questionnaires. A copy of a risk profile outline is included as Appendix 7.1.

ProQuest

ProQuest is a computer-based risk tolerance tool that can be used on the Internet. It is an extension of the client questionnaire and asks a series of multiple-choice questions to provide an analysis of risk profiles. It provides a percentage value for risk tolerance and can be used as a discussion tool by the financial adviser with their client.

If you would like to try ProQuest for yourself, visit www.risk-profiling.com

Legal importance

Establishing, documenting and explaining a client's risk tolerance is an important part of the 'know your client' rule.

ASIC specifically refers to:

The client's personal circumstances and individual values, and aversion or tolerance to risk.

In addition to evaluating the client's risk profile, the adviser should help the clients to understand their own financial risk tolerance so that the client can identify whether the risk associated with any particular investment strategy or product is compatible with their profile.

3.3 ANALYSIS OF INSURANCE NEEDS

The main categories of insurance needs are life, healthcare/hospitalization, education, housing, vehicle for salary/income earners/individuals. On the other hand, insurance needs of entrepreneurs/businessmen are characterised by high income high risk category due to potential losses in business. An analysis of insurance needs identifies the client's current situation and the risks they are exposed to. For example, in the case of Sanjeev and Sanjana Gupta, neither hold enough insurance to provide for their children in the event of either or both of them dying or becoming disabled.

The analysis is a process of assuming Sanjeev dies and determining the financial situation for those who survive him. The process is repeated for Sanjana.

In addition to death, any insurance analysis should also consider the events of disability (temporary or permanent) or health problems such as a heart attack, stroke or cancer. Consideration should also be given to health insurance.

Normally, clients become uncomfortable when these scenarios are discussed. The reasons for their lack of comfort vary but include:

- most people do not like confronting the possibility of their death or disability
- clients often have not provided sufficient funds to ensure that their survivors maintain their current lifestyle
- insurance is generally not a product people want to pay for or use. Some clients refuse to participate in an insurance analysis. If they choose not to, that is their right but they should be warned that limiting your advice might mean they do not get the most appropriate recommendations.

Case study — Insurance needs

Sanjana has no insurance. This is not unusual for women, even if they are working. They do not see themselves and the contributions they make to the family's total financial situation as insurable items.

Sanjeev has some property items covered and a life insurance policy in force, but it is unlikely that he has had a full insurance assessment done. Where he has dual family responsibilities, it might be useful for him to have an insurance policy covering his former wife.

Consider the implications of the death or total disability of his ex-wife for her child- caring responsibilities (depending on the custody assignment). The lack of insurance for both parties will need to be discussed. It might be that they just have never considered insurance as being important. They might have thought it was too expensive or felt that they did not need it. Whatever the reasons for neglecting insurance, you will want to remark on this to ensure they realise the importance of this kind of protection.

3.4 ANALYSIS OF RETIREMENT SAVINGS

Retirement savings relates to the assets the client is gathering to provide an income for when they retire. Again, this is often not popular with clients because it frequently reveals that they will not have sufficient funds at retirement. This means:

- they will need to delay their retirement
- they might need to start contributing more towards their retirement savings
- they might have to reduce their retirement income.

Financial advisers can compound the problem by not identifying the required retirement income and assuming 75% of pre-retirement income when the client might need less.

In other cases, the financial adviser might look only at superannuation savings and ignore other assets such as a rental property.

3.5 ANALYSIS OF INVESTMENT PREFERENCES

What kind of investor is your client? What do they know about investing? Apart from superannuation, have they had any experience in investments that are not capital guaranteed?

Nobody likes to lose money in a stock market correction, but how would they react to such an event?

Determining a client's investment preferences involves questioning them about any previous investment experience, educating them about the characteristics of different asset classes and listening closely to their responses.

A client's lack of experience in making investment choices might require the financial adviser to spend time ensuring that any investment, superannuation or insurance products, are clearly understood.

Reflection

If a client raised any of the concerns that follow, what information could you use to present a counterview?

'I'd never invest in shares because my brother lost a lot of money in 2006 after he withdrew his money when the market crashed!'

'I'd never invest in superannuation because it is too complex!'

'Life insurance is a waste of money.'

'I only want to keep my money in a term deposit where it is safe!'

What are some of the factors that might affect a person's ability or willingness to save?

Case study — Investment preferences

Both Sanjeev and Sanjana completed a risk-tolerance assessment. While both were assessed as having a moderate risk tolerance, Sanjana was a little more conservative than Sanjeev. Both are reasonably well informed about the risks of property and share investments.

3.6 THE CONCLUSION OF THE FIRST INTERVIEW

At the end of the first interview, the financial adviser should be able to outline the initial conclusions from the information provided. Normally, this would be done verbally although some advisers might confirm this in a letter.

Advisers should discuss concepts at this stage and reach some agreement on product structures so that the plan doesn't contain any surprises.

In the plan that is presented to the clients, all information would be included so that there is a written record to support any recommendations made.

Case study — Conclusion

You advise Sanjeev and Sanjana that you can provide a plan to address their goals and the specific issues they have raised.

The recommendations will involve a financial commitment to their future in the form of a savings plan. The recommendations will also address any insurance needs, which would require the payment of premiums.

You advise them that the cost of the plan would be Rs. 4,500 and ask them to confirm if they want to proceed. Both are willing but want to ensure that this does not commit them to any recommendations made. You advise them that it will be their choice whether or not to proceed with the recommendations contained in the plan, after the next interview.

They agree to meet with you next week.

4. MEETING THE CLIENT'S OBJECTIVES

4.1 GENERAL REQUIREMENTS

Your clients have stated some general requirements. It is up to you, the adviser, to assess the current and ongoing financial requirements to consider what outcomes are possible. With a 15-year time horizon and the potential of high earnings, a client has a good base from which to achieve their goals.

Case study — Presenting the plan

Before presenting your recommendations, you should review the information collected in the first interview with the client. You would do this to ensure that nothing has changed that affects the recommendations you are about to propose.

4.2 DISCLOSURE

As you present each recommendation, you must disclose in writing any fees and charges as well as any payments or commissions you receive from making the recommendations. Other benefits that might be received should also be disclosed (*e.g.* prizes, conferences).

Strategies not recommended

Increasing salary sacrificing into superannuation would be a very tax-effective method of saving for retirement. However, with the level of gearing recommended and the current savings plan, cash flow is tight. This strategy could be implemented at later stage.

4.3 RECOMMENDATIONS

First recommendation

Recommendation

Pay off loans.

The first recommendation is to take the funds out of the term deposit and savings account and pay out all loans.

This will leave about Rs. 3,50,000 in their deposit accounts and provide them with extra savings of Rs. 28,990 per month.

Both Sanjeev and Sanjana pay tax at just below the top marginal rate, (*i.e.* 30.0%), so any future borrowing should be for investment where the interest will be tax deductible (*e.g.* a new house whcre the interest will have tax benefits).

Second recommendation

Recommendation

Consider their tax structure and an investment savings plan. Their savings ability is:

◆ Surplus income over expenditure	Rs. 37,000
◆ Loan repayment funds now available	Rs. 28,990
	Rs. 65,990 per month

If they commit to Rs. 5,000 per month, this will be Rs. 60,000 p.a.

To start the investment program, either set up a family trust or establish investments in either or both names with a Rs. 5,000 per month contribution. The funds could be invested in a spread, *e.g.* four managed funds:

- a cash management trust (liquid fund).
- a balanced fund
- an equity growth fund
- a property securities fund.

With changing tax laws affecting trusts, further advice should be taken if a trust is considered. Remember also the provisions relating to clubbing of income.

Third recommendation

Recommendation

See a specialist estate planning lawyer to prepare both wills and review the use of discretionary family trusts and consider using an enduring power of attorney.

Fourth recommendation

Recommendation

Keep some funds in a cash management trust (CMT) liquid fund for short-term liquidity (cash).

Fifth recommendation

Recommendation

Take full insurance coverage to establish a secure base upon which the Guptas can build up their wealth accumulation program.

From the results of their budget, Sanjeev and Sanjana are able to afford appropriate insurance coverage. They are in an early stage of wealth creation and both have considerable responsibilities that need to be covered.

Both Sanjana and Sanjeev are working and the death or disablement of either of them would cause major hardship for the family. Their insurance needs could be broken down as shown in Table 7.

TABLE 7

Owner	Cover	Premiums
Sanjeev	Rs. 5,000,000 term life	Rs. 550 per month
Sanjana	Rs. 5,000,000 term life	Rs. 300 per month
Sanjeev	Income protection policy 75% of salary - 4-week wait - benefit period to age 60	Rs. 1,450 per month
Sanjana	Income protection policy 75% of salary - 4-week wait - benefit period to age 60	Rs. 1,950 per month
Sanjeev	Rs. 30,00,000 crisis	Rs. 1,200 per month
Sanjana	Rs. 30,00,000 crisis	Rs. 850 per month
Total premium		Rs. 6,300 per month

The insurance cover required is calculated by completing a needs analysis using the information gathered at the data collection stage.

If Sanjeev or Sanjana were to die, the loss of income would be significant. So, the level of death cover would need to be at least Rs. 50,00,000. This would allow all debts to be paid and sufficient funds to invest to provide some replacement income.

To fully replace the income a significantly higher level of cover would be needed (assume an 8% yield, therefore Rs. 8,000 per Rs. 1,00,000 of cover). The savings available and the number of sick days available determine the level of income protection required. We have recommended a four-week wait, as the living expenses are quite high. The benefit period selected has been taken to age 60 so that if the client were on claim the payment would continue until age 60.

Level of crisis (trauma) cover has been taken out at Rs. 3,000,000 each so that, in the event of a crisis, this amount would be paid out to cover the cost of extra hospital or rehabilitation costs or simply to compensate for emotional trauma.

Once cover is established, quotes would be sought from several providers to ensure the best cover at the best price.

5. ASSET ALLOCATION

Before selecting investments and once you have established the appropriate risk profile for the client, you will need to ascertain the appropriate asset allocation. Table 8 gives an example of the appropriate weightings in each sector.

(Please note this is only an indicative asset weighting, as there is no one ideal weighting for any particular risk profile — however, the table below is a reasonable indication. Further, international investments have been proposed keeping in mind the government's ongoing liberalisation of foreign exchange convertibility. Visit websites such as www.kotakmutual.com or www.myiris.com and view their fund asset allocations as an example. Revisit Chapter 6 for further explanation.)

Please note it is not unreasonable for a moderate (balanced investor) to hold more than

60% in growth assets. This will depend on the client's investment goals and risk profile.

TABLE 8

ASSET WEIGHTING BY RISK PROFILE

	Conservative	Moderately conservative	Moderate	Aggressive	Very aggressive
Indian shares	12%	26%	35%	45%	55%
Foreign shares	8%	17%	22%	33%	45%
Property	10%	7%	7%	5%	0%

	Conservative	Moderately conservative	Moderate	Aggressive	Very aggressive
Indian fixed interest	18%	13%	12%	4%	0%
Foreign fixed interest	37%	27%	18%	9%	0%
Cash	15%	10%	6%	4%	0%

If clients have existing investments, these will need to be incorporated in the asset allocation. Sanjeev and Sanjana will need to establish where the existing superannuation is to be invested and what the asset allocation split is. Clients' residential property is usually omitted but investment properties are included.

If including significant existing property holdings, it is advisable initially to allocate funds to all other asset classes except property and finally add back existing holdings.

6. SELECTION OF INVESTMENT AND INSURANCE PRODUCTS

Balance benefits with security of income

As the Guptas' wealth increases and their liabilities and responsibilities change, insurance needs and coverage levels will also change. An annual review is necessary.

When considering investment products and appropriate asset allocations, you might find that a product with a higher level of growth assets will fit the income requirements, assist with any tax issues and build up capital assets more quickly. You will have to balance these extra benefits with the required security of income received. The requirement for security of income is relatively low, as sufficient cash flow is obtained from the Guptas' salary income each month. It would, however, probably be unwise to invest in pure growth.

Finally, you will need to consider a negatively-geared equity portfolio. The Guptas' risk profile would indicate that they would be comfortable investing in equities through direct equities. Because of their borrowing capacity, they would have enough to begin funding such a portfolio. Whether you decide to recommend this strategy will depend on the capacity of your dealer group (they might not have a direct equity capacity), relationships with lending providers and your determination of the best outcome for the Guptas. You might decide initially to invest in a unit trust equity product and review the strategy in the next year.

Stability and growth

If it is decided to use borrowed funds for investment, you will need to look for a product (or portfolio) that can provide a stable level of income to help meet interest payments, potential for growth and some level of franking credits although clients should have enough cash flow without relying on income from investments.

Your final selection will depend on these criteria and the products available to you through your dealer's recommended list. Once you have identified specific products, you can provide a projection of the expected return on investment for the plan. A representative must demonstrate a broad understanding of financial products in relation to the market in which they operate.

7. IMPLEMENTATION

7.1 THE WRITTEN PLAN

What the written plan should include as a minimum

Your dealer will have a format which you will be required to use in presenting your written plan. At a minimum, your written plan should contain:

- a restatement of the client's resources and goals
- an assessment of the risk-tolerance profile
- assumptions you have made throughout the plan (*e.g.* inflation, market performance)
- your recommendations for cash flow management (*i.e.* the client's budget before and after plan implementation)
- estate planning review and recommendations
- insurance coverage review and recommendations
- retirement planning

- other strategies considered but not recommended
- taxation strategies and implications
- an initial asset allocation based on the client's risk tolerance, asset class returns and volatility — items that should then be tested for income need, compliance, liquidity, flexibility and risk levels
- recommendations for financial strategies and specific products
- expected outcomes of the strategies and products
- disclaimers and disclosures, including fees and commissions (% and Rs. value)
- a mechanism for review (at least annually) to update personal and financial details
- annual income and tax liability projections
- projected capital growth
- projected monthly cash flow
- the written plan needs to demonstrate the knowledge requirements. Your summary of the financial plan would relate the expected outcomes to the Guptas' objectives and goals. See Appendix 7.3, Financial Analysis, for examples.

7.2 YOUR ACTION PLAN

Implementation step

An action plan should be part of your written plan. The action plan says in essence,

'If you accept the recommendations I've made, this is how we will implement them.'

Your implementation is the natural outcome of the written plan. Before you can take action, it is important that your clients fully understand the plan. When you review the action plan, you should answer any questions the clients ask and ensure that they are satisfied with your explanation. Once all questions and issues have been dealt with, you should get your clients' written approval to proceed with the implementation of their plan. Most dealer groups have standard forms for this purpose.

Your action plan should outline, step by step, the implementation process. It should:

- Ensure that all client sign-offs have been obtained
- Meet all dealer compliance sign-offs
- Ensure that all compliance, disclosure and disclaimer information has been provided
- Ensure that proper benchmarks for each investment and the plan as a whole have been developed
- Ensure proper completion of all application forms and inclusion of cheques for payment of all investments, insurance cover and legal fees
- Ensure that the clients understand your remuneration schedule
- List all the parties who are involved in the full implementation of the plan, such as insurance agents, lawyers and accountants
- Include a time-table for each step required in the implementation of the plan.

There are something's that need to be done prior to the investment stage. Your plan is based on certain assumptions regarding estate planning, insurance coverage and tax management. Once the Guptas have accepted the financial plan, you will need to meet with the referrals (the lawyer, insurance agent and accountant) after each party has reviewed the plan and has agreed in principle with the recommendations.

You will need to set your investment schedule to the next maturity date of the Guptas' term deposit as the funds released at that time will be required to implement the plan. Implementation might include the management of:

- a lawyer
- an accountant
- a real estate agent
- a banking relationship
- fund managers and insurance companies
- your dealer's requirements
- your clients.

Managing your clients during the implementation period is very important. Planning regular communication with clients is important to reassure them that their adviser is working with them and for them.

8. ONGOING SERVICE

In general, you will need to provide a regular review of the Guptas' plan, examining:

- Their insurance requirements
- Superannuation savings outcomes
- The outcome of their investment program
- The performance of the plan against benchmarks and objectives
- Tax management performance
- Budget and cash flows
- Assets and liabilities.

Annual review

The timing of a review will be decided by the financial adviser. The review needs to be regular enough to ensure that the plan can be modified to deal with changing events. Normally, reviews are conducted annually, or more frequently, at the client's request.

At each review, you will want to find out if there have been any changes in the Guptas' finances, lifestyle or goals.

You will also want to make recommendations regarding:

- Level of insurance coverage
- Investment fine-tuning
- Gearing packages
- New strategies or investments.

This review should take a form similar to the original financial plan, so that each year the reviewed plan builds upon previous goals.

REVIEW

As an exercise, use the Guptas' case study to construct a plan, using your dealer's software. In doing so, you will see where assumptions are conservative and where they are generous. You will also be able to gain a better understanding of how each strategy interconnects with taxation and cash flow. If you do not have access to such software, you should consider the suggested plan and look for alternatives. Use the sample financial plan in Appendix 7.3 for details and setting out.

IN SUMMARY

We have developed one set of strategies for the Guptas, which might or might not be accepted. It is important to look critically at our plan.

Are there better alternatives? Some questions you should ask are:

- Would salary repackaging save tax?
- Should Sanjeev cut back on his superannuation savings as he will be paying the superannuation surcharge? Could he use this money more effectively?
- Are they now too highly geared or should they be even more highly geared to take advantage of better interest rates?
- Do they have enough liquidity?
- Have we covered all their requirements?

The final thing to remember is that there is no 'best' plan, no simple solution. You add value and earn your remuneration by working through initial strategies and investments and by ongoing review, keeping the plan on target.

APPENDICES

Appendix 7.1 Risk Profile

Appendix 7.2 How to write a financial plan

Appendix 7.3 A sample financial plan

Appendix 7.4 ASIC IPS (Interim Policy Statement)

Notes

....

....

....

....

....

RISK PROFILE

An important aspect in providing advice is recommending an asset allocation and investment strategy with your risk profile. Each investor is mapped into one of the risk profiles and thereafter an asset allocation appropriate to his profile is suggested. The categories detailed below are more or less a standard classification

Category

Very Conservative

An extremely conservative investor not prepared to accept any capital risk or volatility of return. Prepared to accept low return for security of capital and no volatility of return. No exposure to growth assets is expected.

Conservative

A conservative investor prepared to accept very minimal capital risk with low volatility of return. Prepared to accept lower return for security of capital and minimal volatility of investment returns. Minimal exposure to growth assets is expected.

Conservative to Moderate

An investor who is prepared to accept minimal capital risk with some volatility of return over the short to medium term. Over the medium to long term risk of loss of capital is not expected. Requires some exposure to growth assets.

Moderate

An investor who is prepared to accept some capital risk and volatility of return. An investor who requires protection against inflation and taxation. This investor recognizes the benefit that growth assets can provide over the medium to long-term. Typically, a moderate investor requires a balanced portfolio suited to personal objectives and the economic and investment outlook. Growth assets will always form a part of the portfolio.

Moderate to Aggressive

An investor who is prepared to accept capital risk and higher volatility of return to see portfolio out-performance. An investor who understands the risk/return trade-off with more aggressive investment strategies. Typically, this investor would have an investment strategy biased to growth investments. Some of these investments may not necessarily by 'blue chip'.

Aggressive

An investor who is prepared to accept a high growth/investment return for capital risk and possible high volatility. Typically, this investor will want to seek out high return investment opportunities with consideration of risk and return. The portfolio would primarily be invested in growth assets which would be traded to maximise investment performance. Capital risk is higher and volatility of returns is expected.

Very Aggressive

An investor who adopts a high risk/high return philosophy to investment Typically, this investor accepts the possibility of high losses for high returns and is not concerned about balance in their portfolio.

APPENDIX 7.2

HOW TO WRITE A FINANCIAL PLAN

A comprehensive personal financial plan should contain analysis of all pertinent factors relating to the client. While order and style of presentation may vary depending upon the client's individual circumstances and needs, the plan should include, but not be limited to, the following elements:

1. Client data
2. Client goals, objectives and risk tolerance profile
3. Identification of issues and problems
4. Assumptions
5. Balance sheet/net worth
6. Cash flow management
7. Tax impact
8. Risk management and insurance
9. Investments
10. Estate planning
11. Other strategies not recommended
12. Recommendations
13. Implementation
14. Periodic reviews and plan updates
15. Compliance, fees and commissions

Breakdown of elements

1. *Client data*

   This should include a summary of all the relevant personal and family data, *e.g.* ages, number of dependants, marital status, health and anything else that would influence the recommendation(s).

2. *Client goals, objectives and risk tolerance profile*

   You should list the client's stated goals and objectives so the client, when reading the report, can confirm that you have understood them correctly. You should also assess the client's risk tolerance profile.

3. *Identification of issues and problems*

   You should identify issues facing the client that will affect the recommendation, *e.g.* timeframe of investing, legislation.

4. *Assumptions*

   You will need to make some assumptions throughout the plan relating to the client's situation as well as performance of investments. These should be reasonable and also should be indicated in the report whenever they are made.

5. *Balance sheet/net worth*

   You should summarise the client's current balance sheet, *i.e.* assets and liabilities. These should preferably be laid out in tabular format. Other pertinent information about the assets and liabilities should also be listed.

6. *Cash flow management*

   You should show the client's estimated cash flow position after your recommendations are implemented.

7. *Tax impact*

   The cash flow should include tax calculations. Tax implications of recommended investments should also be discussed.

8. *Risk management and insurance*

   You should discuss the client's current insurance arrangements and suggest changes where necessary, or detail other factors the client should know about.

9. *Investments*

   Discussion of the client's current investments/assets to determine their suitability and whether they should be kept or redeemed.

10. *Estate planning*

    You should discuss issues relating to wills, powers of attorney, testamentary trusts.

11. *Other strategies not recommended*

12. *Recommendations*

    The recommendation should:

    Explain why the recommendation is advantageous

    Summarise the steps involved

    Show the final overall result with respect to:

    (*i*) products recommended

    (*ii*) resultant cash flows

    Discuss the recommended strategy and why specific products have been recommended

    Show resultant asset allocation to the client

    Explain to the client how the recommendation(s) meet the requirements.

13. *Implementation*

    What does the client need to do now?

14. *Periodic reviews and plan updates*

    You should tell the client what to expect with respect to ongoing reviews.

15. *Compliance, fees and commission*

    This is a legal requirement and includes disclosure of brokerage fees and/or commission as well as adequate disclaimers.

A SAMPLE FINANCIAL PLAN FOR NITA AND SOM ARORA

Prepared by Ankit Mehta as Proper Authority Holder for

ABC Financial Planning Private Limited

D-502, Moraj, Navi Mumbai

21 October, 2015

This is an important document which you, the customer, should read. If you:

disagree with, or

do not understand

anything contained within this recommendation, please contact me or my Company for further information.

You may cancel any life insurance policy recommended in this Financial Analysis up to 14 days after you receive your policy document (or equivalent) by contacting the Life Company.

21 October, 2015

Mr. Som Arora and Ms. Nita Arora

49, Nerul, Navi Mumbai

Dear Som and Nita,

Thank you for the opportunity to meet with you to discuss your financial planning goals and objectives.

My recommendations are based on your current position as outlined below. If any of the following statements (or any of the assumptions used in the accompanying plan) do not accurately reflect your current situation please advise me accordingly so I can determine whether my advice is still appropriate.

This plan has been prepared to meet your goals and objectives, and as such no one else can rely on the information or strategies suggested. Please ensure that all information you have provided is correct.

These recommendations are based on your current situation, and if not implemented within 30 days it may need to be reviewed.

This plan is only the first step in managing your financial planning needs — annual reviews will be conducted to cater for changing circumstances.

This information has been compiled from the information as detailed in the Fact Finder completed with you. A copy of the Fact Finder for your own records is available on request. Your current situation is as follows:

> You are aged 45 and 40 years respectively.
>
> You have two children aged 12 and 14.
>
> Som, you will shortly be receiving a compensation payment from an injury sustained around 12 years ago.
>
> Your health is not good.
>
> Your residential property in Mumbai is owned unencumbered.
>
> You have estimated your expenses to be at Rs. 3800 per week.
>
> You each have a will in place which is up to date, but you have yet to establish Powers of Attorney over your affairs.

Assets & Liabilities Rs. In '000

	Approx. Value	**Liability**
Home	20000	Nil
Contents	500	Nil
Car	900	Nil
Motorcycle	100	Nil
Total	21500	Nil

Current Investments	**Approx. Value**
Pending Compensation	2520
Total	2520

Concerns, Issues and Financial Objectives

After legal and other costs, you are looking to invest Rs. 2520,000 from which you would like to generate maximum income from the funds.

You would like sufficient income to generate your required Rs. 3800 per week. You wish to structure your investments in the most tax effective means available.

You wish to spread your assets between a range of investments to maximise the benefits of diversification.

Assumptions

Throughout this plan an inflation rate of 3% p.a. has been used.

Investment returns and growth rates are based on Alfa Market research.

Current marginal taxation rates have been used.

Risk Profile

Following our discussions regarding your investment objectives and attitude towards investment risk, I consider you to be moderate investors. A balanced portfolio looks to invest around 25% in Bank or Government fixed interest securities, with the balance in growth assets, namely property and shares. Further diversification is achieved by investing approximately 29% of the portfolio in overseas markets. This type of portfolio would be expected to generate a reasonable return above inflation and have moderate long-term wealth accumulation potential. However, please note that the value of your capital can move up and down, particularly in the short term. Hence these investments should be considered medium to long-term, with a minimum investment time frame of 3 years. As a guide, you could expect a negative return once in every 8 years.

Recommended Investment Strategy

Introduction

The aim of implementing a financial plan such as this is to ensure that your goals regarding financial security, income needs and diversification by fund manager, product type and class of investment are met. Depending on the state of the economy these funds will have varying levels of performance and this can fluctuate considerably. Generally, over the long-term however, shares have outperformed property and they have both outperformed fixed interest and cash investments.

My recommendations are as follows:

1. We considered using superannuation but because of your concerns with this type of investment we have not used this strategy.
2. With the funds that you are looking to invest, I recommend that they be placed into an area that should provide you with a good level of income. In particular I believe unit trusts to be most beneficial for you. Specifically, for a wide level of diversification through different fund managers and product options, the ABC Investment Solution would be the most suitable. After some analysis, I have identified the following options within this product for you:

ABC International Bond Fund	15% (approx. Rs.374,000)
ABC Equity Trust	15% (approx. Rs.358,800)
ABC Wholesale Diversified Stable	10% (approx. Rs.249,600)
ABC Wholesale Diversified Fund	20% (approx. Rs.499,200)
ABC International Equity Fund	4.5% (approx. Rs.114,800)
ABC Global Equity (ex-Australia) Fund	5% (approx. Rs.124,800)
ABC Wholesale Balanced Fund	20% (approx. Rs.499,200)
ABC Wholesale Industrial Share Fund	10% (approx. Rs.249,600)

3. I have included a section on the share purchases in the 'Share Recommendation' section of the plan. This details our broker's recommendation on the share purchases.
4. Finally, I recommend that you consider establishing a Power of Attorney for each of you. I have included some further information in the plan.

   Please see the relevant page of this attached Financial Analysis for important notices and disclosures concerning these recommendations.

Recommended Investments

The investments I have recommended for you have been carefully selected to meet your investment objectives and risk profile. Some of the things we look at in assessing fund managers is their people and their experience, the performance of their investments, how they manage their investments and the type of assets they invest in. A description of my recommendations follows.

ABC Investment Solution

The ABC Investment Solution is a transaction, administration and reporting service that helps you consolidate your investments into one easy to manage Portfolio. This product helps to build a diversified investment portfolio by offering access to a broad range of managed funds and the ability to invest with a range of experienced Fund Managers. You also have the ability to consolidate new and/or existing shares within the portfolio. This product essentially 'wraps' all of your investments into one convenient package for ease of management. All currency references within Investment Solution are used as a percentage (%). I recommend the funds be transferred to the following trusts:-

ABC International Bond Fund 15% (approx. Rs. 374,000)

This fund's objective is to consistently and competitively outperform the Standard Bond Index , on a rolling 12-month basis. Suggested investment horizon is 3 to 5 years. The nature of the securities this fund is invested in means that fund returns will be vulnerable to changes in interest rates as well as currency fluctuations. Rises in interest rates lower the value of a fixed interest security and hence the value of the fund whilst falls in interest rates raise the value of the fund. Hence, this is a medium term investment (2-3 years), due to volatility in the capital value of the investment.

ABC Equity Trust (Wholesale Unit Class) 15% (approx. Rs. 358,800)

The objective of this option is to provide tax effective income and medium to long-term capital growth. Suggested investment timeframe is at least 5 to 7 years. Performance benchmark is the All Ordinaries Accumulation Index. This fund is recommended to those investors who wish to benefit from the long-term capital gain available from prudent share investment and who are comfortable with short to medium term fluctuations in capital value. Accordingly, the fund has a long-term recommended investment horizon of 5 to 7 years.

ABC Wholesale Diversified Stable 10% (approx. Rs. 249,600)

The objective of this fund is to achieve superior investment performance through providing returns that exceed those from the Diversified Stable benchmark over rolling 3-year periods and maintaining a similar level of investment risk to this benchmark. This fund has a high proportion invested in fixed interest securities, the nature of which makes their value fall when interest rates rise and *vice versa*, although this risk is managed to an extent by the manager. As such, this fund is recommended for a conservative investor wishing an income stream rather than capital growth and the minimum recommended term is 2-3 years.

ABC Wholesale Diversified Fund 20% (approx. Rs. 499,200)

The ABC Wholesale Diversified Fund aims to provide consistent returns with low volatility from a portfolio spread across most asset sectors. Suggested minimum investment timeframe is 4 years. The fund is best suited to those investors with a medium to long-term investment horizon of 3 to 5 years, wanting moderate to high returns that are comfortable with some short-term volatility in returns and capital value of the investment.

ABC International Equity Fund 5% (approx. Rs. 114,800)

This fund's objective is to provide capital growth over the medium to long-term from investments in securities in certain world stock markets. Suggested investment period is 5 years or more. This fund is best suited to an investor able to risk capital loss in the short to medium term in order to achieve high returns in the long-term. The recommended time horizon for investment in this fund is at least 5 to 7 years.

ABC Global Equity (Ex-India) Trust 5% (approx. Rs. 124,800)

The objective of this fund is to seek capital appreciation through investment in the equity securities of non-Indian companies. This fund is best suited to an investor able to risk capital loss in the short to medium term in order to achieve high returns in the long-term. The recommended time horizon for investment in this fund is at least 5 to 7 years.

ABC Wholesale Balanced Fund 20% (approx. Rs. 499,200)

The objective of this fund is to provide investors with a diversified portfolio offering a balance between capital growth over the medium to long-term and a moderate level of income. The fund is best suited to those investors with a medium to long-term investment horizon of 3 to 5 years, wanting moderate to high returns and who are comfortable with some short-term volatility in returns and capital value of the investment.

ABC Wholesale Industrial Share Fund 10% (approx. Rs. 249,600)

The objective of this fund is to provide long-term capital growth and tax effective income. ABC's investment process for selecting companies is built around 4 key criteria — conservative debt levels, recurring earnings/identifiable resources, sound management and quality of business. Their 'bottom-up' research oriented investment style, which emphasises non-Top 50 companies, will combine well with the more 'top down' or Top 50 style of other managers. This fund is recommended to those investors who wish to benefit from the long-term capital gain available from prudent share investment and who are comfortable with short to medium term fluctuations in capital value. Accordingly, the fund has a long-term recommended investment horizon of 5 to 7 years.

Diversification

Diversification for investors simply means 'don't put all your eggs in one basket'. A diversified portfolio is an integral part of building wealth successfully as it enhances the security of a portfolio and the consistency of long-term performance without unduly reducing overall returns, and in some cases, enhancing overall returns. By diversification we mean investing across the main asset classes of cash, fixed interest, shares and property. Within these asset classes there are many sectors that allow further diversification to take place. Such sectors include Government, semi-Government and corporate securities, international investments, industrial and resource shares, and property investments.

Risk Management

It is important to ensure that you are not exposed to financial risk through accident or misfortune, which could jeopardise your present and future plans. In simple terms, if you cannot financially afford to lose something, then you should try to protect your exposure to that potential loss. Insurance can provide a cost-effective method of providing that protection. We therefore recommend you review your house contents and car insurance. Som, we are not able to effect any further life insurance because of your disability and Nita, you have adequate cover at this stage. We will review your cover every twelve months. You should also look at effecting health insurance. However, your pre-existing health conditions may be excluded.

Asset Allocation

The investment portfolio I have recommended for you will provide the following asset allocation:

	Recommended % for Moderate Investors	Actual %
Cash	6	3.3
Indian Fixed Interest	6	9.7
International Fixed Interest	13	17.2
Indian Property	5	4.6
Indian Shares	41	44.8
International Shares	29	20.4
Total	100	100

Please note the Indian fixed interest sector tends to have a higher income yield than that of the international sector (the majority being growth in the international sector). The above asset allocation would be considered fairly aggressive for a moderate investor, though not uncommon.

Taxation

Please note any comments made on taxation are for financial planning discussion purposes. You should refer to your tax adviser for specific taxation advice.

Estate Planning

Wills

It is important that you have properly drafted wills to ensure that your wishes are clearly expressed in the event of your untimely death. When you die without a will, (known as 'intestate') the courts decide what will happen to your estate and this may not be in accord with the way you would want things to happen. The courts use a statutory formula to decide on the way your assets are distributed, and in some cases, it may mean tracking down distant relatives who could be anywhere. Tracking them down can take a long time and can be expensive.

Though you have wills at this time, I recommend that you consult your solicitor and have your wills reviewed as soon as possible. Make sure your wills include provisions that accomplish the following:

Nominate executors and successor executors for your estate.

Make sure that the primary and contingent beneficiaries of life insurance policies are coordinated with the provisions of your wills.

Designate successor beneficiaries who will receive your assets if your spouse should not survive you.

Your wills should be reviewed at least every 5 years in consultation with your solicitor.

Power of Attorney

Consideration should also be given to establishing an Enduring Power of Attorney, so that in the event of your incapacitation the person you nominate *i.e.* each other or some other person can manage your affairs. I recommend that you discuss these matters further with your legal adviser.

Portfolio Review

A review of your portfolio is strongly advised at least on a 12-monthly basis. This is to ensure that your investment portfolio remains consistent with your risk profile and your changing personal and financial situation. In addition it is to assess the performance of individual investments and their continued suitability in your portfolio. I am available anytime in between these formal review dates to answer any concerns or questions you may have regarding your investment portfolio or any other matters in which I may assist.

Concluding Comments

Thank you for the opportunity to present advice on your financial needs. Should you have any questions in regard to the recommended strategies or any other related matter please don't hesitate to contact me. The recommendations are based upon current information and should be considered to be current for the next month only. After that time it may become necessary to review the recommendations accordingly.

Yours sincerely, Ankit Mehta

Certified Financial Planner & Proper Authority Holder of ABC Financial Planning Private Limited

ABC Financial Planning Private Limited (Regn. No.123456), is a Licensed Securities Dealer with its registered office located at Level 11

ABC Building, Lower Parel, Mumbai-400022 .

Client Profile

To assist in the development of an investment strategy appropriate to your particular situation, we discussed your attitude to investment risk and your concerns in the areas of inflation, taxation, safety, liquidity, current income, ease of management and estate planning. Your concerns are shown in the following chart. A higher rating indicates greater concern.

For the purposes of planning a financial strategy we have not yet classified your attitude to investment.

Notes

If you feel that the above profile does not reflect your concerns then we should have further discussions before you implement your investment plan.

Investment Portfolio

We have recommended the investment of your funds after considering your investment profile, your financial objectives, the current economy and economic trends.

Portfolio by Market Exposure

The following table and accompanying portfolio pie chart show the approximate exposure of your recommended portfolio to the primary investment markets. For example, a 'balanced' portfolio seeks to achieve a balance between low risk investments and those having higher risk but the potential for higher returns.

Investment Market	Amount (Rs.)	Portfolio (%)
Cash	83150	3.3
Indian Fixed Interest	244600	9.7
Indian Property	114820	4.6
Indian Shares	1128960	44.8
International Fixed Int.	434310	17.2
International Shares	514160	20.4
Total	2520000	100.0

Portfolio by Market Exposure

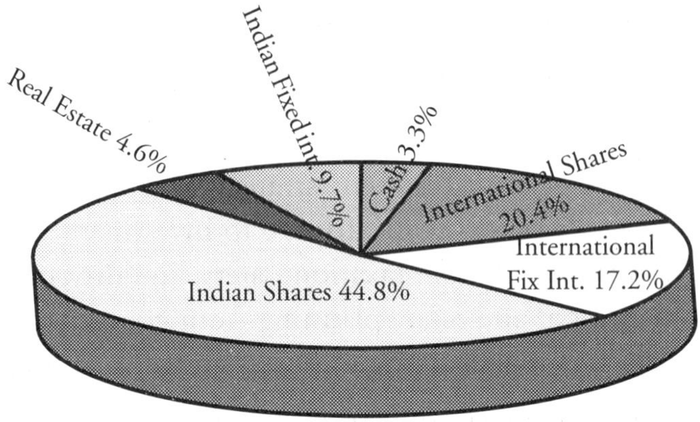

Estimated Tax Liability

To estimate your total tax liability, other sources of income must be added to your investment income.

Based upon the investment income from the recommended portfolio, and other income advised by you and documented in this plan, your total income and estimated tax liability is shown below.

Estimated Tax Liability for Som Arora; The tax liability is estimated to be Nil based on the present and future incomes.

Notes

Your taxable income is subject to a marginal tax rate of 10.0%. Your Medicare Levy is nil.

Estimated Tax Liability for Nita Arora; The tax liability is estimated to be Nil based on the present and future incomes.

Notes

Your taxable income is subject to a marginal tax rate of 10.0%. Your Medicare Levy is nil. Whilst the tax implications of your recommended portfolio have been carefully considered wherever relevant to the preparation of this plan, you are advised to confirm your exact annual tax liability with your tax adviser.

Estimated Cashflow

Adequate cashflow to meet living expenses is fundamental to any financial plan. Based on the estimated income from your recommended portfolio, other income and expenses (inclusive of GST) documented in this plan and estimated tax, we estimate your cashflow to be as follows.

Source Year 1	Client	Partner	Total
Income		0	
Salary	68690		68690
Annuity	2260	0	2260
Consultancy income Payment	0	41700	41700
Investment Income Taxes	61900	31710	93610
Personal	(1550)	(3260)	(4810)
Rebates	1550	3260	4810
Medicare Levy	(0)	(0)	(0)
Net Income	132850	73410	206260
Expenses Living Expenses			200000
Total expenses			200000
Surplus			6270

Action to Proceed

In order to implement this plan, you will need to complete the applications in the following investment documentation and draw cheques for the amounts and in favour of payees listed below. We will be happy to assist you with the completion of all documentation.

Administration Service Investments

Investment Trust

ABC Global Equity	124800
ABC W Divers Fund	499200
ABC W Balanced Fund	499200
ABC (W) International	374000
ABC (W) Share Fund	358800
ABC W Div. St.	249600
ABC W Int'l. Eq.	114800

ABC W Ind Share Fund	249600
Amount: (Rs.)	2470000

Disclosure of Commission - Initial Brokerage

As required under the SEBI Act, it is disclosed that the Authorised Representative and the associated Licensed Dealer in Securities will receive initial brokerage (Establishment or Entry Fees) in relation to the securities recommended by them, up to the rates shown below, either by direct payment or in some other manner. Those payments and their end source are detailed below.

TABLE 1

Investment	Amount Invested	Brokerage	Rebate to Investor	Payment to Auth. Rep.	Payment to Dealer
A	a	g	m0	s0	y0
B	b	h	n0	t	z0
C	c	i	o0	u0	aa00
D	d	j	p0	v0	bb00
E	e	k	q0	w0	cc
F	f	l	r	x0	dd
Average Values (%)		rr	ss	tt	pp0

Notes

The brokerage fee shown is the only initial fee paid by the investor for entry into the applicable investment. Where a fund manager, administrator or other product provider charges an establishment fee then normally the initial brokerage is paid by them from their establishment fee. There is no additional charge to you. In relation to each investment, this fee may be partially or wholly rebated to the Investor as shown in Table 1. If the fee is not rebated or is partially rebated, the balance may be split between the Authorised Representative and Dealer Group as show in Table 1.

Disclosure of Commission - Ongoing Brokerage

As required under the SEBI Act, it is disclosed that the Authorised Representative and the associated Licensed Dealer in Securities will receive ongoing annual brokerage in relation to the securities recommended by them, up to the rates shown below, either by direct payment or in some other manner.

TABLE 2

Investment	Amount Invested $	Ongoing Brokerage $p.a. %	Payment to Auth. Rep. $p.a. %	Payment to Dealer $p.a. %
A	a	g	m	s
B	b	h	n	t
C	c	i	o	u
D	d	j	p	v
E	e	k	q	w
F	f	l	r	x
Average Values (%)		y	z	aa0

Notes

Where the fund manager, responsible entity or other product provider charges an ongoing fee then normally, the above ongoing brokerage is paid from the product provider's ongoing fee, therefore there is no additional charge to you. The ongoing brokerage generally continues until you redeem the investment. The amounts shown in Table 2 may vary over time according to the mix of investments and the total volume of your funds under management. The amount shown is only an estimate for the first year.

Other Fees and Benefits to your Planner and Associated Licensed Dealer

The Authorised Representative may participate in ongoing cumulative reward programs and receive cash and non-cash benefits in relation to specific investment products recommended in this portfolio. If applicable, the products and associated benefits are detailed below.

Management Expense Ratio

The fund manager, responsible entity or other institution operating the recommended investment also charges ongoing fees and expenses for the investment's ongoing management. The Management Expense Ratio (MER) is an estimate of the total of these fees expressed as a percentage of the average net assets held. The MER is used rather than showing an itemised list of all fees and expenses. The investment's MER is not paid to the Planner or Associated Licensed Dealer. You should refer to the Prospectus, other product disclosure document or Short Form Prospectus accompanying your Financial Plan to determine the actual MER (which may be estimated on an annualised basis or expressed as a range).

Buy Sell Differential

Underlying fund managers or responsible entities usually provide a spread between the buying and selling price of the investments they operate. This represents a cost for the buying and selling of investments and will only occur when units in the investment are bought or sold. This cost usually does not exceed 2% and is generally less than 0.5% of an investment's unit price. You should refer to the prospectus or other product disclosure document issued for the investment.

Authority to Proceed

I/We:

Mr. and Mrs. Som Arora

49, Nerul, Navi Mumbai

acknowledge that the products listed in the table below are to be invested in my/our names by:

Ankit Mehta

Certified Financial Planner

Authorised Representative of

ABC Financial Planner Private Ltd.

D-502, Moraj, Navi Mumbai

Licensed Dealer in Securities

Licence No.123456

Client Declaration

I/We have read, accepted and retained a copy of the personal investment recommendations, which includes fees and charges associated with this plan. The client profile, investment strategy and assumptions meet with my/our approval.

I/We acknowledge that the material contained within this plan is solely for my/our use. It is accepted that every care has been taken to ensure the material is accurate and reliable and that no responsibility is accepted for errors or omissions.

I/We understand that a copy of the Data Collection Form or Fact Finder, from which the information in this report has been sourced, is available on request.

I/We understand that the projections on future performances are only a guide and no guarantee is given that investments will meet the expectations stated and where managed or market linked investments have been selected, adverse market conditions may result in capital invested being diminished.

I/we acknowledge that a copy of an Investment Plan, Customer Advice Record or similar was provided to me/us by my/our adviser.

I/We understand that appropriate advice may not be able to be given without complete information and that by not providing sufficient information or choosing to invest in or purchase a life insurance policy other than recommended in this report, I/we risk making a financial commitment to a life policy that may not be appropriate to my/our needs.

Signed...Date...............................

Signed...Date...............................

Adviser Declaration

I/we acknowledge/verify that a copy of an Investment Plan, Customer Advice Record or similar was provided to you, the client.

I/We declare this report is an accurate and complete record of the advice and recommendations that

I/we have given to you, the client.

I/We declare that I/we only provided advice on products for which I/we are authorised to give advice, and that these products are appropriate for the identified needs and objectives of you, the client.

Where advice in this report refers to recommendations for the purchase of products issued by a life insurance company registered by and under legislation administered by IRDA, I am required to advise you that my first obligation is to the life insurance company which has authorised me to sell their products. Where advice in this report refers to recommendations for the purchase of securities issued by a company holding a Dealers Licence issued by SEBI, I am required to advise you that my first obligation is to you the client. In all cases my primary concern is for the financial well being of my clients.

Signed (Adviser)..Date.................................

Know your client

The recommendations made to clients must be consistent with their financial needs and objectives and have a reasonable basis. This Financial Analysis has been based on information, which you have provided. If you believe we have misinterpreted or overlooked some relevant information, it is your responsibility to bring this to our attention before proceeding with this proposal.

In preparing this Financial Plan, we have relied on information supplied to us, which, where reasonable, we have assumed to be correct. Whilst all reasonable efforts have been made to substantiate such information, no responsibility can be accepted if the information is incorrect or inaccurate. This Financial Analysis is prepared solely for the use of the client to whom it is addressed and we do not accept any liability whatsoever to anyone else. The recommendations in this Financial Analysis are based on current information and should only be considered to be current for one month from the date of this Financial Analysis. After that time you should not act on any of the recommendations without further reference to us.

Qualifications

Whilst every effort has been made to include relevant tax and social security considerations, you are advised to discuss your annual tax liability and the tax and social security implications of this Financial Analysis with your tax adviser as the estimates contained herein are intended as a guide only.

Estimates of income and capital growth projection rates are based on assessments of current and likely future economic conditions, as well as investment manager past and likely future performances. Such figures are purely estimates, and are not guaranteed, and may vary with changing circumstances.

Information about the Adviser

Name of the adviser	Ankit Mehta
Adviser's business address	49, Nerul, Navi Mumbai
Telephone number	02 00000000
The companies the adviser represents	ABC Life ABC Financial Planning Pvt. Limited
The products the adviser is authorised to provide advice and sell	Personal savings Personal risk Retirement and investment Superannuation Estate planning ABC Bank
Adviser's employer's or contractor's association with those companies	Agent for ABC Agent ABCFP
Adviser's basis of remuneration	Commission
Who is responsible for the adviser's conduct	ABC Life ABC Financial Planning Pvt. Limited
To whom the adviser owes his or her primary duty	ABC Life ABC Financial Planning Pvt. Limited

Companies whose products the adviser is authorised to sell

List the product group you are authorised to provide advice on and sell, dealing with each life insurance company separately

Agent, sub-agent, indicate for each company

Describe *e.g.*: commission, salary, fee for each company

Life insurance company or

Multi-agent or sub-agents

Life insurance company(ies) with whom you have an agency agreement or sub-agency agreement.

Additional detail of analysis

This section would contain research on shares and managed funds recommended.

ASIC IPS (interim policy statement) 145

"KNOWLEDGE REQUIREMENTS"

[PS 146.118] The following list of ASIC's knowledge requirements applies to a range of products and activities relevant to the financial services sectors to be regulated by ASIC. The core knowledge requirements and the applicable specialist knowledge requirements should be demonstrated by all representatives. However, we recognise that, depending on the nature of the activities undertaken, the extent and scope of the knowledge requirements to be met may vary.

Licensees and principals must first identify the tasks and functions to be carried out by their representatives. They then must determine which of ASICs knowledge requirements should be covered in their training program/s or individual assessments of representatives in relation to those tasks and functions. Note that these content guidelines are not exhaustive.

Knowledge

Generic knowledge

The economic environment

[PS 146.119] A representative should demonstrate a broad understanding of the economic environment in relation to the products and markets in which they operate. This may include coverage of the following concepts:

characteristics and impact of economic and business cycles

interest rates; exchange rates

inflation

government monetary and fiscal policies

Operation of financial markets

[PS 146.120] A representative should demonstrate a broad understanding of the operation of financial markets in relation to the products and markets in which they operate. This may include coverage of the following concepts:

roles played by intermediaries and issuers

structure and inter-relationships within the financial markets

inter-relationship between industry sectors

Financial products

[PS 146.121] A representative should demonstrate a broad understanding of financial products in relation to the markets in which they operate. This may include coverage of the following concepts:

concept of a financial product

different classes and sub-classes of investments (cash, fixed interest, deposit taking accounts, property, equities)

correlation between different asset classes

types of financial investment products

types of financial risk products (*e.g.* general insurance, risk insurance products)

similarities and differences between products

risk factors of product classes

Taxation

[PS 146.122] A representative should demonstrate a broad understanding of the taxation issues in relation to the products and markets in which they operate.

Disclosure and compliance

[PS 146.123] A representative should demonstrate a broad awareness of their disclosure and compliance obligations in relation to the products and markets in which they operate. These may include coverage of the following concepts:

the role of the representative/adviser

relevant legal principles, *e.g.* Corporations Law, ASIC Act, Trade Practices Act, 52 etc.

the relationship between ethics and regulatory requirements, *e.g.* utmost good faith; disclosure of conflict of interest; full disclosure of remuneration/fees and any other matters which may influence the representative's recommendation; confidentiality

relevant industry codes of conduct and practice

regulators guidelines including ASICs requirements set out in this interim policy statement

complaints resolution procedures (internal and external)

Integrity

[PS 146.124] A representative should demonstrate a broad understanding of the following concepts in relation to the products and markets in which they operate including:

ethical advising, *e.g.* the adviser/consumer relationship, conflict of interest, obligations of the individual adviser, full disclosure of interests — refer to disclosure and compliance, etc.

Specialist knowledge

[PS 146.125] A representative should be able to apply the following specialist knowledge within the areas of specific industry or product in which they are operating. The following areas are covered below:

A. Financial planning

B. Securities and futures markets

C. Managed investments

D. Superannuation

E. Insurance — general, life and broking

A. Financial planning

[PS 146.126] A representative providing detailed financial planning services to retail consumers should be able to apply the following knowledge:

Theories of investment, portfolio management and management of investment and risk

investment concepts

investment strategies

identification of types of risk

client risk profile

Advisory functions

the role of financial planner/adviser

participants in the advisory services market

range of services provided

full disclosure of remuneration/commission structures for advisers

Taxation

the Australian taxation and social security systems

relevant taxation laws and regulations

effects of taxation on particular financial products

effects of taxation on financial strategies of individuals and entities

Estate planning

theory of estate planning, *i.e.* allowable investments, enduring and non-enduring powers of attorney, share purchase agreements etc.

management and investment strategies

relevant taxation laws and regulations

B. Securities and futures markets

[PS 146.127] A representative providing financial services on securities and futures products should be able to apply the following knowledge:

Core securities and futures (where applicable)

Operation of securities and futures markets

market participants

roles played by intermediaries

structure and inter-relationships within and between the securities/futures sectors

Types of products

range of securities/futures products

associated risks

investment options using securities products

Theories of investment, portfolio management and management of investment and risk (where applicable)

investment concepts

investment strategies

identification of types of risk

client risk profile

Taxation

awareness of taxation issues relating to securities and futures products (where applicable)

Disclosure and compliance

relevant legislation

relevant codes of conduct/practice

regulators' guidelines

disclosure of fees and charges

role and functions of the regulators

alternative dispute resolution

B.1 Equities

Stockbroking competency standards

ASX Business Rules

B.2 Equity derivatives

ASX Equity Derivatives Accreditation

ASX Business Rules

B.3 Futures

Registered Representatives Examination

SFE Business Rules

C. Managed investments [PS 146.128]

concepts of collective rights

specialist knowledge of the underlying product, *e.g.*

— property trusts; real estate investment strategies; valuation techniques; property management

— equity trusts, fixed interest trusts

— serviced strata schemes

— primary production schemes

— film schemes

— time-sharing schemes

regulatory and legal obligations

taxation implications

D. Superannuation

[PS 146.129] A representative providing detailed financial services on superannuation products should be able to apply the following knowledge:

Operation and management of superannuation markets

Topics may include:

characteristics and structure of a superannuation fund

roles played by intermediaries and issuers

types of superannuation funds

fee structures

administration and management costs

types of contribution

types of products used

annuities/pensions, allocated pensions and income stream products

associated risks

structure of superannuation plans management and administration of superannuation funds

preservation rules

investment strategies within superannuation funds, *i.e.* investment concepts and strategies

restrictions on investment strategies

identification of risk

Taxation

Topics may include:

impact on investment earnings

employer and employee contributions

benefit payments and expenses

tax deductions

capital gains tax treatment

roll-overs

reasonable benefit limits

superannuation surcharge

social security pension eligibility

retirement planning

death benefits

franking credits *Disclosure and compliance* Topics may include:

Superannuation Guarantee (Administration) Act, 1992

Superannuation Industry (Supervision) Act, 1993

role of regulators

adviser fees and commissions

trustee rules

alternative dispute resolution

E. Insurance

[PS 146.130] Given the nature of the insurance sector, the following specialist knowledge category for representatives providing services on insurance products has been divided into core insurance knowledge and type of insurance product. This has been done to recognise industry feedback that there is a body of core insurance specific knowledge (separate to generic knowledge) which should also be understood by those operating within this sector.

Licensees and principals should ensure that their representatives satisfy the requirements relevant to the representatives' tasks and functions.

For example, representatives operating solely within the general insurance market should be able to demonstrate to the licensee or principal an application of the following:

generic knowledge (as applicable)

core insurance

general insurance

generic skills (as applicable)

Representatives operating solely within the life insurance market should be able to demonstrate to the licensee or principal an application of the following:

generic knowledge (as applicable)

core insurance

life insurance

generic skills (as applicable)

Representatives operating solely within the insurance broking market should be able to demonstrate to the licensee or principal an application of the following:

generic knowledge (as applicable)

core insurance

insurance broking

generic skills (as applicable)

Representatives providing services in more than one of the insurance product streams will be required to possess the relevant knowledge and skills in each of the product areas. (See Appendix B for explanation.)

E.1 Core insurance (all categories i.e. general, life and broking)

A representative providing detailed financial services on insurance products should be able to apply the following knowledge:-

Operation of insurance markets (for example)

definition of insurance/risk product

characteristics and participants of the Australian insurance market

roles played by intermediaries

Insurance products (for example)

alternative types of risk insurance products and life insurance products

conditions, exclusions, levels of coverage of risk transfer products

pricing

Taxation

awareness of taxation issues relating to insurance products (where applicable)

Advisory functions (as it relates to insurance)

the role of insurance adviser/broker/agent

participants in the insurance advisory services market

range of services provided

profile and financial information of the client

appropriateness of a risk assessment

remuneration/commission structures for representatives

Disclosure and compliance (for example)

General Insurance Code of Practice

Code of Practice for Advising, Selling and Complaints Handling in the Life Insurance Industry

Insurance Contracts Act, 1984, Insurance (Agents and Brokers) Act, 1984, Life Insurance Act, 1995

legal and regulatory framework for insurance products

role of regulators

alternative dispute resolution

E.2 General insurance (for example)

types of general insurance products/policies

standard cover (and deviations)

policy wordings

taxes and charges

insurance claims

premium rating/risk selection

reporting

product development

underwriting

E.3 Life insurance (for example)

types/classes of life insurance products/policies

standard cover (and deviations)

product development

policy wordings

underwriting

insurance claims

premium rating/risk assessment

investment strategy (investment component of life insurance products)

E.4 Insurance broking (for example)

types/classes of insurance products

standard cover (and deviations)

product development

policy wordings

underwriting

insurance claims

premium rating/risk assessment

types of broking services

ASIC IPS (interim policy statement) 145

"SKILL AND INTEGRITY REQUIREMENTS"

(A) SKILL REQUIREMENTS

[PS 146.131] Representatives providing financial services to retail consumers should be able to apply appropriate skills in relation to their activities and the products and markets in which they operate.

The skill and integrity requirements should be demonstrated by all representatives. However, we recognise that, depending on the nature of the activities undertaken, the skills demonstrated may vary in their level of detail.

Licensees and principals must first identify the tasks and functions of their representatives. They must then determine which of ASICs skill requirements should be covered in a training program or when assessing an individual representative and in what depth. Note that these skill requirements are not exhaustive.

1. Establish relationship with client

This may include:

explaining the representatives role

establishing knowledge level of client

explaining the services offered

identifying the licensee/principal responsible for the representatives conduct

explaining fee and charging methodology

explaining the procedures for complaints handling

2. Identify client objectives, needs, and financial situation

This may include collection of the following types of information from the consumer.

TOWARDS A FINANCIAL

Notes ....

TOWARDS A FINANCIAL

Notes ....

8 CHAPTER

Effective Communication in Financial Counselling

ABOUT THIS TOPIC

This topic focuses on the various types of structured communication in counselling and on the essential components of effective communication. It emphasizes the importance of basic communication skills. Effective communication and counselling techniques are of primary importance in the financial planning process. To develop financial plans tailored to individual clients needs, circumstances, and objectives, financial planners need to be able to know their clients, be sensitive to their individuality, and be committed to a respect for their personhood. It is, therefore, crucial that financial planners develop highly skilled and effective counselling techniques in order to fulfil their commitment to provide a professional service that will meet their clients' needs.

TOPIC OBJECTIVES

At the end of this topic, you should be able to:

- *Define structured communication and explain the differences among three main types.*
- *Describe the primary communication elements in financial counselling.*

- *List and describe the four characteristics of an effective counsellor.*
- *List and explain the basic communication principles.*
- *Describe several ways in which communication occurs through non-verbal behaviour.*
- *Describe the two main skills of attending.*
- *Describe the basic types of responses associated with active listening.*
- *Describe the four types of leading responses.*
- *Compare the advantages and disadvantages of the various types of questions used in financial counselling.*

1. INTRODUCTION

Many people take communication for granted. After all, it is an activity that most of us have engaged in since our childhood years, so why not take it for granted? The sad truth, however, is that many of us are ineffective communicators simply because we make that very assumption. Communication is far too important a skill, especially in the field of counselling, to treat it lightly. It is the single most critical skill that a counsellor brings to a counselling session. The purpose of this chapter is to examine the communication process, as it typically exists in a counsellor-client relationship. Our goal is to enable financial planners to become exceptionally effective communicators in their dealings with clients. Perhaps you already consider yourself to be effective in the area of communication; however, there are probably aspects of the communication process in which you can improve. This chapter will attempt to bring these aspects into sharper focus and provide you with techniques for becoming the very best communicator/ counsellor that you have the potential of being.

1.1 THREE TYPES OF STRUCTURED COMMUNICATION

Lay people often use the terms interviewing, counselling, and advising interchangeably; yet, each term has characteristics that are uniquely its own and that differentiates it from the other two. Let us look at each of these three terms and see how they are alike and how they are different.

Three Types of Structured Communication

- Interviewing
- Counselling
- Advising

1.2 INTERVIEWING

One of the most common forms of structured communication is interviewing. *Interviewing* can be defined as a process of communication, most often between two people, with a predetermined and specific purpose, usually involving the asking and answering of questions designed to gather meaningful information.

For example, a television sports announcer might interview a coach at halftime to get information about what mistakes his team made in the first half, what he plans to do differently in the second half, and how he hopes to win. Or, an interview might take place in a personnel office where a job applicant is interviewed for a position with the firm. The interviewer will want to know the following: What assets will the applicant bring to the job? What is her employment history? Where does she see herself fitting into the firm? What salary does she expect?

In both instances cited, there is a specific purpose to the interview in that relevant information is being sought through a *question-and-answer* dialogue.

Stewart and Cash, in their book, *Interviewing: Principles and Practices,* refer to two basic types of interviews: the directive and non-directive interview.

In the *directive interview,* the interviewer directs and controls both the pace and the content to be covered. It is a much more formalized and structured style of interaction. Often the interviewer even completes a questionnaire form as the interviewee answers pointed questions—for example

What is your age? Where do you live? Where was your last job?

What is the highest level of education completed?

The advantages of the directive interview are that it can be brief and that it provides measurable data. Its disadvantages are that it is often inflexible and does not allow the interviewee to choose topics for discussion.

The *non-directive interview,* on the other hand, allows both the interviewer and the interviewee a wider range of subject areas to be discussed, and the interviewee usually controls the pacing and purpose of the interview. Thus, the advantages of the non- directive interview include greater flexibility, more in-depth responses, and the potential of a closer relationship between interviewer and interviewee. Its disadvantages are that it consumes more time and often generates data that are difficult to measure objectively. All interviews, whether directive or non-directive, share common characteristics. Interviews typically take place in a formal and structured setting. Questions are the primary source of communication used by the interviewer. The subject matter discussed is specific to the overall purpose of the interview, and digressions from the subject are usually not encouraged. Finally, the interview is usually a relatively short-term relationship between interviewer and interviewee.

1.3 COUNSELLING

The second term, *counselling,* is often confused with interviewing, even though they are not synonymous. Counselling implies help giving, often of a psychotherapeutic nature, and the help-giving aspect is more than implied in counselling; it is built in and is an integral part of the process. Simply stated, a counsellor's job is to provide assistance to clients as they explore their present situations, begin to understand where they are in relation to where they would like to be, and then act to get from where they are to where they want to be. Even though this may sound like a simple process, it is not. It usually is a long-term process, typified by struggles, setbacks, and, eventually, insights leading to an ultimate change in behaviour as clients strive to live more fulfilling lives.

While financial counselling takes place over a period of time, the interview is usually a one-time interaction. As such, an interpersonal relationship develops between counsellor and client, something that usually does not occur in an interview. When we discussed interviewing, we stated that the question was the primary stock-in-trade of the interviewer. While questions are also utilized in counselling, they are not the primary response modality. In certain counselling settings, such as mental hospitals and mental health clinics, an intake interview constitutes the first step in the therapeutic process. In this intake interview, many personal questions are asked, either in a written or oral format, but once the intake procedure is concluded, the communication assumes a different form. While questions may still be asked periodically, they are not the predominant form of counsellor response. A counsellor may paraphrase what the client has said, reflect a feeling, share feedback or perceptions, clarify, summarize, interpret, provide information, and confront. In short, counselling is not as stylized as interviewing because the format is less formal and less structured. Much more of the humanness of both the counsellor and the client comes into focus, all with the purpose of providing help to the client.

1.4 ADVISING

Still a third type of structured communication is *advising,* which involves giving specific guidance or suggestions to the advisee. Advising is often confused with counselling. In fact, many people, who are unfamiliar with counselling, think that what they will receive is advice. Perhaps, one reason for this misconception stems from the journalistic proliferation of advice such as is offered in newspaper columns. This is not to say that advice is never offered by counsellors, because it is; but most counsellors believe that the very best kind of advice is self-advice, rather than expert advice.

Several situations might require such advice. A college student, planning a programme of studies, is typically assigned an academic adviser in his or her major field of study. The adviser's role is, simply, to advise the student about programme sequence, course prerequisites, specific course content, graduation requirements, and possible career opportunities in the major area. In short, the adviser is the expert and, as such, provides excellent advice. A tax adviser might provide advice on tax shelters, investments, tax deferral, and so on. In both instances, advisers know much more about their field of expertise than do their clients, and their clients use this knowledge in order to reach decisions.

In financial counselling, there are bound to be occasions when counsellors give advice. After all, financial counsellors are the experts and, thus, their advice has proven value. The danger in offering advice too soon in the counselling relationship is that the client's ability to make decisions is discounted in favour of the expert's opinion. Perhaps the best way to give advice, if advice is given at all, is to hear clients out first in order to understand their situation more completely and to assess their goals, and then to explain what alternatives or options are available.

Advice giving remains a controversial issue in counselling literature. Its critics maintain that advice fosters dependency and robs clients of the right to make decisions for themselves. It is important for each counsellor to question his or her haste in offering ready answers to somewhat complex situations. Is there some inner need like dominance or control being satisfied? Is the advice giver willing to assume the responsibility for another person's life? Is the advice giver projecting his or her own needs, problems, or values into the advice?

So while it is true that many people come to a financial counsellor ostensibly looking for advice or the right answer, it is also true that many people choose not to take the advice when it is offered, or if they do take the counsellor's advice and later discover that it was unsound, they rightfully blame the counsellor.

There is a place for tentative suggestions that leave the final decision about courses of action entirely upto the client. In this manner, clients are free to make decisions that are right for them and, thus, assume the responsibility for their own lives. Advisers who do this are functioning in a wholly professional and ethical manner.

2. ESSENTIALS IN FINANCIAL COUNSELLING

In the preceding section, we differentiated between the three types of planned, purposeful communication, interviewing, counselling, and advising. Each one of these types of communication can be found in the financial counselling relationship. For instance, interviewing in the form of data collection for a fact finder might well constitute the early stages of the communication process. After the data are collected, the second phase would probably consist largely of counselling-listening closely to the client and trying to understand the client's inner world of needs, desires, fears, attitudes, values, and goals. The third and final stage of communication in financial counselling would undoubtedly include giving expert advice, or at least carefully exploring possible alternatives for achieving the client's objectives. Let us look at the dynamics of communication and how it works in actual practice.

2.1 STRUCTURE

In any kind of planned and purposeful communication setting, the first element that needs to be attended to is structuring. Structuring serves to determine both the format and the subject matter of the interaction that is to follow. The counsellor's task is to make the purpose of the session clear to the client at the outset. This would include the inevitable introductions, an explanation of the process involved, a discussion of forms that are used and the amount of time that will be required, a discussion on the confidential nature of the relationship, and some prediction of what kinds of outcomes the client might reasonably expect. This structuring need not be lengthy and cumbersome; in fact, it is far better to structure in a clear, straightforward, and succinct fashion. Consider the following example of structuring:

Example: Counsellor: "In order to be able to provide the best possible service to you, we will probably need to see each other on three or four separate occasions, although I want you to know that I am available to you as often as you need me. Today, I thought we'd start by getting some information about your financial situation. To do this, I shall use the fact finder pages, which will remain confidential between the two of us. As we go about our business together, I am sure that we will be able to come up with a financial plan that will be sensible and help you meet your goals. Do you have any questions?"

The counsellor's approach, in the foregoing example, is friendly and promises co-operation. The client is made to feel important as he/she gets the impression that he or she is the focal point of the counselling situation. The statement offers hope that the results of client counselling will meet the needs and goals of the client. In the early stages of counselling, the client may be apprehensive or uncertain about how to begin, A good guide to follow is to begin where the client is. If the client is, in fact, anxious at the outset, some time should be spent discussing the mere difficulty of getting started. Talking about this will invariably alleviate most of the client's anxieties. It is important to keep in mind that whenever feelings emerge, it is best to focus upon those feelings rather than ignore them. If, for example, a client, in the middle of a session, appears distressed over some aspect of his or her situation (for example, an impending divorce), some time must be given to discussing these feelings. Until the feelings are addressed and expressed, a further discussion of content is unproductive and meaningless.

2.2 RAPPORT

Counsellors should seek to develop rapport with their clients. *Rapport,* another way of describing a comfortable and harmonious relationship, is best established through the personhood of the financial counsellor. Attributes that go a long way toward a rapprochement between counsellor and client would include a friendly and interested concern; an unhurried, leisurely pace; an accepting, non-judgmental attitude; attentive, active listening; and an egalitarian relationship. In such a climate, clients are free to be themselves, since they don't have to be afraid that what they say will be evaluated in a negative way by the counsellor. Furthermore, they begin to realize that the ultimate responsibility for planning, setting goals, and taking action rests with them and not the counsellor.

Perhaps the most important attribute of personhood in establishing rapport is the financial counsellor's acceptance of the client and the client's awareness of this acceptance. This attitude stems from a sincere desire on the part of the counsellor to respect the uniqueness of each client and a genuine wish to be of help. And it might be well to add that accepting others is easier said than done, especially with people who are markedly different from us in terms of their values, attitudes, socio-economic status, and so on. Despite this difficulty, it is absolutely imperative that counsellors accept their clients, because unless a client feels accepted by his counsellor, the relationship will never really become a partnership of equals.

2.3 RECOGNIZING RESISTANCE

Resistance often occurs in even the best of counselling relationships. It can be expressed as either overt or covert hostility toward the counsellor. Open hostility is the easiest type to recognize and, in most cases, to handle. We all know what angry people look and sound like as their faces become blushed; their jaws tighten; they clench their fists; their voices rise; their language becomes more expressively angry. The only effective thing to do, at this point, is to reflect this anger, as in saying, "I can sense your anger. You do not like what I have just said, do you?" This allows clients to vent whatever pent-up feelings of anger they have, and the anger slowly begins to dissipate and then the behaviour becomes more rational.

Covert hostility is more difficult to recognize and can be more difficult to deal with, since clients themselves may not even be aware of their anger. Some indications of covert hostility are missed appointments; being late for appointments; being sarcastic or cynical; being overly genteel or polite; not getting down to business. Whatever the evidence of covert hostility is, the best approach is *not* to interpret the behaviour of the client as latent hostility or passive-aggressiveness but simply to focus on the behaviour itself and let the client analyze or interpret it. For instance, the counsellor might say,

I have noticed that whenever we talk about your spouse's handling of the family budget, you become sarcastic. What do you think might be going on? Again, this helps the client to focus on the feedback received and allows angry feelings to be vented. Resistance must be addressed as directly as possible, if any good is to come of the counselling relationship.

Other types of resistance behaviours, that counsellors might encounter during counselling relationships, would include withdrawal or passivity; dwelling in fantasy or non-reality; ambivalence or vacillation; and the use of inappropriate humour, to name a few. As mentioned, the counsellor should not analyze or interpret a client's resistance behaviour since analysis tends only to raise the client's defensiveness. Instead, the counsellor should be aware of what is occurring, note whether it is a recurrent pattern, and at an appropriate point, share such observations in a non-judgmental manner with the client.

2.4 COMMON AREAS OF RESISTANCE

Client resistance is almost given in a financial counselling relationship, probably because clients, when they enter into a counselling relationship, yield a certain amount of their privacy and personal power over the situation to the counsellor. Resistance is a way of defending oneself, or restoring some of the balance of power to oneself. Certain discussion areas, because of their sensitive nature, seem to be particularly vulnerable to client resistance. One such sensitive subject area is death and dying. Because of its uncertainty, death is extremely anxiety-producing to some people. Dr. Elisabeth Kubler-Ross, an eminent authority on death and dying, postulates that there are five stages that a person facing death passes through denial, anger, bargaining, depression and acceptance. The first four of these stages are all different forms of resistance that the person uses for self-protection. Financial counsellors, when discussing future plans with older people, need to be particularly sensitive to the feelings of their clients. Counsellors must listen and observe very closely what clients communicate when discussing death and dying. Counsellors must be empathetic to feelings and communicate accurately what is heard and observed. A genuine concern for the feelings and attitudes of clients must be manifested. Counsellors must also be aware of their own feelings about death, so that they do not interfere with what clients are feeling and attempting to communicate.

Counsellors can help to restore some control over the future, by involving clients fully in decision making and planning for contingencies. This allows clients to feel useful, worthwhile, and somewhat in control of their situation. Another area where resistance may be encountered involves marital tensions, such as separation/divorce, parent-child disputes, sex, the empty nest syndrome, and midlife crisis. While financial counsellors are not expected to be highly qualified marriage or family counsellors, they should be astute enough to recognize when a married couple is resisting because of an underlying, unexpressed marital problem. And once it is recognized, counsellors should be willing and able to focus with the couple on the problem area. Otherwise, if the problem is ignored, whatever decisions are reached will be less valid than those that would be reached after a full airing of the problem. Besides providing a possibly welcome catharsis for the couple, focusing on the problem can enable them to muster their forces in order to arrive at a mutually satisfactory solution. In counselling couples who are in disagreement on a crucial subject, the counsellor needs to listen closely to what both partners have to say. It is far too common, unfortunately, to let the more dominant partner do most of the speaking and deciding. Since the outcome of the decision affects both partners, both should be involved in the discussion. To do any less, almost guarantees an unsatisfactory conclusion.

Another sensitive area involves the executive who has failed to attain the degree of success he had dreamed of in his profession. His dreams shattered and unfulfilled, he may resort to cynicism, biting sarcasm, or empty humor in an attempt to endure it. Rather than laugh along with him, the effective counsellor *reflects* the underlying feeling to let the client know that he or she understands his disappointment. A simple statement like, "I suppose it is a bitter pill to swallow when you have worked so hard to see your personal hopes go unfulfilled," allows your client to feel understood and appreciated. More often than not, the client will begin to discuss more openly how he feels. And once people are able to express their feelings, they are well on the way to address their problems in an effective manner. Resistance behaviours, in any case, are a certain tip- off that the client is having difficulty subscribing to the counsellor's line of reasoning. It does no good for the counsellor to proceed with business as usual, ignoring the obvious resistance; nothing can be accomplished as long as the resistance continues. The resistance must be dealt with openly and objectively, if there is any chance that it will be diminished, allowing the participants to get on with the business at hand.

3. PROFILE OF THE EFFECTIVE COUNSELLOR

The main thing a counsellor brings to the counselling hour is himself or herself. Financial counsellors, first and foremost, must be themselves in their relation to and interaction with their clients. Each counsellor is a human being, complete with strengths and frailties. But each counsellor is also a professionally trained individual, a person who, ideally, enjoys listening to and trying to understand other people and to accept them as they are. The effective counsellor is also sincere and genuine in attempting to help others learn how to help themselves. This attitude generates interesting, challenging, and highly gratifying work; and it is—more than anything else—hard work, when done professionally.

Carl Rogers, in his classic book, *Client-Centered Therapy,* postulated that there are three conditions necessary to bring about constructive client change: (1) unconditional positive regard, (2) accurate empathy, and (3) genuineness. Most counselling theorists agree that if an effective counsellor client relationship is to exist, the counsellor must value the client as a unique individual (unconditional positive regard), must be able to perceive and understand what the client is experiencing (accurate empathy), and must be open and spontaneous (genuine).

A constructive counsellor-client relationship serves not only to increase the opportunity for clients to attain the goals that are important to them, but also serve as a model of a good interpersonal relationship. Some questions that all counsellors ought to ask themselves, from time to time, are the following:

- Knowing yourself, do you think it will be possible for you to value your clients, especially those who think, feel, and act differently from you?
- How easy or difficult will it be for you to view the world from another's perspective without imposing your own standards, beliefs, and attitudes on that person? Will your own values, ideas, and feelings hinder your understanding of another person?
- How open do you care, or dare, to be with a client? Will you be able to just be yourself, or will you role-play how you think a professional counsellor should be?

These are important questions to consider before engaging yourself in the dynamics of a counselling relationship. Far too many financial counsellors assume that they have the right kind of personality to counsel others without ever scrutinizing themselves in the same way.

Let us examine the three core conditions to which Rogers refers, and a fourth condition, self-awareness.

Four Characteristics of the Effective Counsellor

1. Unconditional positive regard
2. Accurate empathy
3. Genuineness
4. Self-awareness

3.1 UNCONDITIONAL POSITIVE REGARD

Unconditional positive regard is an attitude of valuing the client, or being able to express appreciation of the client as a unique and worthwhile person. Liking and respecting another person have a circular effect. When you value clients, your sense of liking will be communicated to them;

this, by itself, will enhance their feelings for themselves and add to their appreciation of themselves as worthwhile human beings.

3.2 ACCURATE EMPATHY

Accurate empathy means that your sense of the client's world fits the client's self-image. This gives clients the feeling that you are in touch with them. When clients say something like, "Yes, that is it," or "That is exactly right," it indicates that your response was right on target, and that they feel you are closely following and understanding them.

Learning to understand is not an easy process. It involves the capacity to lay aside your own set of experiences in favour of those of your clients—as seen through their eyes, not yours. It involves skillful listening so you can hear not only the obvious, but also the subtleties, of which, even the client may be unaware of.

Developing accurate empathy also means identifying and resolving your own needs so they do not interfere with your understanding of the feelings and concerns of your client. The counsellor who identifies too strongly with the client's state, however, impedes rather than facilitates the counselling objective.

3.3 GENUINENESS

Genuineness means, simply, that the counsellor is a "real" person, that is, there is no facade, no role-playing of what a professional counsellor is considered to be. Professional counsellors are wholly aware of themselves and their feelings, thoughts, values and attitudes. More importantly, counsellors who are genuine are not afraid to express themselves openly and honestly at all times. Financial counsellors do not have to become something different for each client with whom they have a relationship. They are role free; they are themselves at all times.

A counsellor, who is a genuine one communicates in a spontaneous and expressive manner and does not conceal anything, is open and willing to listen to whatever the client is willing to discuss, and is consistent. He or she does not think or feel one thing but say another.

One author suggests that effective counsellors can express directly to others whatever they are experiencing and communicate without distorting their messages, listen to others, be spontaneous instead of planned or programmed, respond openly in a specific and concrete manner, be willing to manifest their own vulnerabilities and frailties, learn how to be psychologically close to others and commit themselves to others.

A tall order? Perhaps. And yet, for a financial counselling relationship to be effective, it is mandatory that counsellors allow themselves to be genuine with their clients.

Otherwise, the relationship deteriorates into a charade of two human beings playing prescribed roles with each other, and this defeats the basic purpose.

3.4 SELF-AWARENESS

There is general consensus among counsellor-educators that counsellors should possess *self-awareness,* especially with regard to their attitudes and values. Counsellors, who are aware of their own value systems, have a better chance of avoiding the imposition of their values onto their clients. This quality is of vital importance since we want to help our clients to make decisions that stem from their own value systems, rather than from ours. The more we know about ourselves, the better we can understand, interpret, evaluate and control our behaviour and the less likely we are to attribute aspects of ourselves to the client, a rather common defense mechanism known as projection. Before we can be aware of others, it is essential that we be solidly grounded in self- awareness.

Barbara Okun, in her book, *Effective Helping,* suggests that counsellors should continually try to determine their own needs, feelings, and values by answering the following questions:

- Am I aware when I find myself feeling uncomfortable with a client or with a particular subject area?
- Am I aware of my avoidance strategies?
- Can I really be honest with the client?
- Do I always feel the need to be in control of situations?

- Do I often feel as if I must be omnipotent in that I must do something to make the client "get better" so that I can be successful?
- Am I so problem-oriented that I am always looking for the negative, for a problem, and never responding to the positive, to the good?
- Am I able to be as open with clients as I want them to be with me? The adage "Know thyself" should apply to financial counsellors and other helping professionals even more than it does to the population at large. A very large part of our responsibility as counsellors is to know ourselves as thoroughly as possible, so that we are then able to provide the very best kind of objective, informed counselling to our clients. A counsellor who has blind spots about himself or herself will surely be less effective in a helping situation than a counsellor who is comfortably self- aware. This is not to say that the counsellor is a problem-free, completely self- actualized individual; rather, it means that the counsellor is a human being, with a multitude of strengths and even some weaknesses, but the weaknesses are known by the counsellor and do not interfere with the dynamics of counselling another person.

Orientation to values

As human beings, we have value systems that are the result of years of living on this planet. Many of our values are inculcated in us by our parents, by schooling, by religion, by our peers, and by society. However they come to us, they are as much a part of us as our physical and psychological characteristics. This is not to say that they are a permanent, static part of our being, because our values can, and do, change.

The point is that values, while deeply internalized, are not immutable. Counsellors need to remind themselves of this fact as they work with clients who are confused and afraid in approaching important decisions. While it is true that we are in many ways a reflection of our past history, we are—or can be—much more than that. There is no need to be shackled to our past. We can, if we choose, overcome our past and live new lives, based upon who we are now and what we believe in and hold to be valuable to us both now and in the future. This is a liberating concept and, as such, frees individuals to think, feel, and behave in ways that are compatible with their present being, rather than dooming them to repeat the past and live in ways that are no longer meaningful.

The financial counsellor's role in this situation is to act as a catalyst rather than as a maintainer of the *status quo.* The implied danger, of course, is that counsellors might try to force change in their clients' values and attitudes where none is desired or sought after, or that counsellors might subtly or not so subtly try to impose their values on clients. Both of these dangers must be consciously guarded against. What counsellors must do is to listen carefully to clients as they sift through the various value choices faced, so when clients finally make the choice, it can be done freely, without encumbrances from the past. Clients must actually be opened up to the freedom of making choices that are relevant and meaningful to their very existence. Good counsellors have a knack for being able to do this.

Differences in values

Each of us has, within us, a hierarchy of values that makes order of our lives. An older executive facing retirement might, for example, rank security above risk taking when deciding how to invest money. On the other hand, a younger financial counsellor might rank risk taking above security in the hierarchy of values. What happens, then, when the risk-taking counsellor sits down to counsel the security-minded pre-retirement executive? If the counsellor is sensitive and understanding, he or she will listen to the older person, and try to get a sense of what is important to the client, what the client is willing and unwilling to do. The effective financial counsellor does not try to sell the client a product that the counsellor believes is right but that the client believes is wrong, unsafe, or risky.

Counselling is caring, and caring means that the counsellor cares enough—has enough faith in the client's worth as a unique human being—to permit that client to make value choices that fit his or her value system. The financial counsellor can and should provide information that will help the client make the choice, but the choice ultimately belongs to the client, not the counsellor. Only in this way, we are counsellors.

In addition to the differences in values, which often are reflective of the differences in age between counsellor and client, we should also consider several other "isms"—sexism and racism—and how they impinge upon the counsellor-client relationship. Let us look first at sex differences. Sexist counselling occurs when the counsellor uses his or her own sex ideology as a framework for counselling. In the field of financial counselling, this might take place when a male counsellor discourages a female client from doing something that has traditionally been thought to be in the man's world, such as returning to work while there is an infant at home to be cared for. This kind of subtle advice giving, besides reflecting the obvious sex-role bias of the counsellor, is not in keeping with what is happening in many households today. Further, it is intrusive in that the responsibility for making that decision is clearly the client's and not the counsellor's. It is critical that counsellors learn to recognize their own biases and sex-role stereotypes and not inflict them upon people whom they are trying to help. In the case of married couples, financial counsellors typically counsel both husband and wife. It is important to understand what both partners have to say. It is far too common to refer to the male of the household, the perceived "breadwinner," without taking into consideration what the female spouse has to contribute. When both husband and wife are in complete agreement, no problem exists. But when they disagree—and this is often communicated through non-verbal signals like a sigh, a frown, or an angry glance—it is important to make a point of bringing the subject up for a full discussion. It is far better to spend whatever time it takes, to bring both partners to a mutually acceptable decision, than to proceed with one person's plan of action, knowing that it doesn't satisfy the other person. Racism, despite notable progress in the civil rights movement over the past two decades, is still with us in many forms. Counsellors engage in racism when they limit the choices of their clients based solely on their clients' race, or when they make faulty assumptions about their clients because of racist stereotyping.

The issue of whether white counsellors can be effective in a relationship with African Americans or Hispanics has been the subject of much research, though no conclusive findings exist. An effective counsellor should be able to work with people of all races, since all people seem to have the same basic psychological needs and problems.

Counsellors need to be conscious of their own biases regarding race and to guard against allowing their biases to adversely affect the quality of the counselling relationship. The counselling strategies employed should not differ with regard to the race of the client, they should not differ on the sex, age, or religion of the client.

4. ELEMENTS OF COMMUNICATION

In the previous section, we discussed the attributes of an effective counsellor. In this section we will explore communication as a process and attempt to relate fundamental principles of communication to effective financial counselling. An effective counsellor is also an effective communicator.

Communication is often thought of as one person sending a message through both verbal and non-verbal channels to another person or persons with the intention of evoking a response. A speaker asks, "How are you?" and the listener (or receiver of the communication) answers, "Just fine— except for my back." Effective communication takes place when the receiver interprets the sender's message in precisely the same fashion in which the sender intended it. Difficulties in communication arise when the receiver misunderstands and/or misinterprets the sender's message. Since any individual's intentions are private and rarely clearly stated, the receiver of the message has the difficult job of decoding the message without knowing for a fact what the sender's intentions are.

In addition, communication failures can also be attributed to the wide variety of stimuli with which individuals are bombarded during the course of a conversation. People try to communicate while watching television or listening to the radio, or they attempt to conduct two conversations simultaneously. But, all noise is not auditory; some is emotional in nature. For example, labour-management negotiations are often fraught with suspicion and mistrust. Prejudices and biases, then, are emotionally built-in stimuli that interfere with objective listening and effective communication. Related to this communication failure is the sad but simple truth that individuals listen in order to evaluate and render judgment about the speaker, which, in turn, makes the speaker guarded and defensive about what he or she is attempting to communicate. Perhaps the best example of this type of ineffective communication is a city council meeting, where one side advocates the raising of taxes, while the other side interrupts, casts aspersions, and generally fights for all it is worth, against the tax hike. Whenever there are two people, or two groups, each with a strong vested interest in an emotional issue, the likelihood of there being clear communication is virtually nil. Communication, even in the best of circumstances, should not be taken for granted. Some of the basic principles of communication are as under:

4.1 BASIC COMMUNICATION PRINCIPLES

Communication is learned through experience, but experience itself does not necessarily make one an effective communicator. As children, we learn how to communicate by imitating our models— parents, brothers, sisters, neighbours, playmates, babysitters. Unfortunately, not all of our models are effective communicators; thus, we acquire poor habits of communication early, and those habits, like all habits, are difficult to break. A child, reared in a home where everyone talks at the same time and no one listens, carries this model upon leaving the home.

The meaning of words is illusory; words do not mean—people do. Words are merely symbols. Consider, for example, a simple word like rock. The teenager immediately thinks of loud music; the geologist thinks of a hard object created millions of years ago; the burglar thinks of a diamond ring; the old person thinks of a favourite chair, and so on. The point is that a word can have almost as many meanings as there are people who use it.

Language is learned; thus, in a sense, we are programmed, and the meaning of words stays within us for future reference. This programming is extremely helpful since, once we learn a word, it usually remains ours for a lifetime. However, this programming can also serve as an impediment to open communication with others, in that we often refer back to our original conceptions of words without thinking how others might interpret them. For example, the word girl, once used to refer to any female, is now clearly inappropriate in referring to an adult woman in this age of women's rights.

No two people are programmed alike; therefore, no symbol can always be interpreted the same way. Individuals differ in the nature and degree of their understanding. We perceive things differently, from our own frame of reference, so meanings differ.

It is impossible for any individual to encode or process all parts of a message.

Besides the fact that words are often inadequate in describing accurately what we are feeling or thinking, there is also the problem of distortion, that is, an individual's altering the event to suit his or her own purposes. But even if we have the precise word and communicate it without distortion, we still are faced with the problem of the receiver's receiving it in the same way in which it was intended.

Some experts claim that the single greatest problem with communication is the assumption of it. Too many people assume that their messages are automatically understood. We also sometimes assume that our perceptions are more right than the perceptions of someone else.

Where human communication is concerned, no assumptions can or should be made.

We always communicate. Anything we say or do can be interpreted, in a meaningful way, as a message. Even during periods of silence, communication takes place. Non-verbal behaviours (which are discussed in some detail in 4.2 below) such as eye contact, facial expressions, gestures, body posture, voice inflections, hesitations, and the like, all speak volumes. In fact, most sociological research claims that approximately two-thirds of the total message is communicated *via* non-verbal channels, especially where human emotions are concerned.

Listening is communication, too. Unfortunately, not everyone is a good listener; yet, that should not be too surprising, since listening as a communication skill is rarely, if ever, taught formally. To speak precisely and to listen carefully present a real challenge to all of us. The way in which we listen and respond to another person is crucial for building a fulfilling relationship. When we listen carefully, with understanding and without evaluation, and when we respond relevantly, we implicitly communicate to the speaker, "I care about what you are saying, and I would like to understand it."

The most effective communication occurs when the receiver of a message gives understanding responses, sometimes called paraphrases. A client might say, "I do not know I doubt that we can afford to send both of our kids to college." A financial counsellor using an understanding response would respond to the above statement with, "So you're just not sure you have the resources for a college education right now." While it might be tempting to try to convince the clients at this juncture that there is a way to finance their children's college education, the understanding response communicates a desire to understand the clients without evaluating these statements as right or wrong. It also helps the counsellor to see the expressed ideas and feelings of clients from their point of view.

Personalizing messages enhances the communication process and the counselling relationship. The hallmark of personal statements is the use of the personal pronouns, I, me, and my. Using generalized pronouns such as everyone, anyone or somebody to refer to your own ideas only tends to confuse clients and, hence, results in ambiguity and faulty understanding. Personal statements like, "I can appreciate your concern over not having adequate resources," reveals your own feelings to clients and increases the personal quality of the relationship.

4.2 ELEMENTS OF NON-VERBAL BEHAVIOURS

As mentioned above, clients communicate many feelings and attitudes to counsellors through non-verbal behaviours, including (but not limited to) fear, anxiety, sincerity, confusion, anger, aggression, happiness, hostility, interest, boredom, and concern. In the counselling context, *non-verbal behaviours* refer to those aspects of communications other than the words themselves. The two main sources of non-verbal behaviours are the *body* and the *voice*. From these two sources come seven types of non-verbal signs of meaning: *body position, body movement, gestures, facial expressions, eye contact, voice tone,* and *voice pitch.* Each of these types of non-linguistic signs conveys a wealth of information to the observant financial counsellor.

It should be noted that the counsellor's first impressions of the meaning or significance of any body language must be checked out against other clues given by the client.

Elements of non-verbal Behaviours

The body

- Positions
- Movements
- Gestures
- Facial expressions
- Eye contact

The voice

- Tone
- Pitch

4.2.1 The body

When learning to improve one's ability to observe the non-verbal behaviours of clients, it is important to notice the various ways by which the body actually communicates, either in agreement or in variance with what is actually said. In particular, the counsellor should notice and learn to interpret the communications that are transmitted by the client's body positions and movements.

Body positions

Overall body posture is the first thing the observant counsellor notices. Clients who sit erect and comfortably are usually relaxed. If they lean slightly forward, it is usually a sign of interest and involvement in the counselling session. If they slouch or seem to draw away from the counsellor, they may have no interest or trust in the counsellor— or they may be bored. Good client posture may indicate self-assurance and positive self-esteem. Poor posture may signal a lack of self-assurance or low self-esteem. The counsellor should also notice the position of the client's arms and legs. When the legs are uncrossed and the arms are positioned comfortably at the sides, the client is usually relaxed and open. Tightly crossed arms and legs, on the other hand, may indicate distrust or unreceptiveness. The facial position of the client should also be noticed. Most people's faces are expressive of a wide range of ever-changing feelings. The client whose face appears frozen in one position may be signalling fear, anxiety, or anger, or some other pre-possessing feeling that could become a block or obstacle to open communication with the counsellor.

Movements

The client who frequently changes body positions may be indicating physical or emotional discomfort, or a lack of interest. The counsellor should take note of such movements and try to relate them to information gleaned later. There is reason to believe that body language may be more honest or pure than verbal communication. In certain positive, straight forward human experiences we know that it is. The impulsive hug or kiss of greeting for people we care for is the most obvious example. But people also communicate through the body when they do not want to communicate, or when they are hiding or contradicting themselves. For example, a client may say, "No, I am not nervous about investing in a tax shelter," while biting his nails, pulling at his hair, or fidgeting distractedly. People often say what they think they may be expected to say in a given situation or context, not realizing what they may actually be communicating through body language.

Gestures

Hand and arm gestures are usually used to illustrate or accent verbal statements. Hands clasped so tightly that the knuckles are whitened and taut certainly signify something, perhaps fear or anxiety. While jerky hand and arm gestures may indicate anxiety, smooth and flowing gestures usually mean that the client is relaxed and interested in the counselling session. Frequent crossing and uncrossing of the legs, or bouncing a leg that is crossed, may indicate nervousness, boredom, or lack of interest.

Facial expressions

The financial counsellor can learn much from a client's facial expressions. Look for frowns, smiles, or nervous habits, such as biting the lips. Look especially to see if the client's facial expressions change as topics change, and note whether the expression is appropriate or incongruent. For example, if the client talks about anger, does she appear angry? If she facially expresses disgust about her husband's spendthrift ways, do her intentions in her last will and testament reflect that feeling by providing for her children through a trust, rather than leaving everything outright to her husband?

Eye contact

Eye contact, or the lack of it, in the counselling session can indicate the client's feeling. If the client's eyes are downcast and rarely meet the gaze of the counsellor, the client could be shy, anxious, or fearful (though not necessarily toward the counsellor). On the other hand, if the client stares or glances constantly at the counsellor, anger or hostility could be indicated. If the client's eyes rove all around the room, looking at the walls and ceiling while the counsellor is filling out the data-gathering form, there could be a serious lack of interest in the relevance of data gathering. A client who is open and interested in the counselling session will usually meet the gaze of the counsellor. This eye contact of the client usually indicates interest in the session and a positive and concerned attitude toward counselling. Needless to say, reciprocity from the counsellor is likely to be perceived by the client in the same way.

4.2.2 The voice

Non-verbal voice clues can be observed in the tone and pitch of the client's voice. Tone and pitch are qualities of the voice that may indicate the speaker's feelings, quite apart from what is actually said. They should be observed closely.

Voice tone

Voice tone is loudness or softness. The client who talks very loudly or shouts may be indicating anger or hostility. The client who talks very softly may be exhibiting fear or shyness.

Voice pitch

Voice pitch is the quality of a voice that indicates how high or low the voice is on a musical scale, A high-pitched voice may indicate anxiety, fear, or anger. A low-pitched voice may indicate either comfort or control of strong emotions. Obviously, some people's voices are naturally louder than others. The natural pitch of different voices also varies greatly. The point is not to type these differences but to observe and determine which vocal qualities are natural to a particular client so as to recognize variations.

If these vocal qualities do vary during counselling sessions in relation to personal and financial details, they can be important clues to the strong emotions that often affect a client's motivations, needs, and objectives. The counselling sessions themselves are often an inducement to clients to open up and give vent to feelings about their financial condition. Thus, voice tone and pitch are important factors for counsellors to observe and consider in relation to all other clues that characterize the client and reveal the individual's self-image.

4.2.3 Interpreting the meaning of non-verbal behaviours

It is important for financial counsellors to note that in all the descriptions above of non-verbal behaviours, of body language, we have stated that a behaviour may or usually does indicate one or more feelings. Non-verbal behaviours are clues that must be clearly observed and compared with what the client says in order to determine whether they are appropriate or compatible with their actions. For example, if a client blurts out, "I am furious with the broker who sold me that bunch of junk bonds last year! "and strikes the desk, the gesture is compatible with the verbal message—it agrees with what the client says. If the client makes the same statement and sits calmly smiling, however, there is incompatible behaviour—the body language does not jibe with the verbal message. When the financial counsellor observes incompatible behaviour of this sort in a client, it should be mentioned to the client in order to clarify the element of the communication that is correct.

Non-verbal behaviours are clues or indicators. While they signify something, their meanings can be clouded by incompatibility, distortion, or vagueness. Premature assumptions about what they really mean would be as unprofessional as failing to notice them altogether. For example, a client's palsied hands might be due to one or more of the following causes: nervousness, fear, Parkinson's disease, too much coffee, chemical poisoning, or alcoholism. The client who always talks loudly may be either angry or hard of hearing, or merely an over-bearing individual. The client who shows no interest in counselling may be worn out with worrying whether his recent commodities futures trading is going to wipe him out with margin calls, or whether he should buy term or whole life for estate liquidity, or whether he will have an estate. He may be on tranquilizers over worry about a son and heir who himself abuses drugs. For any number of reasons, the client may need psychological counselling or therapy before he can undertake financial counselling. In short, not all the problems that clients may bring to financial counselling sessions are financial in origin or nature. When present, these non-financial problems will distort client messages and add to the difficulties of clarifying them.

Observant counsellors need to be astute enough to discern from among all the verbal and non-verbal clues and be aware that in most client cases there will be a mixture of compatible and incompatible evidence. Counsellors thus understand who clients are, where they are, where they want to go; and can then suggest the optimal ways to help each one get there. *Do not assume that you know what a given behaviour means.* Check it out and clarify your perception with each client.

And do not forget that as a counsellor *you* communicate in both verbal and non-verbal ways, too, just as the client does, and that your communication behaviour very much affect the client. This is particularly true of non-verbal messages. Therefore, any of the communication and psychological considerations in this chapter that you may agree with are important with respect to the client and are also important for you. As a financial counselling professional, you will want to remove from your own behaviours those elements that present obstacles and barriers to successful communication with the client and with other professionals with whom you deal with. The client is then more likely to accept your role in the counselling situation and, ultimately, the plan you develop for meeting his or her financial needs and objectives. Similarly, other professionals whose expertise you will often need to call upon in developing and implementing a plan will respect your role as a financial counsellor and planner.

5. ATTENDING AND LISTENING SKILLS

Paying attention to clients is the first necessary component in good communication. No matter how expert your other communication skills are, if you are inattentive to your clients' verbal and non-verbal behaviours, you are apt to lose them at the very outset. How often have you been in the company of another person who shies away from looking at you, who glances nervously at his wristwatch, who interrupts you, and who, literally and figuratively, turns his back to you? Surely, if you have had this kind of experience, you can recall how uncomfortable and ill at ease you were with this inattentive behaviour.

If a counsellor's goal is to understand clients, the counsellor must first pay close attention to or focus on their verbal and non-verbal messages. Poor attending and poor listening lead to poor understanding.

5.1 PHYSICAL ATTENDING

Gerard Egan, a renowned counsellor-educator, categorizes attending behaviour into *physical attending,* or using your body to communicate and psychological attending, or listening actively. He uses the acronym, SOLER, as a reminder of the five basic attributes associated with physical attending. Let us look at these five attributes.

'S': Face the other person squarely

When there is face-to-face, direct contact, the communication process is enhanced. You communicate non-verbally to the other person, "I am here with you; I am tuned-in and ready to face the issues with you head-on." Turning your body away lessens your involvement with the other person.

'O': Adopt an open posture

There is something to be said about receiving a person with open arms. Crossed arms and crossed legs can inadvertently communicate a holding-off of the other person. An open posture—open arms and uncrossed legs and an open smile—communicates receptiveness to the other person and, hence, increases good communication and decreases defensiveness.

'L': Lean toward the other person

This is another physical signal of interest, involvement and caring. Two people who care about each other, when involved in conversation, almost always can be seen leaning toward each other. On the other hand, two people who are observed leaning away from one another, or sitting rigidly straight in their chairs, seem to be either bored or disinterested, or extremely cautious and defensive about getting involved with each other.

'E': Maintain good eye contact

Good eye contact consists of looking at another individual when you are in conversation. Poor eye contact consists of rarely looking at the other person, or looking away when he or she looks at you, or staring constantly with a blank expression on your face. The eye contact should be natural and spontaneous. Since you are interested in your client, you will want to use your eyes as a vehicle of communication.

'R': Be relaxed while attending

It is possible to be both intense while focusing on the client and relaxed at the same time. A nervous, fidgety, or rigid counsellor communicates these feelings to the client. A counsellor who sits in a casual fashion, who speaks naturally and spontaneously, and who uses natural gestures has the advantage of being free to focus intently upon the client and his or her communication, as well as helping to facilitate naturalness and spontaneity in the client.

As has been mentioned previously, it is impossible not to communicate, so as a counsellor you might as well use your body—gestures, posture, eyes—to communicate whatever message you wish to communicate. Otherwise, the body may communicate something you do not wish to communicate. In other words, try to make your body work for you on behalf of your counselling relationship.

5.2 ACTIVE LISTENING

So far, attending has been described as a physical activity; active listening brings in the psychological activity involved in attending. Many of us take listening for granted, but there is a distinct difference between simply hearing and actively listening. Hearing means the receiving of auditory signals. A person says, "I have a bad headache" and we hear that message and respond, "That's too bad" or "Here, have a couple of aspirin." An active listener on the other hand, might respond, "You look as though it is really getting you down." In short, the active listener responds not only to the verbal message received through the auditory channel, but also to the unspoken, or non-verbal message, communicated by the sender's body, facial expression, or tone of voice.

Active listening, then, means putting the non-verbal behaviour, the voice, and words together—all the cues sent out by the other person—to get the essence of the communication being sent. An active listener is an understanding listener, one who attempts to see the world from the other's frame of reference. If you can state in your own words what the other person has said, and that person accepts your statement as an accurate reflection of what he or she has said, then it is safe to say that you have listened actively and understood with accuracy.

But it must be stated that active listening is not merely parroting another's words—a computer can be (and has been) programmed to do that. Active listening means involving yourself in the inner world of another person while, at the same time, maintaining your own identity and being able to respond with meaningfulness to the messages of that other person.

5.3 RESPONDING DURING ACTIVE LISTENING

As indicated above, active listening is hard work and requires intense focusing and concentration. Years of not listening have made most of us poor listeners. We are distracted easily; we tend to evaluate and judge what is being said while it is being said, so that we are framing our own responses to the speaker's statement before the speaker is finished talking and, thus, we miss the message.

There are several simple ways of responding to people so that they feel accepted and understood. Let us look at some of these response modalities. Perhaps the simplest response modality is what Allen Ivey refers to as *continuing responses.* Non-verbally, if you want someone to continue talking, you might smile or nod your head to communicate agreement and/or understanding. Equally as effective in communicating your under- standing is a minimal encourager like "uh-huh," "mmmm," "then?" "and... ?" These relatively unobtrusive responses encourage the speaker to continue talking.

They communicate to the speaker, "Go on, I'm with you."

Another type of response that enhances communication is the *restatement-of-content* response. The rationale for restatement is to let speakers hear what they have said on the assumption that this may encourage them to go on speaking, examining, and looking deeper. Restatement communicates to the client, "I am listening to you very carefully, so much so that I can repeat what you have said."

The most effective restatements are those that are phrased in your own words, a paraphrase of what the speaker has stated. To do this effectively, we must temporarily suspend our own frame of reference and attempt to view the world from the other person's perspective.

Suppose the client says to you, "I'm really in a financial bind, what with taxes, inflation, fuel bills; I don't know how we make it from one month to the next." An accurate restatement might be expressed, "So things are tough for you financially. It seems like you can't make ends meet." The client, hearing this understanding response, is encouraged to delve more deeply into the situation, feeling that the counsellor has, indeed, heard the message on the same wavelength upon which it was transmitted. The bond between client and counsellor is, thus, strengthened, and greater opportunities for creative problem solving are opened up.

Just as we manifest understanding for our clients by responding to the content of the message, so may we also show our understanding of the client's experience by responding in a way that reflects the feelings expressed. Sometimes feelings are expressed directly, and at other times they are only implied or stated indirectly. In order to respond to a person's feelings, we must observe the behavioural cues like tone of voice, body posture, gestures, and facial expression, as well as listen to the speaker's words.

Consider this client statement, "Within the next few months, we need to buy a new refrigerator and another car. [Sighs] I just don't know where the money is going to come from." A *reflection-of-feeling response* might go, "You sound pretty hopeless about your financial state. It sure is hard to break even, let alone get ahead, these days." Again, by responding in an empathic way to the client's statement, you communicate a deep understanding of the person's experience; in addition, you progress one step further by addressing the non-verbalized feelings. We illustrate to the client that we understand so well what he or she is stating that we can paraphrase both words and feelings.

It is helpful to both the client and the counsellor to struggle to capture in words the uniqueness of the client's experience. The most effective types of understanding responses capsulize both the feeling and the content of the client's message. The basic format for this type of response is "You feel ______________[feeling] because __________[content]." This response enables clients to get in closer touch with the feelings that are an outgrowth of their situations. And that, in turn, facilitates the working through of the problem, because the counsellor involves clients in exploring themselves in the problem. Because you have accurately understood and responded to them, clients will go on to share other personal experiences that bear upon the presented problem. A word might be added here about the difficulties that some people have in dealing with feelings, either their own or the feelings of others. Problems often arise in interpersonal relationships because one or more of the involved persons choose to repress, distort, or disguise their feelings rather than admit that feelings are present and then discuss them openly. This is particularly true of so-called negative feelings like anger, sadness, anxiety, frustration, discomfort, and confusion. In actuality, no feelings are negative since they all are part of being human. In any case, counsellors who wish to communicate effectively need to address their own feelings as well as those of their clients. The mutual expression of feelings is an integral part of building a close, trusting, caring relationship.

Two other types of understanding responses need to be mentioned. Each is related to the restatement-of-content and the reflection-of-feeling responses; yet, there is a subtle shade of difference. First is the *clarifying response* that tends to amplify the speaker's statement. The clarifying response does not add anything new to what the speaker has said; it simply expands what has already been stated. The counsellor attempts to restate or clarify for the client that the client has had some difficulty in expressing clearly. It is akin to a translation of the client's words into language that is more familiar and understandable to both client and counsellor. Suppose a client says, "I'm not sure. Nothing makes sense anymore. Things get more confusing the more I think about them. It's a real puzzle to me." A counsellor, by way of clarification, might say, "I can sense your bewilderment. Let me see if I can help out. From what you' ve said previously, I get the impression that you want to get your mortgage straightened out before you increase your monthly savings. Is that it?" If the financial counsellor has, indeed, been following the flow of the client's experience, this statement will help to clarify the client's confusion over the situation to the extent that the counsellor's response is on target, the puzzle becomes suddenly clear and more readily solved.

Another side to the clarifying response concerns the counsellor's need to have things clarified. When the counsellor is puzzled, then it is certainly legitimate to ask for clarification as, "I'm sorry. I don't follow what you're saying. Can you make that more clear for me?" Clarified responses are helpful because they:

- facilitate client self-understanding
- attend especially to the client's feelings
- communicate the counsellor's understanding
- move the client towards a clearer definition of the problem

The other type of understanding response is the *summarization response.* Summaries are especially helpful toward the end of an interview, since they focus and capsulize a series of scattered ideas to present a clear perspective. The summary has the effect of reassuring clients that you have been tuned in to their many messages. For the counsellor, it serves as a check on the accuracy with which the various messages have been received.

It is often better to have the client do the summarizing. In this way, the client maintains the responsibility for bringing the messages together into a meaningful conclusion. As in clarifying, themes and emotional overtones should be summarized, and the key ideas should be synthesized into broad statements reflecting basic meanings. An example of an effective summary might be: "So today you described your overall financial situation as bleak, although you think you might be able to increase your savings if you could refinance your mortgage. I know you're rightly concerned about that." If the financial counsellor has accurately summarized the essence of the interview, the client then has a better handle on the intricacies of the situation, and a resolution is closer at hand.

What we have covered thus far are the basics of non-verbal behaviours, the skills of attending and active listening, and the five basic types of responses associated with active listening: continuing responses, restatement of content, reflection of feeling, clarification, and summarization.

Five Types of Responses Associated with Active Listening

1. Continuing responses
2. Restatement of content
3. Reflection of feeling
4. Clarification
5. Summarization

The element common to all five of these response modalities is that the counsellor follows, or tracks, the client's lead. This response communicates a high level of understanding and enables the client not only to experience what it feels like to be understood, but also to progress further toward an ultimate resolution of the situation.

SELF ASSESSMENT EXERCISE 1

1. Describe the importance of structure in financial counselling.

   ....
   ....
   ....
   ....
   ....

2. List several sources of resistance behaviours encountered in counselling

   ....
   ....
   ....
   ....
   ....

3. List basic principles of communication theory.

   ....
   ....
   ....
   ....
   ....

6. COUNSELLOR LEADING RESPONSES

A *leading response* is one in which the counsellor, to a certain extent, takes the lead and deviates somewhat from the client's preceding responses. When the financial counsellor decides to make a leading response, it is the counsellor's frame of reference that comes into focus. Up to this point, the counsellor's responses have followed from the client's statements, but here the emphasis shifts. An obvious danger of this shift is that the counsellor may move in a direction in which the client is not yet ready or willing to move. Despite this danger, if the counsellor has followed the client closely so far, and if a good relationship has been established, then this different kind of response should not threaten the client, as long as it is interposed carefully and tentatively.

The first of the leading responses is known simply as *explanation.* Explanation is a relatively neutral description of the way things are. It deals in logical, practical, factual information. It is often offered at the client's request, although there are instances when the counsellor will offer an explanation without its being requested. A client may be confused by some terminology that the counsellor has used and ask, for example, "Exactly what is an annuity?" The counsellor's explanation should be simple, concise, and comprehensible. Long-winded explanations tend to become vague and hard to follow. The counsellor should also guard against explaining things in a condescending, patronizing, or pedantic tone. The best explanations are those that are exchanged between equal partners (not superior-subordinates) in a relationship.

Another type of leading response is the *interpretive response.* Interpretations can be particularly risky when the counsellor goes too deep too soon, or when the interpretation is off base. Interpretations often come across as sounding overly clinical, diagnostic, and authoritarian. Despite these drawbacks, interpretations can be extremely effective responses because they often cut to the heart of the matter. When the interpretation makes sense to the client, it definitely accelerates the interview. We should keep in mind that the goal of all interpretive efforts is self-interpretation by the client in order to increase the client's ability to act effectively. The following is an example of a facilitative interpretation:

Client: "I m not sure whether I want to retire early. I like to keep busy, and I don't know what I'd do with all that free time,"

Counsellor: "So the prospect of an early retirement is a bit frightening. Maybe you're afraid that you'd just waste your time away?"

Notice that the financial counsellor's interpretation did not stray too far from what the client had said. The counsellor used the words "frightening" and "afraid," but probably did so on the basis of some fear or trepidation detected in the client's voice. Further, the counsellor responded tentatively, using qualifiers like "a bit" and "maybe," and converted the second statement into a question by a raised voice at the end of the sentence. This enables the client to assimilate the counsellor's response without feeling as though it has been offered as a fiat from above. The client, thus, is free to accept, modify, or deny the counsellor's interpretation, and this is very important. If the counsellor's interpretation is inaccurate, it is far better to discover that early than to proceed indefinitely along the wrong path.

A third type of leading response frequently employed by counsellors is *reassurance, or encouragement. A reassuring response* is designed with the intention of making the client feel better, to bolster his or her spirits, and to offer support in a time of need. It communicates clearly to the client that "I am here by your side, ready to aid you in any way that I can." As a means of helping, however, the reassuring response tends to be merely a temporary measure. It is akin to offering a tissue to someone who is crying; the crying may stop temporarily, but the underlying causes have been left untouched.

For this reason the counsellor must be careful not to use reassurance indiscriminately. The understanding (reflection-of-feeling) response discussed in the previous section on active listening is far more effective when emotions surface. The understanding response communicates accurate empathy; the reassuring response offers only sympathy, and very few people like to feel pitied. Contrast the effect of these two different kinds of responses on our hypothetical client:

Client : "I get so furious whenever my broker ignores me! It's almost as though I don't exist!"

Counsellor : (using reassuring response): "Well, don't feel so bad. It doesn't do much good to get so worked up. Try not to worry about it, and you'll feel better."

Counsellor : (using reflection of feeling): "I can feel the rage as you speak. You feel like a non-person around your broker, that you are not getting adequate service for the money you are paying, and that makes you angry." The first counsellor response patches a band-aid on a deep wound and is, therefore, ineffectual. The second response reflects the deeply felt anger and, in so doing, helps the client work through the anger. Reassurance, while not a harmful response, promises pie in the sky and delivers nothing. The final type of leading response is called *advice, or suggestion.* Many people actively seek the advice of others, possibly hoping that the advice giver will make the difficult decision for them, or solve their problems for them. And, as chance or human nature would have it, there is certainly no shortage of people in this world willing to dole out free advice. In a financial counselling relationship, however, the best kind of advice is self-advice. Counsellors who have been responding in an understanding fashion are already well on their way toward helping clients discover, in their own way and in their own time, what advice is best for them. There are times within a counselling relationship when proffering advice is acceptable, but these times are few. When advice is given, it should be offered tentatively, in the form of a suggestion, or several suggestions, about which the client has the final decision. Otherwise, the counsellor not only leads, but takes over the ultimate responsibility for the client's financial plan, and each person has the right to formulate his or her own plan. Advice giving robs the client of this right.

Counsellor Leading Responses

- Explanation
- Interpretive
- Reassurance/encouragement
- Advice/suggestion

7. THE QUESTIONING PROCESS OF A FINANCIAL COUNSELLOR

The question is surely one of the most timeworn response modes used by financial counsellors. Many counsellors see their main role as an interviewer or an interrogator. The question seems appropriate only when it is an honest attempt to gather information that the counsellor requires and to which the client has access. Unfortunately, the question is not always used in this fashion. Moreover, the question-answer dialogue sets up a pattern of communication that is difficult for the participants to break: the client waits for the inevitable question; the question comes, followed by the answer (and not much more); and then comes the wait for the next question. Questioning almost always casts the counsellor in the role of authority figure and the client in the role of a somewhat passive subordinate, certainly not the type of interpersonal relationship conducive to effective counselling.

Despite the disadvantages of the question mentioned above, there are times when only a well-phrased question will suffice, particularly when we are seeking data from the client. Even here, though, there is a qualitative difference among the various types of questions that might be asked. Several categories of questions are discussed in the following section.

7.1 OPEN-ENDED VERSUS CLOSE-ENDED QUESTIONS

Ideally, questions posed by the counsellor should be *open-ended* and should call for more than just a yes or no response on the part of the client; otherwise, they tend to stifle interaction. The open-ended question allows the client to select a response from his or her full repertory. The *close-ended question* limits the client to a specific, narrow response, often either a yes or a no. The open-ended question solicits the client's opinions, thoughts, ideas, values, and feelings. The close-ended question typically solicits singular facts or one-word replies.

Contrast the differences in the following sets of questions. The first question in each set is close-ended; the second question in each set is open ended :

1. *a.* Are you ready to start an investment program?

   b. How do you feel about starting an investment program?

2. *a.* Have you given any thought to retirement?
   b. What thoughts do you have about retirement?
3. *a.* Are you afraid to start saving something now?
   b. Why have you decided to wait to start saving?

As can be readily seen from the above examples, the open-ended questions ask for more complete, comprehensive information. In a way, they force the client to formulate thoughts, ideas, and feelings into fully rounded responses. On the other hand, the close-ended questions solicit only a one word or short-answer response, requiring little thought and offering virtually no feedback.

7.2 LEADING QUESTIONS

Other types of close-ended questions that are not only ineffective but also manipulative are those termed *leading questions.* These questions usually begin with, "Don't you think...," or "Do you really feel" More often than not they lead the client towards a conclusion that the counsellor (not the client) has already formulated, so that there is the element of dishonesty in even asking the question. It is far more effective, and honest, for the counsellor to rephrase the leading question into a declarative statement in the form of sharing a perception or opinion with the client.

Consider the following leading questions:

"Don't you think you should start an investment program now?" "Do you really feel that $ a month is enough?"

"Are you sure you've considered all possibilities?"

With just a bit of reflection, we can see that the counsellor is actually saying: "I think you ought to start an investment program now."

"I don't feel that Rs. 1000 a month will be enough."

"I'm sure there are other possibilities you haven't considered."

The latter statements are much more honest and to the point than the questions from which they stem. Generally speaking, declarative statements communicate far more clearly than the manipulative leading questions. A good rule of thumb to follow in everyday intercourse is to make as many statements as possible and save the questions for honest information seeking.

7.3 THE EITHER/OR OR TRUE/FALSE QUESTION

Another kind of relatively ineffective question is of the *either/or* or *true/false* variety. While this question is not quite as close-ended as the leading question, it is only slightly less closed, since it limits the client to only two options. For example:

"Do you plan to stay in this house or move to an apartment?" "Are you more apt to take a risk or play it safe?"

Clients might prefer both options, or neither, or a third or fourth option; but here they are forced to choose from what we have offered them. The world is not simply black or white; there are various shades of gray; yet, when we phrase questions so that clients are forced to choose from one of two-options, we are restricting the clients' responses. We can improve on the preceding examples by asking:

"What are your plans after retirement regarding housing?" "How do you usually make your decisions?"

Again, we see that by opening up the question we allow clients to respond freely from their own frame of reference, and not from ours. And this is what good interviewing is all about.

7.4 WHY QUESTIONS

Even though *why questions* can be classified as open-ended questions and, thus, theoretically sound, such is not the case. On the surface, questions beginning with why appear to be legitimate enough, signifying the inquiry into causal relationships, as in, "Why are you planning to retire at age 62?"

Unfortunately, why questions carry with them a connotation of implied disapproval by the questioner, thus forcing the person being asked the question to justify or defend his or her thoughts, ideas, or actions. Even when that is not the meaning the questioner intends, that is generally how the why question is received. The why question tends to question the client's motivation (or lack of motivation) and, thus, creates a certain defensiveness.

Perhaps the chief reason that why questions are received so poorly dates back to the manner in which parents put children on the spot: "Why didn't you pick up your room?" "Why don't you have your shoes on?" "Why can't you be more careful?" And, of course, this line of inquiry is later picked up by teachers with students: "Why don't you have your homework?" "Why didn't you study for this test?" In short, as children, we learned that when an adult asked us a question beginning with why, it meant, "Change your behaviour; think as I think; behave the way adults do." And we carry that lesson with us throughout life, usually responding to why questions in a defensive, negative manner.

So unless there is a valid reason for asking a why question, and when no other type of question will suffice, it is generally better to avoid why questions.

7.5 QUESTION BOMBARDMENT

Still another kind of faulty questioning technique, called *question bombardment,* occurs when we ask double, triple, or even quadruple questions without waiting for a response. This is frequently referred to as question bombardment. As absurd as this may sound, it occurs far too frequently in interviews to escape comment. For example: "What type of investment program appeals to you most—stock, municipal bonds? Or would you rather look into annuities? When do you think you'd be ready to begin?"

The first question in the series is open-ended in nature and can stand by itself quite well; yet the interviewer isn't content to let well enough alone, but instead tacks on other, more restricting close-ended questions. The result is that the client is caught in a hailstorm of questions all at one time and, more often than not, gets the opportunity to respond to only one of the several questions asked. If more than one question needs to be asked, it is better to form separate questions, waiting for a full response to each question before going on to the next one. The other issue to be addressed, though, is whether so many questions need to be asked in the first place.

Concluding Remarks

Questioning is a major component in the repertory of most interviewers. Yet that need not be so. If we wish to become better communicators, one thing that we can do is to convert some of our questions (especially close-ended, leading, either/or, and why questions) into statements. With a statement, we assume responsibility for what we say. With a question, we shift the responsibility to the other person, which may sometimes be necessary. Far too often, however, we simply shirk our own responsibility for, and involvement in, the interaction when we revert to questioning. As stated previously, counselling is not the same as interviewing. If we hope to do counselling, we need to do far more than simply ask one question after another.

Categories of Questions

Open-ended Either/or and true/false

Close-ended Why

Leading Bombardment

How Ethical Behaviour Improves Communication

Sometimes words are insufficient. Many clients misunderstand the specifics of the plan recommended by a financial counsellor. This problem is compounded when complex financial instruments are required to implement the plan. It is much like drivers and automobiles. Most drivers really need transportation, and cars solve this problem, however, that doesn't mean that drivers understand how their cars operate.

A financial planner once stated that there are two essential rules for effectively dealing with a client. The first is to earn his/her trust because trust breaks down communication barriers. Different counsellors may accomplish this in different ways, but the counsellor must feel free to ask the challenging questions and continue to probe until a satisfactory level of understanding is achieved. When there are limits to what the client can understand, earned trust is essential.

The second rule is to maintain trust, a critical factor in the counsellor-client relationship. Although clients do not fully understand, they should not fail to act. Indeed, if they understood every aspect of financial planning, they would not need a planner. Clients often make decisions based solely on their trust in their financial adviser.

There is no better way to earn and maintain trust than to develop an unassailable reputation for ethical and professional behaviour. A valuable side benefit is improved communication.

REVIEW

QUESTIONS

1. Describe three forms of structured communication.
2. Describe the importance of establishing rapport with the client in financial counselling.
3. List four characteristics of an effective counsellor.
4. What is the importance of self-awareness in the counselling relationship, especially concerning value orientations and differences?
5. List and briefly describe the ways in which non-verbal behaviours are communicated by the body and the voice.
6. Why is it important to assess the meaning of both verbal and non-verbal behaviours?
7. Describe five important attributes associated with physical attending.
8. What is the type of response made during active listening that is illustrated in each of the following examples?
    a. "Well, let's see what we've concluded then. You want to set aside about Rs. 30,000 per year to save for a down payment on a time share house at the beach, and safety is your prime consideration in the investment of that money."
    b. "I'm not sure I'm following you. Tell me again what your plan is for disposing of your interest in the partnership."
    c. "From what you just told me, then, I gather that you want to stay away from the partnership and put the money into the stock market instead."
9. Describe four types of leading responses.
10. The questions listed below are examples of which of the following concepts? (More than one concept may be illustrated in each case.)

    why question

    question bombardment leading question close-ended question open-ended question.

    true-false question

a. "Why haven't you started converting some of that term insurance to whole life?"

b. "Don't you think your present portfolio of investments is pretty illiquid?"

c. "What goals do you have with respect to the education of your children?"

d. "Do you plan to hold on to your mutual fund?"

e. "Don't you think you should put Rs. 20,000 into an Provident fund this year? That isn't much money for you, is it? After all, don't you have at least that much in your passbook savings account right now? Or am I mistaken on that point?"

f. "You were born in 1966, right?"

SELF-TEST QUESTIONS

T F 1. The single most important skill financial counsellors have is their technical expertise.

T F 2. Interviewing, counselling, and advising are all similar to and different from each other.

T F 3. The purpose of advising clients in financial counselling is to convince them to do what counsellors think they should do.

T F 4. It is not particularly important for the counsellor to convey an attitude of acceptance toward the client.

T F 5. There is usually a certain degree of client resistance to counselling because the client must relinquish to the counsellor some privacy and personal power.

T F 6. Financial counsellors are frequently confronted with the personal problems of clients as apart of their total financial situation.

T F 7. The client's resistance behaviours are unimportant to a successful financial counselling relationship.

T F 8. Counsellors must be aware of themselves before they can be aware of others.

T F 9. A word is a universally understood and agreed-upon symbol of a thing.

T F 10. A client's non-verbal communication conveys more information than verbal messages.

T F 11. There is no reason to believe that body language is more honest or open than verbal communication.

T F 12. When financial counsellors perceive incongruencies between a client's verbal and non-verbal messages, they should clarify what the real message is.

T F 13. Non-verbal behaviours are positive statements or messages that can either be taken at face value or be freely interpreted.

T F 14. An element common to all responses in active listening is that the counsellor follows the client's lead.

T F 15. All advice offered in counselling should be tentative, with the client making the final decision.

T F 16. Asking the client questions is usually appropriate only when it is an honest attempt to gather information that the counsellor needs and the client can provide.

T F 17. "Why" questions carry a connotation of implied disapproval by the questioner.

ANSWERS

1. *a.* Interviewing can be defined as a process of communication with a predetermined and specific purpose, usually involving the asking and answering of questions designed to gather meaningful information.

   b. Counselling implies help giving, often of a psychotherapeutic nature. The help-giving aspect is built in and an integral part of the process. A counsellor's job is to provide assistance to clients as they explore their present situations, begin to understand where they are in relation to where they would like to be, and then act to get from where they are to where they want to be.

   c. Advising involves giving specific guidance or suggestions to the advisee.

2. Establishing rapport creates a climate in which clients are free to be themselves, since they don't have to be afraid that what they say will be evaluated in a negative way by the counsellor. They begin to realize that the ultimate responsibility for planning, setting goals, and taking action rests with them and not the counsellor.

3. *a.* unconditional positive regard

   b. accurate empathy

c. genuineness

d. self-awareness

4. Counsellors who are aware of their own value systems have a better chance of avoiding the imposition of their values onto their clients. This quality is of vital importance since we want to help our clients make decisions that stem from their own value systems, rather than from ours. Values, while deeply internalized, are not immutable. Counsellors need to remind themselves of this fact as they work with clients who are confused and afraid in approaching important decisions. Counsellors must have enough faith in the client's worth as a unique human being to permit that client to make value choices that fit his or her value system. The financial counsellor can and should provide information that will help the client make the choice, but the choice ultimately belongs to the client, not the counsellor.

5. *a.* Body positions—Clients who sit erect and comfortably are usually relaxed.

   Slouching may indicate lack of interest or trust. Poor posture may signal a lack of self-assurance or low self-esteem. When the legs are uncrossed and the arms are positioned comfortably at the sides, the client is usually relaxed and open. Tightly crossed arms and legs, on the other hand, may indicate distrust or unreceptiveness. The client whose face appears frozen in one position may be signaling fear, anxiety, or anger, or some other prepossessing feeling that could become a block or obstacle to open communication with the counsellor.

   b. Body movements—Frequent body movement may indicate physical or emotional discomfort, or a lack of interest.

   c. Gestures—Hand and arm gestures are usually used to illustrate or accent verbal statements. Hands clasped so tightly that the knuckles are whitened and taut certainly signify something, perhaps fear or anxiety. While jerky hand and arm gestures may indicate anxiety, smooth and flowing gestures usually mean that the client is relaxed and interested in the counselling session. Frequent crossing and uncrossing of the legs, or bouncing a leg that is crossed, may indicate nervousness, boredom, or lack of interest.

   d. Facial expressions—The financial counsellor can learn much from a client's facial expressions. Look for frowns, smiles, or nervous habits, such as biting the lips. Look especially to see if the client's facial expressions change as topics change, and note whether the expression is appropriate or incongruent. Facial expressions can reinforce the spoken words or suggest a lack of commitment.

e. Eye contact—If the client's eyes are downcast and rarely meet the gaze of the counsellor, the client could be shy, anxious, or fearful (though not necessarily toward the counsellor). If the client stares or glares constantly at the counsellor, anger or hostility could be indicated. If the client's eyes rove all around the room, there could be a serious lack of interest. A client who is open and interested in the counselling session will usually meet the gaze of the counsellor. This eye contact of the client usually indicates interest in the session and a positive and concerned attitude toward counselling.

f. Voice tone—The client who talks very loudly may be indicating anger or hostility. The client who talks very softly may be exhibiting fear or shyness.

g. Voice pitch—A high-pitched voice may indicate anxiety, fear, or anger. A low- pitched voice may indicate either comfort or control of strong emotions.

6. Both verbal and non-verbal behaviours communicate. If the two types of communication are not consistent with each other, the counsellor must delve further to determine the true meaning. Non-verbal behaviours are clues or indicators of the client's true feelings. Most sociological research claims that approximately two-thirds of the total message is communicated *via* non-verbal channels, especially where human emotions are concerned.

7. *a.* Face the other person squarely.

   b. Adopt an open posture.

   c. Lean toward the other person.

   d. Maintain good eye contact.

   e. Be relaxed while attending.

8. *a.* Summarization

   b. Clarification

   c. Restatement of content

9. *a.* Explanation is a relatively neutral description of the way things are. It deals with logical, practical, factual information.

   b. Interpretations can be extremely effective responses because they often cut to the heart of the matter. When the interpretation makes sense to the client, it definitely accelerates the interview.

   c. A reassuring response offers sympathy. It is designed with the intention of making the client feel better, to bolster his or her spirits, and to offer support in a time of need.

   d. Advice, or suggestion, essentially involves telling the client what he or she should do. In a financial counselling relationship, however, the best kind of advice is self-advice.

10. *a.* "Why haven't you started converting some of that term insurance to whole life?"

    Open-ended question, why question

    b. "Don't you think your present portfolio of investments is pretty illiquid?" Close-ended question, leading question

    c. "What goals do you have with respect to the education of your children?" Open-ended question

    d. "Do you plan to hold on to your mutual fund?" Close-ended question

    e. "Don't you think you should put Rs. 20,000 into Provident fund this year?

    That isn't much money for you, is it? After all, don't you have at least that much in your passbook savings account right now? Or am I mistaken on that point?" Question bombardment, leading question, close-ended question

    f. "You were born in 1966, right?"

    Close-ended question, true-false question

ANSWERS TO SELF-TEST QUESTIONS

1. False. The ability to communicate is the financial counsellor's most important skill.
2. True.
3. False. The purpose of advising in counselling is to persuade clients to do what clients perceive is in their own best interest, all things considered.

The best advising is self-advising, since it encourages clients to assume responsibility for their own well-being.

4. False. Without the counsellor's acceptance of the client, rapport will not be established, and the client will not offer the required information.
5. True.
6. True.
7. False. Resistance behaviours are always indicators that the client is having trouble relating to the counsellor, the counselling relationship, Or some of the sensitive topics being discussed.
8. True.
9. False. Words are symbolic, but their meanings are as varied as the people using them.
10. True.
11. False. There is reason to believe that body language is more honest or pure than verbal communication as evidenced by certain positive, straightforward human experiences such as greeting someone with an impulsive hug or kiss.
12. True.
13. False. Non-verbal behaviours are clues or indicators; therefore premature assumptions about what they mean are unprofessional. Do not assume that you know what a given behaviour means. Check it again and clarify your perception with the client.
14. True.
15. True.
16. True.
17. True.

IN SUMMARY

The topic begins with a delineation of the various types of structured communication: interviewing, counselling, and advising. From there it proceeds to some of the essentials inherent in financial counselling: structuring the counselling relationship; establishing rapport; and dealing with resistance. Next it looks at some of the characteristics of effective counselling: unconditional positive regard, empathy, genuineness, and self- awareness. The second part of the topic focuses on basic communication principles and skills such as non-verbal communication, using the skills of attending to a client, listening and then responding to a client, and asking effective questions.

In this topic we understood differences between three main type of structured communications *i.e.* interviewing, counselling and advising. We also understood need for unconditional regard of client with accurate empathy which comes out of genuineness to help and self knowledge of the counsellor. We discussed various ways of non-verbal communication and responses associated with active listening. In last section we compared advantages and disadvantages of various types of questions used in financial counselling.

SUGGESTED ANSWERS TO SELF-ASSESSMENT EXERCISE 1

1. Structuring serves to determine both the format and the subject matter of the interaction that is to follow
    a. Death and dying
    b. Marital tensions, including separation/divorce, parent-child disputes, sex, the empty nest syndrome, and midlife crisis
    c. Failure to attain the expected degree of professional success
2. *a.* Communication is learned through experience, but experience itself does not necessarily make one an effective communicator.

    b. The meaning of words is illusory; words do not mean—people do. Words are merely symbols, and a word can have almost as many meanings as there are people who use it.

    c. Language is learned; thus, in a sense, we are programmed, and the meaning of words stays within us for future reference. This programming is extremely helpful since, once we learn a word, it usually remains ours for a lifetime.

    d. No two people are programmed alike; therefore, no symbol can always be interpreted the same way. Individuals differ in the nature and degree of their understanding. We perceive things differently, from our own frame of reference, so meanings differ.

e. It is impossible for any individual to encode or process all parts of a message.

Besides the fact that words are often inadequate in describing accurately what we are feeling or thinking, there is also the problem of distortion, mat is, an individual's altering the event to suit his or her own purposes.

f. Some experts claim that the single greatest problem with communication is the assumption of it. Too many people assume that their messages are automatically understood. Where human communication is concerned, no assumptions can or should be made.

g. We can never not communicate. Anything we say or do can be interpreted in a meaningful way as a message. Even during periods of silence, communication takes place. Non-verbal behaviours such as eye contact, facial expressions, gestures, body posture, voice inflections, hesitations, and the like, all speak volumes.

h. Listening is communication, too. Unfortunately, not everyone is a good listener; yet, that should not be too surprising, since listening as a communication skill is rarely, if ever, taught formally. To speak precisely and to listen carefully present a real challenge to all of us.

i. The most effective communication occurs when the receiver of a message gives understanding responses, sometimes called paraphrases.

j. Personalizing messages enhances the communication process and the counselling relationship. The hallmark of personal statements is the use of the personal pronouns, I, me, and my. Using generalized pronouns such as everyone, anyone, or somebody to refer to your own ideas only tends to confuse clients and, hence, results in ambiguity and faulty understanding.

CHECKLIST

Below is a checklist of main points covered by this topic. Use this checklist to test your learning :

- Interviewing, counselling and advising are three different forms of structured communication.
- Rapport, recognizing resistance and overcoming resistance forms bed rock of structured communication.
- Effective counsellor will have unconditional positive regard for client, use 'accurate empathy' to be with client in emotional plane, will seek

genuine information and translate them correctly due to his own self-awareness.

- Communication takes place by combinations of verbal and non-verbal means.
- Effective communication needs to be a two way process and requires response and feedback
- "Intention" and "Attention" are essential for active listening
- Continuous response, paraphrasing, reflection of feeling, clarification and summarization improves active listening
- Counsellor supports ongoing communication with explanation, interpreting agreed communication, encouraging client to open up and provides advice
- Open questions are another useful skill for communicators. However, questioning is usually best kept to a minimum when listening.
- Either/Or questions help to focus around facts. True/False question also help in speeding up the process
- Why question are open ended and difficult for clients to answer easily. They may deal with issue for which client may not have rational answer or any answer at all.